The Way to the West

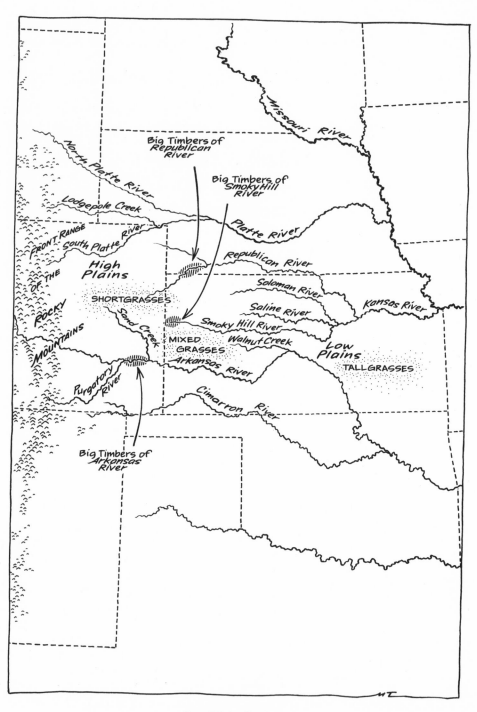

Central Plains: Physical

The Way to the West

Essays on the Central Plains

Elliott West

CH

*A Volume in the Calvin P. Horn Lectures
in Western History and Culture*

University of New Mexico Press
Albuquerque

14 13 12 11 10 09   4 5 6 7 8 9

ISBN-13: 978-0-8263-1653-0
ISBN-10: 0-8263-1653-0

LIBRARY OF CONGRESS CATALOGING-IN-PUBLICATION DATA
West, Elliott, 1945–
The way to the West: essays on the Central Plains
Elliott West
1st ed.—p.cm.
(Calvin P. Horn lectures in western history and culture)
Includes bibliographical references and index.
ISBN 0-8263-1652-2 (CL)   ISBN 0-8263-1653-0 (PA)
1. Great Plains—History.
2. Great Plains—Description and travel.
3. Natural history—Great Plains.
1. Title. 11. Series.
F591.W453 1995
978—dc20 95-4351
CIP

Designed by Sue Niewiarowski

*To the memory
of Robert G. Athearn,
teacher and friend*

Contents

Maps

Acknowledgments

It's hard to know where to start and when to stop in thanking those who have helped with this book. I'll begin with the Department of History and the Center for the American West at the University of New Mexico. Their invitation gave me the chance to pursue my curiosity. Three other institutions provided indispensable help. A fellowship from the Newberry Library of Chicago, Illinois, allowed me to spend the academic year of 1992–93 working in its incomparable archives. Part of that year's funding came from the National Endowment for the Humanities, which also has my deep gratitude. I also offer my special thanks to the Fulbright College of the University of Arkansas. My college has given me resources and encouragement with equal generosity, and I greatly appreciate both.

Individuals at those institutions deserve more than my thanks, but thanks are all I can offer. Dean Bernard Madison of Fulbright College has been a good friend and as fine a boss as I could want. Special thanks go to staff members of the Newberry Library: Fred Hoxie, Jim Grossman, Helen Tanner, Dick Brown, Dick Sattler, David Buiserret, and the wizard of the archives John Aubrey. Their mix of rigorous criticism, insightful suggestions, good humor, and encouragement has inspired an army of researchers, and I am glad to have been among them. Visiting and resident scholars at the Newberry—Henry Drewel, Eli Zaretsky, Alfred Young, John Marino, Henry Dobyns, Ganady Dubovitsky, Fr. Peter Powell, Fritz Jennings, and many others—also helped make that research year the most intellectually rewarding of my life.

Three scholars of western history—Richard White, John Mack Faragher, and James Sherow—read parts of the manuscript and offered extremely helpful criticism. Thanks to each of them, and to Richard Etulain, who applied his shrewd eye to an entire version of an early draft. Friends and colleagues helped along the way, especially Fred Limp, Elaine Williams, and Tom Green. I am particularly indebted to specialists in plant and animal sciences,especially Edward Everett Dale, Jr., Glenn Plumb, Larry Rittenhouse, and Tim Seastadt, who served as guides through a complex maze of writings. Four graduate students have helped along the way with both thoughtful comments and dirty work: David Dawson, Jeff Woods, Michelle Davidson, and Brian Miller. In the summers of 1993 and 1994 I participated in the Institute of the American West in Boulder, Colorado, created by the Social Sciences Education Consortium and funded by the National Endowment for the Humanities. In hashing through some of this book's issues, I profited enormously from two other faculty, Patricia Nelson Limerick and Gary Holthaus, from the institute staff, Jim Giese, Barbara Miller, and Lori Eastman, and especially from the sixty high school and middle school teachers who taught me more than I could have imagined about the West today.

My family carried part of this load of work. I thank my children, Elizabeth, Bill, Richard, Garth, and Anne, for their patience with my distractions. My mother, Betsy West, as always gave her encouragement and confidence, and my brother Richard helped me laugh my way through the low points. With her usual limitless generosity, my wife and closest friend, Suzanne Stoner, kept me going with her ideas, understanding, and her unfailing sense of humor.

I dedicate this book to Robert G. Athearn, who introduced me to western history while I was a graduate student at the University of Colorado. He was a son of the northern plains, and he wrote and spoke on many of the themes in these pages: continuities of the frontier and the recent West, environmental limits, the power of stories and illusion, and above all the complexity and slipperiness of the lessons that the West offers us. I still learn from him, and so should we all.

The Way to the West

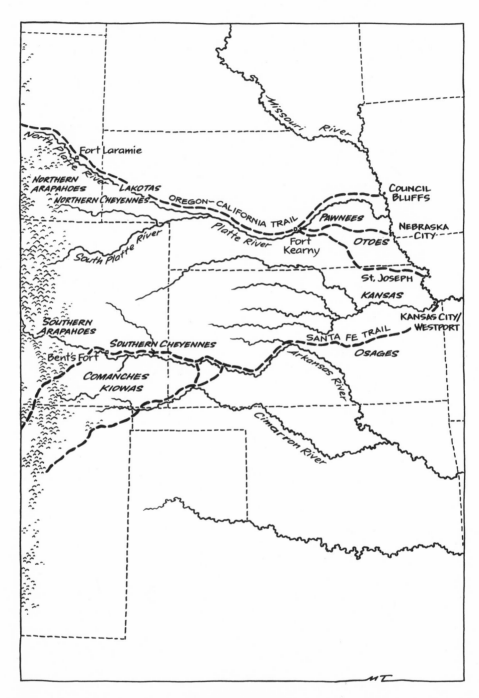

Central Plains: Historical

Introduction

These essays are expanded versions of the ninth annual Calvin Horn Lectures on Western History and Culture, given at the University of New Mexico in the fall of 1993. The invitation to take part in that series came from Richard Etulain, director of the university's Center for the American West. When I asked Dick what I would be expected to speak about, he told me, "Whatever you want." That stunningly rash answer was a kind of goad. Because I am basically lazy, I tend to persist on an established course, like a ball rolling across a floor, unless something deflects me. The invitation from Dick the Deflector has been a chance to explore some aspects of western history in which I have not worked before.

In particular I have reached a bit into environmental and American Indian history. The essays also touch, to some degree, on social and literary history and on the West of popular culture. My larger purpose has been to suggest the rewards of studying the history of the West from multiple angles of view and with the help of insights of different disciplines.

In doing that I have kept my focus primarily on one part of the American West, a subregion that historians have studied in plenty of detail already. The setting is that part of the North American Great Plains that lies west of the 98th meridian, east of the Front Range of the Rocky Mountains, south of the Platte River, and north of the Arkansas River. This country, called here the central plains, covers most of central and western Kansas and eastern Colorado, part of southern Nebraska, and a dollop of southeastern Wyoming.

Today, if you drive across this region east-to-west, you will first
see ranchland and irrigated farms, then drier and flatter country with
plenty of sagebrush but fewer cattle and virtually no crops. There
will be long stretches that seem, when viewed at fifty-five (or seventy, or eighty) miles an hour, to have no uses at all. Your passage
will be punctuated by small and medium-sized towns. Some of the
names have a vague historical resonance to the casual tourist: Hays,
Goodland, Sharon Springs, Kit Carson, Las Animas, Cheyenne Wells,
and Chivington. Mostly you will see highways, their medians and
shoulders, off-ramps, on-ramps and other roads crossing overhead,
state "rest areas," and, every twenty or forty miles, mercantile clusters where you can buy fuel, meals, magazines, selected groceries,
soft drinks, pecan logs, postcards, tee-shirts, adjustable caps, and a
broad selection of *chotchke*, western-style.

It's a familiar encounter with the contemporary West, but this
car-window view of the plains can also be understood as a recent
expression of some old, persistent themes. Some of the people you
see, the occasional rancher or farmer in his tractor cab, are trying
hard to live there and get what they need from a stingy land, like
nomads and homesteaders of the last century. A lot more, like overland marchers heading for Oregon, look on this country simply as
something to get across. A few others combine the first two perspectives, making a living off transients in a hurry.

As in this case, so many obvious lessons of the plains are easy to
pass by and miss. The country seems to have a lot of very little.
Unlike rural New England or the deserts and villages of the southwest, one can move through here without much sense that anything
has happened. The landscape seems overwhelmingly empty. Gertrude
Stein wrote that in the United States there is more space where
nobody is than where anybody is. Here, you think, is the country
she was talking about.

That easy impression, however, is wholly misleading. The plains
are as historically dense and as geographically, botanically, and
zoologically complex as most other parts of the nation and the
world. Anyone who stops his car and walks around for an hour
will get some inkling of the range of topology and life forms within
even an acre or two, and a little reflection will conjure up at least
a few famous events and characters associated with this country:
George Custer, Wyatt Earp, and Buffalo Bill Cody, cattle drovers

and railroad workers, Roman Nose, Black Kettle and the Sand Creek massacre, Marshal Dillon and Festus, Dorothy, Auntie Em, and Toto.

These are hints of a far greater ecological, historical, and mythic complexity. The central plains cover a little less than a hundred thousand square miles. They rise gradually in altitude from about a thousand feet above sea level in the middle of Kansas to more than six thousand feet about fifty miles east of the Rockies, then they dip slightly into a trough at the base of the mountains. The eastern portion is called the "low plains," and the western, beyond about the 100th meridian, the "high plains." As one moves westward and upward, the terrain gradually levels out, and the dominant indigenous grasses and forbs (where they are allowed to grow) are progressively shorter and sparser. Timber is common in the east and especially thick in the creases between the rolling hills, but on the high plains trees are usually found only along the more dependable streams. The long, low swells of land have reminded many outlanders of the ocean. When an army unit came in sight of the timbered bottoms of the Republican River after riding for four days in 1849 without seeing a tree, an Irish private called out joyfully, *"Be Jesus* we're in sight of land again!"[1]

Travelers traditionally have been impressed, and sometimes stultified, by the apparent topographical sameness of the central plains, especially the western reaches, but in fact every part of this country, high plains and low, is an intricate mosaic of smaller, quite varied environments.[2] Seven percent or so of the land is part of an elaborate system of watercourses.[3] The main rivers flow generally eastward. The largest are the Platte and the Arkansas. Between them, the Kansas River is formed by the convergence of the Saline and Smoky Hill Rivers, both of which rise near the Colorado-Kansas border. Downstream from that confluence, the Kansas is joined by the Solomon and Republican Rivers, both of them formed by several forks flowing through southwestern Nebraska and northwestern Kansas. Other streams—the Big Sandy (or Sand Creek), the Purgatory (or Purgatoire) River, Walnut and Pawnee Creeks—drain into the Arkansas in eastern Colorado and western Kansas. These rivers and streams take much or all of their water from many small, erratically flowing creeks, some of them spring-fed.

Thus, besides the broadscale differences between the low plains to the east and the high plains to the west, there is this other fundamental division throughout the region: there are lowlands and uplands, scores of watercourses, from wide rivers to nameless gulches and seeps, and drier terrain above that drains into them. The soil composition of the uplands and lowlands usually differs considerably, as does the vegetation. The contrast in plant life is especially striking on the high plains, where the drier uplands support only the more stunted grasses while the moister stream bottoms provide a welcoming environment for lusher, taller flora that normally are found well to the east. Lowlands and uplands are quite different habitats that offer their own distinct opportunities and threats to plains creatures—including, as will be seen, people.

These are only a few of the grander and more obvious distinctions. Terrain can vary considerably within an acre or so. Even on the seemingly uniform shortgrass plains, there are significant variations in the soil's composition and its ability to hold water. The slopes running down toward streams have different drainage and often different soils from both the flatter highlands and the riverine bottoms. Much of the uplands is dotted with depressions, some quite large, that fill with rainwater during the spring and summer. Gullies and springs have their own distinctive natures. The central plains are a topological and ecological patchwork.

Every part of the plains, however, can change profoundly from year to year in response to one vital resource—rainfall. The famous "line of semi-aridity" falls roughly along the 98th meridian, just beyond present-day Salina, Kansas. West of it the average annual rainfall drops below twenty inches. However, this generalization, while revealing, is also extremely deceptive. Within a typical year it rains far more in some months than in others: the average for July is usually six or seven times that of January. The average annual precipitation, furthermore, is figured from numbers that can vary wildly from year to year. The upper Arkansas River valley near Pueblo, Colorado, for instance, received an average of 1.87 inches in July between 1905 and 1958. The yearly totals for that month, however, ranged from 0.13 to 5.26 inches.[4] Not even that tells the whole story. Summer rains often arrive as violent, torrential storms. It is not unprecedented for an area to receive a third of its annual rain in a day and up to a fourth of it in one hour. Most of that water washes away, worthless to whatever or whoever depends on it. In other words, as you move west, rainfall both declines and becomes more erratic. You get less of what you have to have, and you cannot depend even on that.

These variables—altitude, topology, soil, precipitation, and others—combine in numberless ways. The varied results offer broad ranges of opportunities and difficulties for plants and animals. There are floral "communities" and "societies," some in patterns as complex as the human minglings in ethnically diverse neighborhoods of Chicago and New York City. The dominant blue grama of the short-grass plains often is interspersed with buffalo grass, false buffalo grass, hairy grama, squirreltail, little barley, western wheatgrass, needlegrass, sand dropseed, red and purple three-awn, sun sedge, yucca, side-oats grama, and little bluestem, not to mention prairie cat's-foot, milk vetch, gumweed, blazing star, velvety goldenrod, and the occasional prairie coneflower and puccoon. Living over, among, and under these plants is an equally diverse menagerie of mammals, birds, reptiles, amphibians, insects, rodents, and invertebrates—from bison, the largest land animals in the western hemisphere, to pocket mice and nematodes. How these various life forms respond to their particular surroundings in turn affects these creatures' relationships among themselves as well as the shape and makeup of the land. All those plants and creatures and all their intertwined relationships in turn are affected by variations in rainfall and by longer swings in climate.

It's complicated, and making it much more so has been the presence of people. Humans have been living on the central plains for at least twelve thousand years.[5] The earliest, so far as we know, were hunters of the Clovis and Folsom cultures, from about 12,000 to 8000 B.C., who preyed on the vast congregations of mammoths, bison, horses, deer, elk, and camels that flourished during the Pleistocene era. With the waning of the Pleistocene came a warmer, much drier period, the Altithermal, 6000 B.C. to 1500 B.C. Most of the larger Pleistocene species vanished, and plains peoples turned to more diversified means of feeding themselves. They stayed more in villages, foraging among a wide variety of wild plants and hunting "almost anything . . . that walked, crawled, flew, or swam."[6] For the first time pottery appears in the record. At the end of the Altithermal, moister conditions returned. Beginning around A.D. 1000, the first plains farmers appeared along the Smoky Hill, Republican, and Solomon Rivers. Over the next few centuries there flourished a remarkable agrarian culture that spread eventually into the Colorado high plains and over much of Nebraska and western Iowa. These farmers lived in large rectangular wattle-and-daub houses. They hunted deer, pronghorn, bison, and other game, gathered plants and mussels, and cultivated corn, beans, squash, and sunflowers. The population boomed. In fact, the Native American population during these years seems to have been larger than at any time before or after, including the later years of mass invasions from the east by the Lakotas and others. After about A.D. 1200, the archeological record once again begins to grow sketchy, probably reflecting the dramatic slackening of rainfall over the next three centuries and more.

This general chronology barely suggests the rich, varied patterns from these millenia. There are clear and recurring signs of an erratic climate forcing major adjustments, especially on the high plains to the west. At Signal Butte, along the North Platte River in southern Wyoming, excavations have revealed three successive occupations, the most recent three to five hundred years old and the earliest from at least three thousand years ago. In the layers showing a human influence, the detria of daily life—knapped flint, animal bones, charred cobs of maize, bits of pottery—are embedded in dark humus produced during relatively rainy times. Separating these strata are quite different ones, each made up of eighteen to twenty-four inches of windblown sand signifying deep droughts. These layers are "culturally sterile," empty of any hint of people's presence.[7]

Perhaps these tell of a general evacuation, but more likely inhabitants were simply turning to alternative lifeways to survive. Eyewitness accounts from more historically accessible periods tell of plains peoples relying on diverse and complex means of subsistence that would leave little or no evidence for archeologists. Early Spanish explorers found not only village-dwelling farmers but also drifting hunters, whom they called *Querechos*, nomads who had no pottery, lived in painted tents, used dogs as beasts of burden, and hunted bison with arrows tipped with flint that they chipped with their teeth. In winter the *Querechos* fled to the more hospitable edges of the high plains. A leading authority on the period just prior to European contact argues that Indians of that time were able to live year-round even on the arid, stormblown high plains by shifting residence with the seasons, from the grassy highlands in the summer to protected winter camps along the streams.[8] However they coped with their surroundings, various peoples also expanded their grasp of resources through trading networks within and beyond the plains. Some villages apparently provided chert and dolomite to neighbors. Hunters exported bison hides, and probably meat, southwestward to Pueblo country and east to the Mississippi valley. In exchange they received a variety of items. Burial sites contain marine shells from the Gulf coast, snail shells from the Ohio valley, and mica from the Appalachians.[9]

Thus, for dozens of centuries plains peoples had worked out intricate arrangements for living within the complex, changing, and sometimes precarious world of the central plains. Then, in the mid-1500s, a new element—the arrival of Europeans—brought far greater complications. The consequences can be divided crudely into two categories. First, Native American groups were displaced, directly and indirectly, by pressure from expanding white societies. The Euro-Americans, pressing on the plains from the south, north, and especially the east, remade the land for their own needs and pushed Indians before them, deepening old rivalries among native peoples and triggering new ones. Second, however, the newcomers brought the Indians unforseen opportunities. In particular they carried with them a remarkable array of goods and life forms that native peoples could put to their advantage. The Euro-American invasion, that is, had countervailing results. It severely reduced the land and other crucial resources available to Indians; it simultaneously introduced other resources and dramatically expanded the possibilities of what could be done with them.

Several Indian groups were shoved onto the plains from the east by the intensifying competition for land. When he was a young man, a fifty-year-old Lakota told a government agent in 1859, he had visited settlements of his kinsmen as well as Sac and Fox in Wisconsin, Michigan, and Illinois. Only a handful of whites were there. "But see!" he went on, "the whites [now] cover all of these lands . . . and also the lands of the Poncas, Omahas, and Pawnees." The same would soon happen to his own country, he predicted. That "stated pretty accurately" the trend of events, the agent thought.[10] The same compacting force, however, introduced manufactured cloth for dress and housing, metal blades, points, awls, scrapers, guns and ammunition, iron pots, pipes, beads, and paint, and a long menu of potables and edibles, from coffee and whiskey to sugar and rice. Whites also brought horses. This one addition expanded enormously the geographical range and pace of trade and the capacity to hunt and wage war. Before horses had actually done much work, they had, in a sense, already made over the region. The plains as potential living space—as an area of imagined possibilities—was transformed.

The "push" of displacement and the "pull" of new opportunities combined to scramble the tribal populations on the plains. The Lakotas, who by the 1850s were mourning their own dispossession, forced others into the mountains as they fought to control the bison herds on the northern plains. Some of these displaced persons may have been the Shoshonean peoples who would become the Comanches. In any case, the Comanches migrated from the northern Rockies and Great Basin onto the southern plains by the early 1700s. By 1800, having acquired huge numbers of horses, they dominated the country from below the Arkansas River to the Edwards Plateau in Texas. Although the Kiowas seem to have linguistic and cultural affinities to southwestern groups, their tradition tells of their moving from the northern Rockies to the Black Hills, from which they were in turn driven southward by tribes crowding in from the east. There they turned increasingly to trading and raiding on horseback with their new allies, the Comanches. Less powerful tribes of the upper Missouri valley, such as the Arikara, were pressed inexorably onto the plains and found themselves virtual wards of the more numerous Lakotas.

The Cheyennes, who play prominent roles in the essays that follow, moved westward from the Missouri River in the late 1700s and early 1800s, somewhat later than the Lakotas. Stopping first at the Black Hills, they next migrated southward around the Platte River, pressured by the Lakota and drawn to the role of middlemen who shuttled between the horse-rich tribes to the south and the Missouri's farming and trading villages.[11] Along the Missouri's middle reaches and on the eastern plains were sedentary groups. Some, notably the Pawnees, Otos, and Omahas, had been there for generations. Others, like the Sac and Fox and Potawatomies, were driven there from the Great Lakes country and Ohio valley. All of these now felt the pressure from tribes newly arrived on the western plains.

Accompanying the Indians were Euro-Americans, tugged and shoved by forces similar to those moving the Indians. French traders were testing the possibilities on the central plains by the early 1700s. By the last decades of that century British agents, operating out of upper Missouri villages, were sending goods throughout the region. New Mexican *comancheros* ranged from the south plains northward to the Platte, where a party was seen doing business as late as 1858. Following Lewis and Clark, American firms began feeling their way into the trade, first on the upper Missouri and then in the central Rockies and on the plains. Whites in far larger numbers moved back and forth across this country, some of them emigrating to the Pacific coast and others carrying goods to and from markets in the southwest. By the mid-1800s white farmers, compelled partly by diminishing land and rising prices to the east, were edging onto the eastern plains and looking covetously toward central Kansas and Nebraska and even farther.

This extraordinary shuffling of human power and populations naturally required equally sweeping adjustments by everyone involved. Facing new challenges in unfamiliar settings, natives and whites all had to devise new means of supporting themselves and of dealing with the stresses of new circumstances. As people moved about and adapted to their changed situation, they in turn had profound effects on the non-human world of the central plains—the natural setting that was changing anyway by the dynamic of its own parts and through regional climatic swings.

Varied peoples of unequal power adapted in their own ways while contesting with each other for shrinking resources and expanding opportunities within diverse and changing environments shaped by an erratic climate: this was not a simple story. The tangle and weave of events and influences make the history of the central plains as complex as that of any place on earth. Historians ought to approach it with a healthy trepidation.

At the very least, anyone trying to understand that history should begin with a few ground rules. First, the famous episodes of the 1800s were not the opening of the region's history. They were accelerated changes in a place that was centuries-deep in dynamic developments. Second, the events of those years were made by a large cast of human groups that included white pioneers and diverse Indian peoples, each with an individual story but all of them caught up the process of emigration, adaptation, accommodation, and conflict. Third, those human actions in turn are incomprehensible apart from the environment in which they happened. Plants and animals were not just the backdrop for the peopling of the plains or merely motivators for the acts of nomads and sodbusters. They were, in some sense, actors themselves. They pursued their own needs, and so doing they helped define the terms of others' actions and influenced the course of human events.

These four essays are a modest attempt at considering a few connections at work among the historical changes on the central plains. This is a paradoxical enterprise. Obviously no one can come close to knowing all the parts—the peoples and their environments—and the relationships among them. Constructing a narrative necessarily requires choosing and stringing together only a few pieces of what **is** known. In other words, to tell a story arguing for inclusiveness, you have to be exclusive.[12] Nevertheless, it is worthwhile to work within that paradox to encourage a broader perspective in writing the history of the American West. These essays argue the wrongheadedness of the tendency to separate and categorize too cleanly the elements of that history—people and nature, whites and Indians, and the West of prehistory, the frontier, and the modern day.

The approach I am suggesting demands at least some attention to work done in other disciplines. From time to time I have brought in a smattering of scholarship from the fields of anthropology, environmental and animal sciences, literature, and literary criticism. I hope my dabbling will suggest a few of the ways the insights of others can expand our historical understanding of the West.

The first essay, "Land," concerns the interaction among people, their ambitions, and the environmental settings in which they pursued those goals. Specifically, it looks at some of the consequences of new peoples moving onto the central plains in the previous century. The second essay, "Animals," builds on the first by trying to explain one of the most famous changes of that time and place—the precipitous decline in the population of the plains bison. "Families," the third essay, considers how this ubiquitous human institution, the family, adapted to the new and changing world of the plains, even as it shaped profoundly its physical and social environmnent. The final essay, "Stories," speculates on how human perception and imagination have had a sweeping and continuing influence on the West, including the environment, creatures, and institutions that are at the center of the other essays. The theme throughout is the intricate weave of ecology, human actions, and people's mental reading of the world around them.

1
Land

For it is he who gave me unerring knowledge of what exists,
to know the structure of the world and the activity of the elements;
the beginning and end and middle of times,
the alternations of the solstices and the changes of the seasons,
the cycles of the year and the constellations of the stars,
the natures of animals and the tempers of wild animals,
the powers of spirits and the thoughts of human beings,
the varieties of plants and the virtues of roots . . .
Wisdom of Solomon, 7:17-20

For every atom lost to the sea, the prairie pulls another out of decaying
rock. The only truth is that its creatures must suck hard, live fast,
and die often, lest its losses exceed its gains.
Aldo Leopold, *A Sand County Almanac*

"The astonishing thing about the earth. . .," according to Lewis Thomas, "is that it is alive."[1] He was writing about our planet as seen from the moon—a useful perspective for reminding ourselves of the connectedness of things in the world around us. No one would deny that people and their environments have something to do with one another; but, just as obviously, we pay too little attention to the implications. Humans and non-humans are bound together in intricate webs of mutual influence. So are their stories.

Western historians have always paid plenty of attention to the environment. Usually, however, their approach has been doubly misleading. They treat people and their surroundings as if they were separate and independent. The line between "man" and "nature" is

13

clear and distinct; and the physical world outside people has been mostly something that inspires human action. Families sell farms and pile into wagons after hearing tales of Oregonian wonders. Men look hungrily at herds of bison and untilled soil, then go to work. The environment in these stories is essentially passive.

The land has always been more of a participant than that. It is not a matter of imagination and volition—grasses do not wonder whether they ought to bloom—yet plants and animals do pursue their needs. They fashion accommodations with their surroundings. When impinged upon, they respond. Even soil is both a medium and a collaborator in intricate interchanges with organisms and chemical compounds. In short, every part of an environment interacts with whatever is around it, setting limits for other life and having limits set for itself. When people act, they do so within this infinitely larger set of dynamic, related associations.

The theme of this essay is the interaction among people, the plants and animals around them, and the natural processes at work on all of them. The setting is the central plains in the middle of the last century, years greatly consequential for all actors—nomads and freighters, mules and horses, grasses and cottonwoods.

In the summer of 1840, great numbers of plains Indians gathered in a broad bottom along the Arkansas River a few miles below Bent's Fort. These bands of Cheyennes, Arapahoes, Kiowas, Comanches, and Plains Apaches came together to seal a peace ending years of bloody, bitter conflict. Kiowas and Comanches, led by Little Mountain, Sitting Bear, Bull Hump, and Shavehead, celebrated the new alliance by giving the Cheyennes and Arapahoes so many horses that their former enemies lacked the ropes to lead them away. The Cheyennes, with their leaders, High Backed Wolf, Little Old Man, and White Antelope, responded with gifts of brass kettles, calico, blankets, and guns, and with a feast of bison, venison, rice, dried apples, and corn meal sweetened with New Orleans molasses. This assemblage at a spot the Cheyennes still call "Giving Presents to One Another Across the River" was one of the great moments in the history of these peoples. It was their equivalent of the Congress of Vienna or the Treaty of Versailles—with the difference that this alliance has lasted a good bit longer.[2]

As that peace-making was taking place, another event was occurring about five hundred miles to the northeast. Residents of far-western Missouri formed the Platte County Western Emigration Society, dedicated to organizing the first overland party to California. Encouraged by tall talk from a returned trapper, Antoine Robidoux, members of the society spread the word, put their farms up for sale, and prepared to rendezvous the next spring in Sapling Grove, Kansas. From there they planned to take the road westward up the Platte River to the promised land.

Except for their timing, these two episodes would seem to have nothing in common. In fact, they were pivotal moments in the entwined histories of the peoples who together were transforming the central plains in the mid-nineteenth century.

This is the story of two invasions. Between the 1820s and the 1860s, two peoples whose lifeways could hardly have been more different moved into and across the central plains. Both were drawn westward by alluring opportunities. Both set in motion complicated chains of changes in the world around them. Those changes rippled outward in space and time; in some ways the consequences are still with us. Tracing those developments, we can learn much about the plains and their history—and, beyond that, about the West at large.

In the first of those invasions, a large and growing population of Native Americans moved into the central plains between 1820 and 1850. The most important of these groups, the Cheyennes, followed a long, looping path from villages in present North Dakota, first to the Black Hills and then farther south by the 1820s into the country along and below the Platte River. Along the way they formed a close alliance with the Arapahoes, then with the Lakotas, another group of invaders who ranged south of the Platte but who concentrated north of that river.

The Cheyennes were pushed into this country by pressure from the east, but they were also one of many peoples over the last two hundred years who have been lured onto the plains by what they believed were grand opportunities. They were drawn by the vast herds of bison, but they also saw the chance to become middlemen in a sprawling trading system that reached from New Mexico to Canada. Positioned in the country south of the Black Hills, they could move goods and horses from the Comanches and other tribes below them to the trade fairs of the Missouri valley, then carry other items back to rendezvous in the south. The Cheyennes became key figures facilitating the flow of trade over a region as large as that

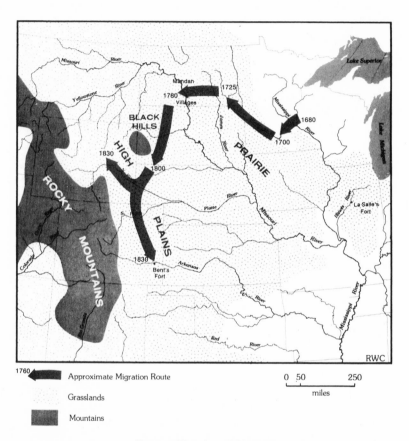

Cheyenne Migrations, 1680–1850

(Map from E. Adamson Hoebel, The Cheyennes: Indians of the Great Plains,
New York: Harcourt Brace Javanovich College Publishers, 1978)

between Georgia and New York. By 1820, when Steven Long visited a large Indian trading camp near present-day Denver, Cheyenne middlemen had been meeting annually for at least a few years with Arapahoes and Kiowas to exchange British goods for horses. The next year Jacob Fowler reported from the Arkansas that Arapahoes had sent large numbers of horses north with Cheyenne traders.[3]

To exploit that opportunity, Cheyennes were pulled steadily southward. They were attracted both by the large herds of wild horses and those kept by the Comanches and by a warmer climate more congenial for themselves and their animals.[4] By the late 1820s they had another reason to stay as close as possible to the Arkansas valley. Charles and William Bent and their partner, Ceran St. Vrain, began trading there, and once Bent's Fort was built in 1833, the Southern Cheyennes directed their business mainly through that post.

As they gravitated to the south, however, the Cheyennes and their Arapaho allies naturally found themselves increasingly in conflict with Indians already there—the Kiowas, the plains Apaches, and the Comanches, as well as Pawnees who periodically made hunting forays into this country. Throughout the 1820s and 1830s, these peoples wrestled for control of the upper Arkansas valley. The peacemaking of 1840, culminating with the exchange of gifts along the river near Bent's Fort, marked the end of that warfare. The invasion of the Cheyennes was accomplished—although their troubles were hardly at an end.

Thus, the period between 1820 and 1840 was one of the most momentous and complex in the history of the Great Plains, a time of migration and displacement, competition, territorial struggles and diplomatic maneuvering. Of the many results, one was especially important: a dramatic rise in population. This might seem odd, since most Indians, battered by diseases introduced by Euro-Americans, were suffering devastating declines in their numbers; but on the central plains there were *more* Indians, not fewer, not because plains Indians were exempt from those scourges but because so many newcomers were arriving in the country. Diseases hit the region hard after 1849, but nonetheless the effective population—the number of people, that is, who were living in and using the resources of this area at various times of the years—may have doubled between 1820 and the 1850s, from about eight thousand to as many as twenty thousand.[5] Those are not large numbers by our standards; there are nearly twenty thousand people living today in Garden City, Kansas, for instance. By the terms of life among plains people of that time, however, this rise in population was a stunning development. It was an invasion of major proportions and an event heavy with implications for this land and its people.

Simultaneous with this Native American invasion was another, this one of Euro-Americans—the great overland migration toward the Pacific coast and the growing surge of freighting to the southwest. This second wave of newcomers did not occupy the area in the same sense as the Indians. They were transient invaders, but invaders nonetheless. They crowded temporarily into parts of the country, moving up and down the two rivers, the Platte and Arkansas, that formed the northern and southern boundaries of the central plains. They used some of the land's most vital resources during several months of each year; and in numbers, at least, this invasion dwarfed the other.

It began in the 1820s, with the start of the Santa Fe trade. For the first ten years or so, the number of wagons moving along the Arkansas River road between Missouri and New Mexico fluctuated between twenty-five and 130. Trade and military traffic picked up in the 1840s, especially with the Mexican War in 1846. More than 350 wagons made the trip that year. Up until then shipments from the United States were mainly calico, groceries, leather goods, and *bayeta*, (a heavy scarlet cloth New Mexican women used to make petticoats), and in return the southwest sent mules, furs, and some specie. With gold strikes in the southwest the trade diversified, and by 1850 five or six hundred wagons were carrying the usual loads, plus ammunition, whiskey, flour, and hardware. As southwestern wool production increased, herds of sheep were taken westward and cargoes of raw wool and skins were carried back. By the end of the 1850s more than eighteen hundred wagons were lumbering back and forth along the road with all the old loads, plus mining equipment, canned goods, and bottled beer.[6]

In the meantime emigrants to the Pacific coast were moving up the Platte River road. About twenty thousand of them made the trip between 1841 and 1848. Then the gold rush sent a huge surge over the trail—as many as 185,000 persons between 1849 and 1852. "One could look back for miles and miles on a line of wagons, the sinuous line . . . resembling a great serpent crawling and wriggling up the valley," an overlander wrote in 1852.[7] The human tide then slackened, but still nearly ninety thousand more made the crossing during the next six years, for a grand total of nearly three hundred thousand men, women, and children plodding their way up the Platte valley between 1841 and 1859. This was one of the continent's greatest human migrations of the nineteenth century. Its pilgrims roughly equalled the population in 1850 of all of Wisconsin, or West Virginia, or Arkansas and Florida combined.[8]

These two developments—the overland flow of Pacific-bound settlers and the emigration of Indian peoples onto the plains—are among the most familiar in western history. Almost always, however, they are considered separately, as if they had only a glancing relation to each other. Somehow an obvious point has been largely overlooked—that these were simultaneous, interrelated events with wide-ranging consequences for that part of the West where they overlapped, the central portion of the Great Plains.

Once we think of these twin migrations as part of the same story, at least one implication quickly becomes obvious. The coming of the Indian and white invaders represented a massive intrusion of new life forms onto the central plains. It was a varied assemblage: people, mules, oxen, horses, dogs, sheep, and a selection of other minor players. Some of these humans and animals tried to make the plains their permanent home; others passed through to somewhere else; all tried to draw what they needed from the country. Taken together, this wave of new arrivals created one of the greatest potential forces of environmental change in the region's recorded human history.

The repercussions were profound for much of what lived on the plains, but most obviously for those people, the new Indians and old, who called the plains home and who relied most heavily on that environment. Their story can tell us a lot about what it meant—and continues to mean—to live on the plains.

When the Cheyennes left the Missouri valley to take up a life as pastoral hunters and traders, they learned a lesson familiar to students of western history. If you chase opportunity into new country, this lesson goes, you will have to commit yourself to a new way of life, and that commitment, regardless of how plentiful the opportunity, will almost certainly involve new and probably unforeseen limitations. In seeking new things that you *can* do, you are almost certain to find that there are also new things you *cannot*.

Some of these new limitations were essentially social and political. In the more humid east, large numbers of Cheyennes had been able to live together in permanent villages. The plains, however, required them to break up into smaller groups and to move around as they pursued game and used different parts of the region at different times of the year. Emigration, in other words, brought with it fragmentation, a kind of social fission. In high summer the Cheyennes could reassemble in something resembling the old numbers. It was then they conducted their great hunt and observed rituals of renewal. The rest of the year was spent in much smaller gatherings— bands and "camps." A few of the implications of this social fracturing will be discussed in the next two essays. Here, it's worth noting that the pursuit of opportunities carried with it a threat to the Cheyennes' collective identity, their sense of who they were.[9]

Other limitations—the ones emphasized in this essay—concerned the Cheyennes' ways of making a living. When they moved on the plains, the Cheyennes adopted a dual economy of hunting and pastoralism. Their commitment to that way of life brought with it two obvious limitations. As hunters, they had to remain within striking distance of an adequate amount of prey—deer, elk, antelope, bear, and above all bison—that provided their food, shelter, trade, and other needs. Despite the apparent abundance of game, this requirement led to considerable difficulties, as will be seen in the following essay.

The second aspect of the Cheyenne economy, its pastoral side, also demanded considerable adaptations. There is a substantial literature on nomadic pastoral cultures that have operated, some of them for ten millenia, in settings that vary from the Sahara and the Asian steppes to mountain plateaus and northern Scandanavia. For all their differences, these peoples all have lived by a delicate balancing of three sets of needs: their own, their herds', and those of their environmental settings. Survival has depended on an exceptionally dense ecological knowledge and the ability to adjust within circumstances that allow very little room to maneuver. Such delicate arrangements, in turn, imply that each people endured a long and chancy period of trial and error as individuals learned how to make it in their own peculiar world.[10]

The Cheyennes were attempting what would have been, under ideal conditions, a complicated and potentially treacherous transition in lifeways. As their most fundamental demand, they had to be mobile enough to hunt and to seek out those parts of the plains best suiting the opportunities of the moment. That in turn left the Indians closely reliant on their horses. Substantial numbers were needed, given the heavy losses from disease, theft, and harsh weather; the tribes of the central and southern plains supported from five to thirteen horses per person.[11] Consequently, the Cheyennes and their neighbors were left closely dependent on the resources those horses had to have. The shift, as James F. Downs has emphasized, was much more than adopting an efficient means of hunting and moving about. More than simply a tool, a horse was "a large animal with distinctive patterns of behavior to which man must adjust before [its] various potentials . . . can be made useful . . . ."[12]

Such a statement might seem ridiculously obvious, but in fact its implications are enormous and as the Cheyennes discovered often troubling. As they pursued their new lifeways, the pastoralists found themselves restricted by the requirements of their animals.[13] Most important, the Cheyennes had to follow a particular annual cycle. In the spring they fattened their horses in the grasses along the rivers. That forage was a remarkably diverse collection of flora. There were buffalo grass and grama grass, the dominant covering of the high plains, as well as a mix of low shrubs and different kinds of forbs. There were also "midgrasses" and "tallgrasses," little bluestem the most prominent but also big bluestem, side-oats grama, and others. Plants like these were common on the lower plains of eastern Kansas and Nebraska, but on the higher plains to the west they were found almost entirely along streams, where they were protected from the harshest weather and were supported by moister soil and a shallower water table. River valleys were protected corridors where these dominant eastern grasses extruded much farther westward than they normally could. In spots these eastern river grasses grew in lush profusion. On Bear Creek, south of Fort Laramie, soldiers once cut the head-high "slough grass" with butcher knives and laid it down to make a causeway across a bog for them and their horses.[14]

The eastern grasses growing along the rivers sprouted quite early, often by the first day of March. The Indians' horses, weak from winter's deprivations, could begin to build back their strength by grazing the river bottoms in March and April. In late spring and early summer Indian pastoralists moved their animals onto the highlands between the streams. This was shortgrass country, dominated by buffalo grass and blue grama. These grasses had adapted to the erratic high plains weather by greening out later, biding their time, thus avoiding a killing blow from storms that often bellowed onto the high plains after an early warm spell. Shortgrasses were not nearly as dense as the river cover—an early traveler said he could spot a rattlesnake at fifty yards—but once they had begun to grow, by May or early June, they became highly nutritious.[15] The highlands then became a gigantic pasture where the Indians could congregate in large numbers and their horses graze throughout the summer. Those also were the months of the great bison hunt and the season when the many camps and bands drew together for religious ceremonies. In the fall, Indians broke up into small camps and drifted back toward the stream valleys.

We are used to thinking of plains Indians as nomadic hunters who patterned their lives to follow the herds of bison that provided so many of the Native Americans' own immediate needs. It is just as accurate to imagine them as arranging their movements according to what their horses had to have. They spent the year chasing grass, basically.

Another lesson can be learned here. Historians today are quick to say that there is no such thing as "the West." The land west of the Missouri is better understood as a collection of subregions, including the Great Plains, and within those, sub-subregions, like the central plains. However, as the Cheyennes discovered, it goes well beyond that. Even those smaller areas are composed of quite different parts—microenvironments—each with its own opportunities and its own limitations. In this case the central plains are made up of rivers and valleys and highlands, very different settings with different resources and different dangers. Unless it is closely adapted to one of these particular parts, any species will have to learn to rely on most or all of those varied habitats, using each as best it can. When all goes well in every one of those microenvironments, life can be grand; but if any one of them fails, things get complicated.

Thus, the Cheyennes soon found that their move to the plains was in a way paradoxical. In one sense they were liberated into a country where they could range over a far larger area; but at certain times they were forced to depend on a few limited parts of that huge new home. They discovered that the Great Plains, those wide open spaces, were sometimes one of the most confining places to live on the continent.

That point was made most dramatically during the plains winter. From November through February, the Great Plains could be (and still can be) one of the harshest and most dangerous environments in the United States.[16] Periods of moderate temperatures are punctuated by storms with thick swirlings of snow and powerful frigid winds that sweep across the landscape and threaten even the best-adapted creatures. Winter's danger was largely unappreciated by whites at the time because few whites were on the plains when the weather turned nasty. The earliest accounts of the cold time came from soldiers, like Dodge, and from freighters who were sometimes caught far from home. Teamsters struck by early storms burned their wagons to keep warm but still arrived in the settlements looking "more like icicles of the north pole than human beings."[17] Survival away from shelter for more than a few days was unimaginable. "It snowed all the afternoon. Blew up awfull cold in the evening. . . . River froze nearly across," a freighter told his diary. Three days later his mood darkened: "Last night it snowed all night. . . . We are 80 miles from wood and no buffalo chips. If we get away from here you will hear from me."[18]

He made it, but like many others in the same situation, he watched some of his animals freeze to death. On two separate occasions between 1844 and 1854 freighters along the Arkansas lost more than three hundred mules when caught in early winter storms.[19] During the Mexican War the army took over Fort Mann, an outpost near the future site of Dodge City built to provide protection and repairs for freighters. Of seventy-five horses there in November 1847, only about a dozen, "barely able to stand," were alive in mid-January. All but one hundred of the eight hundred oxen had died, and only a half-dozen of 144 mules remained. Scurvy-ridden soldiers watched packs of grateful wolves gorging themselves on the frozen carrion.[20]

One of the most vivid descriptions of winter conditions comes from a most unlikely source: Damon Runyon's father. In 1868, twelve years before siring the famous journalist whose stories inspired the musical and movie *Guys and Dolls*, Alfred Runyan wrote a newspaper dispatch from the field while serving with a volunteer Kansas cavalry unit on the highlands north of the Arkansas River:

> Our horses were now so weak for want of corn that we had to
> walk nearly all the time. The only food they got was by
> digging under nearly fourteen inches of snow; and as the men

were also weak for want of proper food, we had to march
very slow. We camped that night on Round Pond Creek, a
small stream, but with a great deal of timber on it. Here the
men suffered more than at any other time; and as it snowed
all that night and the next day, it being also very cold, and
the men being starved, a great many almost barefoot, they
suffered almost beyond human endurance. Hundreds would
have given anything they possessed for one good meal. I
have seen five dollars offered for one small piece of buffalo
meat, the size of a silver dollar. One man gave a good pair of
buckskin gloves for one hard-tack. . . . Hunters went for
buffalo, but returned unsuccessful, as there were none to be
seen. . . . [The men] were all exposed to the bitter fury of the
storm, without tents, and some of them froze their almost
naked feet very badly that night. The men began to talk of
the good qualities of horse and mule meat.[21]

Runyan and his fellows were learning some hard seasonal truths.
For anyone hoping to live on the plains during the winter, the most
immediate danger came from the vicious storms like the one that
caught Runyon's unit, the "northers" that swept over the land rapidly and with little warning. They lasted up to a few days, sometimes
dropping considerable snow, and they were usually followed by several days of deep, killing cold. Survival ultimately depended on finding some kind of shelter, which was no simple task in that huge,
mostly flat and treeless region.

Besides this dramatic threat, there was another nagging problem.
During the colder weather from October to March, Indians and horses
all required more energy, particularly on the exposed uplands. Unfortunately, the fuel for that energy was being partially withdrawn.
Rainfall virtually stopped in winter, and the splendidly adapted grama
and buffalo grasses took a good portion of their nutrients underground, so by December this dominant forage offered less than half
of its summer protein. Shortgrass, to be sure, was still the horses'
best available food by far. Unlike the midgrasses and tallgrasses of
the streambeds, which lost virtually all their nutritive clout by
autumn's end, grama and buffalo grasses, even with their reduced
protein, cured naturally into nourishing fodder. They were like God's
hay. Nonetheless, that winter pasture was a lot less valuable than in
summer. Every square yard of grass was providing fewer calories just

at that point when each animal had to have more, simply to keep pace with the cold. This nutritive crunch naturally was greatest during storms and the coldest snaps. Horses had to cover more ground merely to keep the inner fires burning—movement that cost more energy when they could least afford it. Spending calories by hunting or hauling freight or marching only deepened the deficit.

Here was the winter dilemma. It was the season posing grave periodic threats to life; and beyond that—all animals, people included—had to have dependable access to more energy resources at the time when such resources were least available. Whites mostly avoided this dilemma simply by staying away, unless they were caught on the plains by their own foolishness or, like Runyon, were ordered there against their will. Indians, however, could not flee to the fringes of the country or import large supplies of food for themselves and their animals. They turned to another strategy, one described by Colonel Richard Dodge:

> In winter the Plains Indians, who are very susceptible to cold, remain in their teepees nearly all the time, going out only when forced to do so, and getting back as soon as possible to the pleasant warmth of their homes. Their ponies are wretchedly poor, and unable to bear their masters on any extended scout or hunt. . . .A day which would be death on the high Plains may scarcely be uncomfortably cold in a thicket at the bottom of a deep narrow canyon. Indians, plainsmen and all indigenous animals understand this perfectly, and fly to shelter at the first puff.[22]

The plains pastoralists, that is, met the annual crisis by breaking up into small groups and retreating to certain locations around the region. Those places had to meet four criteria. They had to have adequate forage. They had to have water for people and animals during the driest months of the year. They had to have timber that would provide fuel. Finally, these places had to be in terrain protected from the vicious wind that sucked the life out of anything warmblooded and unlucky enough to be on exposed ground during a storm.

Somehow Indians and their horses had to find those spots within the thousands of square miles of the central plains where those four conditions—forage, water, timber, and sheltering land forms—over-

lapped. All such places had one thing in common: they were lo-
cated along watercourses. The meandering rivers and creeks had
carved out protective bluffs and cutbanks. The riverine systems had
reliable water and grasses for winter forage. They also had stands of
trees that could be used both for fuel and as supplemental food for
horses. Not all parts of every stream had what the Indians needed,
of course. Winter camps were possible only where Indians found the
right combination of factors.

The most famous of such spots were the three "big timbers." The
largest and best known was the Big Timbers of the Arkansas, a band
of cottonwoods stretching up and down the river from the grove's
thickest point near modern Lamar, Colorado. The other two "big
timbers" were on the Smoky Hill (called by the Cheyenne the
"Bunch-of-Timber River") close to the present Kansas-Colorado line
and on the Republican River near present McCook, Nebraska. Besides these, there were other locations scattered along the Arkansas
and Platte Rivers and on such tributaries as the Purgatoire River,
Walnut Creek, Lodgepole (or Pole) Creek, and Sand Creek.

By now the Cheyenne's problem should be fairly clear, at least in
broad outline. Moving to the plains had offered them a great bounty
of the most alluring resources spread out across those great grassy
steppes; but to survive there the Cheyennes had to depend on a
portion of that country, to hunker down each winter in selected
parts of the riverine lowlands. Of those hunkering spots, two things
were immediately obvious. First, there were not many such places.
Those microenvironments represented only a tiny portion of the
millions of acres of the central plains, and they were limited as well
in their essential resources, especially grass and wood. Second, many of
those vital shelters of the Cheyennes were in precisely those parts of the
plains that the other wave of invaders, the overlanders, were using too.

In other words, the double invasion of mid-century, that unprecedented force of ecological change, came to be focused on one of
the country's vital microenvironments. This fact was missed by virtually all white observers—and it has been overlooked almost entirely by historians ever since—probably because of timing. Indians
moved into the river timberlands during the late fall, when whites
were secure and warm back in St. Louis or out in the Willamette
valley; when white emigrants and teamsters began plodding up the
river trails in mid-spring, Indians were heading for the high, open

plains. Whites in the summer, Indians in the winter: it was a kind of shuttle system of land use along the river bottoms. Once we recognize that pattern, and then begin to look for the results, one point becomes clear: Indians, white travelers, and their horses and oxen and mules were gobbling and burning the very bejabbers out of one of the most vital, vulnerable, and limited habitats of the Great Plains.

It is not easy to reconstruct an earlier plains environment and to trace its changes. What interests today's historian is not necessarily what caught the eye of a diarist a century and a half ago. The element of chance, from short-term fluctuations in rainfall to whether an observer happened to look at a certain stretch of road, can complicate the job considerably. Fortunately, the central plains were one of the most frequently traveled parts of the West during these years. Explorers, trappers, traders, army officers, sportsmen, businessmen, and scores of thousands of overland emigrants moved up and down the river trails and occasionally over the land between. Enough of these passers-by left accounts of their trips to offer at least some sense of the more noticeable changes under way.

Take, for instance, descriptions of the river woodlands. Along the Arkansas, the Big Timbers early in the nineteenth century seem to have stretched from close to the Purgatorie River (about La Junta, Colorado) nearly to the Kansas border, a total of nearly sixty miles.[23] For nearly 150 miles downstream from there, the sandy soil, the prairie fires in the broad and open basins unprotected by scarps, and the heavy springtime flooding kept the valley relatively timber-poor.[24] Even here, however, were stutterings of cottonwoods and sometimes heavy growth on the river's islands. Both Zebulon Pike and Jacob Fowler, in 1806 and 1821, noted remains of numerous camps along this part of the river, and passing through on their way to Santa Fe in 1825, Thomas Mather and Joseph Brown found that "the traveler . . . will always be sure of wood ."[25] At the eastern end of this thinly wooded part of the Arkansas, thick stands of elms, ashes, and other hardwoods grew along two prominent tributaries, Pawnee Fork and Walnut Creek. Upstream from the Big Timbers, between that great grove and the foothills of the Rockies, James noted "considerable" timber in 1820, and fifteen years later Dodge found skirts of cottonwoods lining the Arkansas and the creekbeds feeding into it.[26]

That picture was changing by the 1840s. Thomas J. Farnham wrote in 1839 of only occasional willows and "a few decrepit cottonwoods . . . at intervals of miles" in the valley below the Big Timbers.[27] Soldiers marching upriver in 1846 saw very few trees through here until they reached the mouth of Sand Creek. All sources indicate that the Big Timbers reached no farther than this spot, roughly thirty miles west of the state line at what is today Lamar, Colorado.[28] After another ten years the basin below the Timbers had lost its last noticeable growth; David Lindsey and Charles Post both called the Big Timbers the first shade they had seen for 175 miles—that is, since about Pawnee Fork.[29] By then the famous stand of cottonwoods itself was being thinned. In 1846 Susan Magoffin compared its taller, denser growth to that along the banks of the Mississippi, but seven years later Lieutenant E. G. Beckwith found the scattered trees across the bottoms "not thick enough to obstruct the view," and in five more years Charles Post found the two or three hundred cottonwoods low and scrubby.[30]

The changes along the Platte were even more striking. At the eastern end of the great valley of the Platte was Grand Island, about fifty miles downstream from the future site of Fort Kearny. In the 1830s this sixty-mile-long island held a mass of trees, including mulberry, oak, and other hardwoods. Above Grand Island, Edwin James wrote in 1820 of the broad Platte "embosoming many islands, some of which are broad and considerably extensive, and all of them covered with a growth of cottonwood and willows."[31] Henry Dodge found woods abundant on the south shore of this stretch in 1835. Farther on the high bluffs on both sides of the valley were cut by ravines that were "covered with timber of small growth" as well as wild plums and other fruits. At the forks of the Platte, Dodge climbed a hill for a loftier view of the trail he had just traveled. Looking back toward the east he saw that the hills rising above the river were "covered with scattered groves of timber; and we saw the feathery outline of some tall trees, at an immense distance, just shooting up above the horizon."[32]

However, when Osborne Cross traveled this same route in 1849, he thought that any tree "might be looked on as a curiosity." Over the next ten years travelers told of boiling tea with dry knotted grass and of finding "not a stick in that distance large enough for a switch."[33] Along the South Platte in 1842 John Charles Fremont remarked on the dramatic degeneration of timberlands.[34] Some timber could be found away from the Platte bottoms—cedars grew high on the bluffs, and there were stands of cottonwoods, occasionally quite thick, well up the feeder canyons—but along the main valley there was little to be found. Above Fort Kearny Richard Francis Burton in 1860 could squint and see some dwarf cedars, "distant black dots . . . which are yearly dimishing," but as he proceded "the vegetation dwindled, the river islands were bared of timber, and the only fuel became buffalo chip and last year's artemesia" (which he thought "a hideous growth").[35] The few surviving specimens naturally caught a traveler's eye. The South Platte had its "lone tree crossing," and along the North Platte in Nebraska were four other "lone trees," the most famous a large cedar near Ash Hollow that was hacked up badly over a few years before being felled around 1853.[36]

By then travelers almost never mentioned another source of fuel common in earlier years—driftwood. Pike, Long, Dodge, and Fowler all had been thankful for dead timber washed out of the tributary streams and left along the Platte and Arkansas, sometimes in considerable amounts. What today is called Two Butte Creek, entering the Arkansas from the south at Holly, Colorado, was called "Piles of Driftwood" by the Cheyennes because of the great tangle of trunks and branches near its mouth. By the latter 1850s emigrants mentioned such debris only as a rare and lucky find.[37]

Getting some feel for changes in pasturage is much trickier, but as with timber, a trend is clear enough. Early travelers on the Santa Fe trail generally found adequate or good grass for their teams. By the time Stephen Watts Kearny's Army of the West marched up the river in mid-summer of 1846, reports were mixed. Soldiers noted a variety of flora, including horsetail and virgin's bower, and forage that was sometimes plentiful; but in other places grazing was much poorer. George Rutledge Gibson complained that forage around the river's great bend "afford[ed] but scanty pasturage," and a bit farther the cavalry was "riding in all directions . . . in search of grass." He compared the area, suggestively, to "the sod of an old common." Prospects improved upriver, but as he approached the welcome shade of the Big Timbers, he once again noted sparse dry grass, then only the rarest forage mixed heavily with weeds, cacti, vines, sage, and poison oak.[38] By the late 1850s a traveler approaching the Timbers wrote that pasture had been failing for a hundred miles and an emigrant wife worried to her diary that her "cattle were nearly starved for grass."[39]

The Platte valley, one of North America's great pasturelands, showed a similar wear. In the early 1840s Thomas Jefferson Farnham thought that the Platte "assumes unequal importance" among western rivers: "But for it, it would be impossible for man or beast to travel those arid plains, destitute alike of wood, water and grass, save what of each is found along its course."[40] However, even before the gold rush the grass was starting to fade, and in 1849 two army officers told of some spots with grass up to the mules' eyes but other places where the covering was "very indifferent," "pastured . . . completely," or "eaten bare."[41] In subseqent years travelers were swimming their teams to islands and driving them as much as a mile from the road to find even the scantiest forage.[42]

When the questions move from the changes to their causes— when we shift from *what* to *how* and *who*—answers become more slippery. A lot of the damage certainly came from the white emigrant traffic pouring through the Platte and Arkansas valleys. Trouble began with the act of movement itself. The many thousands of iron-rimmed wheels bearing scores of thousands of tons of cargo, the hundreds of thousands of hooves of straining oxen and mules, the millions of booted steps of the overlanders—all these crushed and tore at the earth and the grasses. This was no narrow path across the plains. Wagons traveled in parallel columns as many as twelve abreast for protection and accommodation of traffic. As ruts wore dangerously deep, wagoneers steered slightly to one side, setting one set of wheels on the relatively protected center of the previous trail. This gradually widened the emigrant highway and its erosive effects. An aerial photograph from the 1950s of the Santa Fe trail west of Dodge City shows remnants of the old ruts forming a pathway gnawed into the land, a corrugation twenty-five or thirty times as wide as a nearby paved highway.[43]

Along the Platte the traffic by 1849 had formed a "whitened . . . trail as far as the eye could reach." This thoroughfare in 1854 had become "as broad as eight or ten common roads in the States." In spots the results were remarkable. "It appeared as though each train passing over had broken the roots of the grass, and the wind, blowing in only one direction, had blown the sand away, leaving a chasm seventy or eighty feet deep," an emigrant wrote in 1855, and added: "I should judge that about every train made a new road."[44] The long-term consequences of this sheer abrasion of migration were considerable. A modern study of a much smaller wagon road showed that the wheels' crush quickly killed off the dominant grasses. After the road was abandoned, revegetation proceeded slowly through a succession of weeds and short-lived grasses, from prostrate pigweed and Russian thistle through tumblegrass and squirreltail. It took at least twenty years, and in some cases fifty, for the nutritious blue grama, a staple of plains forage, to reappear.[45]

Much more damaging was grazing by oxen, mules, horses, cattle, and sheep. It is easy to underestimate those animals' impact if one reads the usual accounts. Every history of the Oregon Trail points out that the emigration peaked in 1850 and 1852, then quickly receded. By "traffic," however, these writers mean people and nothing else. In fact, as the number of human emigrants declined, that of animals rose steeply as drovers began supplying military posts with beef and pushing seed herds of cattle and sheep toward the Pacific and the southwest. During the gold rush there were perhaps two animals for every person who headed up the Platte trail, or between 100,000 and 150,000 head of stock. By 1853, the ratio had shot up to eleven animals for every human (15,219 people, according to the register at Fort Kearney, and 162,000 cattle, horses, mules, and sheep). By 1856 a Mormon looked over the herds along the Platte and wrote that "it seemed as if Missouri would be totally drained of cattle." The next year, when only about seven thousand people made the trip west, a diarist watched a single herd of nine thousand sheep crossing the South Platte on the way to Oregon. As the number of two-legged travelers declined, the number of four-legged ones was going way up.[46]

To the south, traffic on the Santa Fe road was dominated by commercial freighting, except for the gust of forty-niners and the crowds of Colorado-bound goldseekers ten years later. Freight wagons were gargantuas next to the emigrants' converted farm wagons. "They make us think . . . of a line of white elephants lumbering along," a diarist wrote of the canvas-topped prairie schooners.[47] Organizers typically took along ten or twelve oxen or mules for every freight wagon, counting animals in harness, replacements, and cattle driven to market. By the late 1850s nearly two thousand wagons a year were using the trail, most of them making at least two trips annually. A single outfit usually consisted of twenty-five wagons and more than three hundred draft animals. Each train stopped twice a day to rest and graze its herds. Trains had to camp well apart from neighbors, since their animals' feeding left each place useless for any others.[48]

It all added up to two gigantic streams of horses, mules, oxen, sheep, and milch and beef cattle lumbering and bawling and chewing their way up and down the Arkansas and Platte basins, eating away forage by the thousands of acres. Emigrants, freighters, and drovers were felling and burning trees by the thousands and trampling the sod and grasses, wearing an ever-widening road into some of the finest natural pastureland of the plains. Here, surely, was part of the cause of the changes along the rivers.

But, as always, it is tempting to see all big changes, bad as well as good, as primarily the doing of white pioneers. Indians, too, were playing a part. They were keeping as many as a 100,000 to 150,000 horses year-round on the west central plains, occasionally coming together in huge camps. In 1821, *before* the large-scale arrival of Cheyennes, Jacob Fowler guessed that there were twenty thousand horses in a winter trading camp on the upper Arkansas. George Bent remembered as a child seeing Indian herds grazing for fifty miles along the Arkansas near Bent's Fort. In 1854 experienced observers estimated forty thousand to fifty thousand horses in a gigantic gathering farther downriver.[49]

During the summer, these herds grazed on the shortgrass highlands, with little noticeable impact; but when the cold came, Indians retreated to those select spots along the streams. Between storms their horses could find shortgrasses to graze within a reasonable radius from camp. When the blizzards struck, people and animals crowded under the sheltering bluffs and within groves of trees— timber that also provided fuel for cooking and warmth. Native herders also trimmed the new growth of older cottonwoods and cut down fresh seedlings for another purpose. "We were astonished at seeing great numbers of fallen trees," J. W. Abert wrote of his tour along the Purgatory in 1845, "but afterwards [we] learned that the Indians are in the habit of foraging their horses in winter on the tender bark and young twigs of the cottonwood."[50] This harvesting alone must have taken a considerable toll. Rufus Sage, wintering along the South Platte with a small party of trappers, cut down two or three small trees every day to feed a remuda that was only a tiny fraction of the size of a typical Indian winter herd.[51]

In early spring, after the long and debilitating winter, the Indians were in position to take advantage of the early-sprouting midgrasses and tallgrasses, largely worthless during the coldest months but invaluable now, the best available forage to begin the job of fattening and strengthening the horses that had survived the annual ordeal. The natives loosed their herds on the greening pastures of the river swards, once again calling on the valleys' unique gifts for what they had to have.

Native American pastoralists bore down on some parts of the river systems more than on others. Cheyennes, Arapahoes, Comanches, and Kiowas probably were mostly responsible for the loss of the vital Big Timbers, where in November 1848 an estimated six thousand Indians camped in weather "cruelly, bitterly cold, . . . snowing and freezing." Such a clustering could easily have included twenty to twenty-five thousand horses. Likewise, the South Platte was a favorite region for wintering and springtime fattening. In the spring of 1848, Thomas Fitzpatrick found a string of Lakota and Cheyenne villages with thousands of horses strung out for nearly eighty miles along the South Platte, plus another twenty miles up Lodgepole Creek.[52] In some areas—the forks of the Platte, the North Platte above the forks, and the Arkansas below the Cimarron cutoff, for instance—Indians and whites both relied heavily on the river resources. There the impact from the two invasions naturally was the greatest. Throughout these two crucial riverine environments, the ecological consequences were profound. Never before, and arguably never since, had the appetites of so many new creatures been set loose so quickly onto these limited, vulnerable, and critically important parts of the central plains.

Both invading forces, then, had a hand in changing the country and wearing away its resources. This did not mean, however, that the implications were the same for each. To the contrary, the Native Americans paid a far heavier price. Most obviously, they relied on the plains environment for most (but not all) of what they needed to survive. When that environment failed them, they were in deep trouble because they had no alternative sources of support. White overlanders, by contrast, could call on vast reservoirs of outside help. If necessary they could—and as the years passed they did—bring along supplements of fodder and fuel to get them through. White emigrants, furthermore, caught this country during its most livable months of spring and summer, when the grass was best and the weather the kindest. Indians, on the other hand, were staking their lives during the harshest turn of the year on what they could get from an increasingly battered, deteriorating environment.

There was yet another way in which this environmental crisis worked more against the Indians. To get at this point, we have to call on the insights of another discipline—that of plant sciences. The literature on grasslands ecology is vast and sprawling. It includes thousands of sources on plant and animal life, soil and drainage, drought and flood.[53] Most useful here are the dozens of studies done during the environmental disasters on the plains during the twentieth century, especially those of the 1930s and 1950s. Much of that work concerned overgrazing and its effects, and a lot of those lessons can be applied retrospectively to that earlier time when animals were taking an extraordinarily heavy toll on the grassy corridors across the plains. The results are instructive.[54]

Part of what was occurring would have been easily misinterpreted at the time. When forage like that along the river roads—the shortgrasses, midgrasses, and tallgrasses—is eaten down in early spring, for instance, the first result is a profusion of new growth, and if there has been enough rain, the grazed ground cover springs up twice as high as the ungrazed. Thus, travelers heading west fairly early in the travel season probably found *more* forage than those who had come a few weeks before them. However, if that new growth in turn is eaten away more than a time or two, the results are different. Each plant's response becomes increasingly feeble. After half a dozen grazings, all species begin to falter, and some send up only sparse and wispy blades. After a couple or three years of heavy springtime use, all types of grasses are severely depleted. The result is the devastated look described in dozens of overland diaries from the end of the travel season.

What was happening here? Grazed grasses send up that first vigorous regrowth because they have their priorities straight. Their most immediate need is for the essential equipment for photosynthesis—thus that second rapid growth of fresh green shoots sent above the surface to soak up sunlight—but because grass, like the rest of us, has only so much energy, every plant that produces regrowth is "borrowing" resources from another part of itself: its roots. That diversion of energy is no problem if surface matter is eaten away only once or twice; but repeated loss and replacement, with roots denied what they need over and over, is disastrous. Part of the root systems is going to die anyway, even under the happiest circumstances. That lost part must be replaced if a plant is to survive. If grass keeps sending its energy upstairs, it cannot afford those replacements. The plant's underground support systems shrink, often dramatically, and then, because they cannot pull enough water and sustenance from the soil, they cannot sustain and expand growth either below or above ground. By then they are approaching nutritional bankruptcy. The subterranean atrophy poses another danger. A healthy matting of roots is essential to surviving the most challenging time of year— winter—when rainfall is sparsest and when hard freezes kill some roots of the healthiest plants. Thus, heavy summer grazing brings first a withering then often a slightly delayed death.

Consistent overgrazing, in other words, leads to short-term problems that compound into long-range calamities. The effects differ among the various species. The midgrasses and tallgrasses are the first to feel the worst. If eaten down several times, they lose much of their bulk and fail to spread. After only one summer of heavy grazing, the amount of surface material of some grasses can drop by as much as eighty-five percent, and their root systems shrink by half. Grama and buffalo grasses fare a lot better initially, enough so that they actually increase their territory into soil that had been dominated by its taller competitors now suffering badly; but if those short-grasses are overgrazed for two or three consecutive years, they too show devastating losses. They produce far less vegetation on top of the ground; their roots thin out dramatically; their stolons (the tendrils sent out to expand their cover) are feeble or entirely absent.

The consequences are twofold. First, the composition of grasses is drastically altered. In particular the taller species, the special favorites of cattle and the essential fodder for Indian horses during the springtime season of strengthening, are no longer much to be seen. In one study big bluestem made up fifty-eight percent of modestly grazed lowlands along a stream; in similar terrain that had been heavily grazed for several years, it composed only one percent of the cover. The disturbed soil is also invaded by weeds and other plants far less useful to grazing herds of any sort. Second, the overall production of forage grasses of all kinds declines catastrophically. The tallgrasses virtually vanish. The shorter grass may compose a larger portion of what grass can be seen, but its yield—that is, what it has to offer animals to eat—is far, far less. Where cattle and horses have eaten down the pasture heavily for a few years, the surface matter of buffalo and grama grass is barely one-third of what can be found in modestly grazed terrain. The grass that does survive is far more susceptible to occasional threats of drought, trampling, insects, and unseasonal heat and cold.

When we take this understanding of how grasses work, and what they can and cannot do, then project these lessons backward to the mid-nineteenth century, a couple of points become clear. White overlanders probably would not have grasped the damage they were causing because the full effects of their overgrazing did not become apparent until the end of any given travel season. After all, the most baneful damage was happening out of sight, literally underfoot, among the roots that were the key to the grasses' long-term survival. (On the other hand, emigrants were intensely aware of what may have been another result of the overland invasion. A recent study showed that the number of insects on overgrazed land can be nine times that on modestly grazed ground. Emigrant traffic, thus, might have triggered a population boom of the buzzing, biting, stinging creatures that travelers thought were the worst aspect of plains life.)[55]

The full consequences of overgrazing would have been appreciated only by those whites who saw the results of the river pastures being eaten down several times—that is, those who tried to use these routes *after* the last travelers had passed. The effects were especially clear at the end of a succession of seasons of heavy use. In 1857 Philip St. George Cooke tried to lead a military expedition heavy with herds up the Platte route in mid-October. The corn carried for extra feed was quickly exhausted, and forage was so rare and puny that he ordered his men to unharness the older mules and to dismount and lead their weakening horses for two hours a day. By the Platte forks, grass was found only far from the road, if at all. "After this the horses began to die and necessarily be left on the road," Cooke told his journal. As the weather worsened and his losses mounted, he found himself in charge of a fullblown disaster: "The earth has a no more lifeless, treeless, grassless desert; it contains scarcely a wolf to glut itself on the hundreds of dead and frozen animals which for thirty miles nearly block the road . . . ; they mark, pehaps beyond example in history, the steps of an advancing army with the horrors of a disastrous retreat."[56]

This was the time when Indians were ending their highland hunting and were returning to spend the winter in the river lowlands, and these were the conditions they would have found in many of their sanctuaries along the Arkansas and Platte. The trees were mostly cut, leaving little fuel or cottonwood sprigs to help feed their horses. Other forage was reduced as well. The midgrasses and tallgrasses, which were little use in the winter but would be crucial several months later, suffered heavy losses. So did, apparently, the shortgrasses, eaten over and over, reduced to the slimmest remnants and struggling to survive. Survival for the plants would not be easy, for the grasses were moving into the most treacherous time of their own annual cycle. The cold of winter always will kill a portion of their roots. The winter months are also far and away the driest; the average rainfall of January, for instance, is only about a sixth that of July. With their underground matting of roots starved and thinned from the ravages of the overland herds, the river pastures of the 1850s would have had a tough time of it, even if left alone; but at this, their most vulnerable turn of the year, the other invaders, the Indian pastoralists and their horses, settled in. People, animals, and plants were bound up in a mutually desperate fight for survival. Indians turned to the river valleys when their horses needed them most, and that was exactly the time when those environments could least afford to feed them.

Given this, the descriptions of barren trails and vanishing woodlands are hardly surprising. As the 1850s wore on, this crucial microenvironment—the foraging grounds and timbered bottoms along the plains rivers—was showing the impact of the one-two punch of the overlanders, then the Indian pastoralists. It was a gathering ecological crisis that would have proved deeply troubling under the best of circumstances.

Circumstances were not the best, however. In fact, they were getting worse. Two other developments during the 1850s brought even greater pressure to bear. The first was the arrival of still more people and animals. From the south, out of Texas, Comanches and Kiowas were moving northward, pushed by an expanding white settlement and by other Native Americans, Cherokees, Creeks, and others who had been removed from the southeastern United States into the Indian Territory south of the Arkansas. Comanches and Kiowas had long used the Arkansas valley and central plains, of course, but the pressure from the south forced them to rely more heavily on that country, especially in the winters when they could no longer turn to their traditional ranges in central and southern Texas. In 1849 Indian agent Thomas Fitzpatrick estimated that the effective Indian population along the Arkansas might soon increase as much as fifteen thousand; this guess was surely exaggerated, but just as certainly the use of the river by pastoralists during the coldest months increased substantially during the years that followed. In 1859 Comanches and Kiowas told agent William Bent that from then on they would be spending every winter camping on the river and asked that their annuities be delivered there.[57] An already congested, overstressed country became yet more crowded.

Second, the weather changed. Between 1848 and 1862, the central plains were scorched by some of the worst droughts of the century. Looking back, it must have seemed as if nature had played an especially black joke. According to a remarkably ambitious study by Merlin Lawson, rainfall in this region between 1825 and 1849 was extraordinarily generous—the wettest stretch, in fact, during the 350 years between 1600 and 1950. So much rain fell during that time that Lawson calls this twenty-five-year period "the monsoon." This was precisely the period, of course, when the twin invasions of Indians and overlanders were getting under way. When Indians made their commitment and cast their future with the plains, drawn by the sweep of grasslands and basins deep in pasture, they were seeing this country lusher and greener than at any other time over three and half centuries, from before Jamestown to the time of Joe McCarthy. Then, about 1849, just as overcrowding had begun to take its toll, and just as the goldseeker juggernaut began devouring wood and grass, the rains slackened. Drought hit the Arkansas valley in 1849. Rain was modest to poor throughout the region during the next several years, then devastating droughts struck between 1859 and 1861.[58] With that, the Indians were left to make it in a very different world.

Drought tightens the circle of what is possible for everything living on the plains. For the Indians, most obviously, it took away much of the food normally available for their horses during the summer hunting season. High-plains shortgrasses are marvelously adapted to periodic shortages of water. Their most effective response has been to develop an extraordinarily dense system of shallow roots which can exploit the merest sprinkling of rain; a square yard of grass might have twenty miles of roots in a foot of its topsoil. When rainfall slackens, shortgrasses invest more of their energy and water in maintaining this underground system and less on sending new shoots above ground. During full drought they became virtually dormant. This rerouting of resources quickly reduced the nutritional usefulness of forage for grazers. When horses tried to take the grasses' energy for themselves, they found that it had been pulled mostly out of reach, into the dirt. As a dry spell deepens, weaker members of the grass community die and the basal cover—vegetation on the surface—shrinks considerably. In a study in western Kansas, twenty percent of a test area was without grass in 1932; after four years of drought, ninety-seven percent of the ground was bare.[59]

With that, each horse had to cover more ground to find enough food to stay alive. In a wet year a herd of seven hundred horses needed about five acres of feed a day; in a drought they needed twenty-three. Horses, furthermore, had shallow reserves of strength going into the crisis, since drought had denied them the full richness of the springtime river grasses. In short, the Indians' horses were ill-prepared for the search for food, much less the rigors of the hunt. As they moved around more and more for less and less, their energy ebbed steadily. The Kiowas' pictorial calendar for 1855, an especially dry year, is a curious one—a seated man with his legs straight out in front of him. It depicts "the summer of sitting with legs crossed and extended," so called because that year's drought and dreadful heat left the Kiowas' mounts so feeble that their riders had to stop frequently even on modest marches to let the animals recover. White soldiers told the same story. "Horses much worn, and lean from scarcity of grass," Jeb Stuart wrote in another drought year. Near the Smoky Hill, in country normally graced with waterholes and ample feed, he had to divide his small troop in half to find enough forage.[60]

Ironically, the blistering summer droughts had the same practical effects as the brutally cold winters. They made the vast shortgrass highlands useless, indeed dangerous, to Indian hunters. The Indians, predictably, responded just as they did in winter: they headed for the rivers. Even those watercourses suffered during drought, of course. The Arkansas occasionally went dry, and a freighter recalled having to sink barrels in the Platte's quicksand in 1863 to find enough seep for his animals and men.[61] In those valleys, at least, the pastoralists could find the best of a bad situation. Water usually was there and more grass worth eating. Indians might also turn to another winter strategy—cutting cottonwood shoots for their horses when no feed was to be found.[62] By abandoning the highlands, Indians were moving away from the normal summer haunts of bison, but many of those animals, too, drifted to the streams when rains stopped and short-grasses failed to develop.

In any case there are some indications that with the onset of drought at least some among the Cheyennes and other central plains tribes were spending more of their usual hunting season not on the uplands but along the streams. In 1849, a wet year along parts of the Platte but dry along the Arkansas, Indians remained in camps along the Arkansas thoughout the summer freighting season. Cheyennes and others were all along the road again in the summer of 1855, according to agent Jonathan Whitfield, and during the following two seasons there were frequent reports of Indians on the Santa Fe route, sometimes in considerable numbers, from just past Council Grove to the upper Arkansas.[63] The disadvantage of this response, of course, was that it redoubled the wear on the river systems. Having pastured their horses along the streams in the winter, Indians were drawn close to the rivers in the summer as well, and at the very time when the pace of white traffic was rising dramatically. By 1856, the Missouri *Republican* reported freight trains were having to go miles off the road to find even thin feed for their teams. This overburdened grassland would have to support the Indians once again in a few months, after the white emigrants had passed and the killer cold had settled in.

Indians of the central plains were a people in crisis. Their troubles arose partly from historical developments—the emigration of Native Americans and whites and the crowding of more animals into the region—and partly from environmental cycles that have always played a prominent role in the deep history of the plains. These changes brought with them the destruction of pastures and timber essential to the Indians' pastoral lifeways (see figure on p. 41). The pastoralists' problems did not stop there. Intricately bound up with this calamity was another one (considered in the next essay), a disastrous decline in the number of bison. By mid-century the Chey-

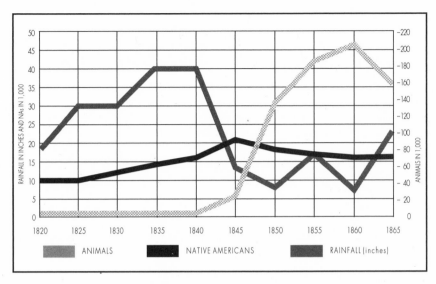

Population and Resources, 1820–1865

This figure traces three vital elements in the history of Indian peoples of the west central plains: the year-round Native American population, rough estimates of animals, Indians, and overlanders using the river valleys, and annual rainfall.

ennes were facing a bitter irony. Having moved onto the plains, they watched the steady disappearance of what had brought them into this new country in the first place.

This crisis was part of a shuffling of populations and power that altered dramatically the relationships among people and the land's resources. Indians knew that this crowding and bumping was affecting the world around them. In 1835 along the Platte, Henry Dodge met a group of Arikaras, people recently pushed westward by the Lakota into the valley now used by the Lakota, Cheyenne, Pawnees, and others. Their leader, Bloody Hand, worried about the consequences. "I am traveling all over this country, and am cutting the trees of my brothers," he told Dodge. "I don't know whether they [the valley's other occupants] are satisfied or not," he added, "but we have no land of our own. I am traveling on their land and killing their buffalo before my friends arrive so that when they come up, they can find no buffalo."[64]

The Indians' alarm was mounting by the mid-1840s, although by now they placed the blame wholly on the whites marching across the land. "Our women and children are suffering for food, . . . [and] we are now weak and poor . . . ," the Cheyenne Old Bark told J. W. Abert in 1845. "The whites have been amongst us, and destroyed our buffalo, antelope, and deer, and have cut down our timber. . . ."[65]

Four years later Superintendant D. D. Mitchell reminded his superior that the central plains tribes considered any depredations "perfectly justifiable as a retaliation for the destruction of their buffalo, timber, grass, &c, caused by the vast numbers of whites passing through their country without their consent."[66] During the 1850s warriors along the roads were complaining angrily to overlanders that travelers had destroyed their woodlands and pastures, that "they [the Indians] were hungry and our cattle were eating their grass and traveling through their country."[67]

To make matters worse, the Cheyennes and their allies could not find relief by pushing into new areas. To the east were the oncoming whites and the Pawnees, Otos, and other Native American enemies; to the north were the Lakota, who were also suffering depletion of resources; to the west were the Rockies and more enemies, the Utes; to the south the Comanches and Kiowas were being pushed onto the central plains by Texans and tribes newly arrived from the southeast. Until 1846 it was possible to acquire food, horses, and captives by raiding into New Mexico, but with the Mexican War, Indians were told that villagers to the southwest suddenly had become valued citizens who must have full respect and protection. Lifelong raiders, Comanches especially, were understandably confused.[68] The pastoral hunters found themselves progressively constricted within a deteriorating environment. "Our ground," Old Bark told Abert, "[is] diminished to a small circle."[69] The central plains region, that vast, open country that had seemed a liberation, was rapidly becoming a cage.

The Cheyennes had few options to meet this crisis. One was to rely on government aid. Annuities from the Treaties of Fort Laramie (1850) and Fort Atkinson (1853) might make up for vanishing resources; but these subsidies were hardly munificent. A rare document scribbled by an agent (who thankfully had lost the original invoice) lays out in detail what was given to his charges along the upper Arkansas for 1858. Besides bales of dry goods, casks of beads, and bundles of hoop iron, the Indians received 32,500 pounds of flour, 13,400 pounds of rice, 15,500 pounds of sugar, 4,800 pounds of coffee, and 1,761 pounds of hardtack, or "pilot bread." This allotment might seem considerable; but when it was spread among the tribes, each person would have received 2.9 pounds of flour, 1.2 pounds of rice, 1.4 pounds of sugar, less than half a pound of coffee and about a sixth of a pound of pilot bread.[70] To put these figures into context, freight companies typically allowed their employees a daily ration of a pound and a half of flour and up to a pound of bacon.[71] The annual allotment of a Cheyenne or Comanche was roughly equal to a teamster's ration for two days.

Where was the rest to come from? To find the difference between what they needed and what they were getting, plains peoples really had only one other possibility: white travelers and freighters. The Indians who drew close to the rivers during the 1850s were after more than water and grass during a drought. Over and over, emigrants wrote of crowds who wheedled and pestered them for bacon, sugar, bread ("beeskit! beeskit!"), coffee, and other foodstuffs as well as whiskey and tobacco. Travelers usually became irritated or angry. Some responded with what passed for humor. A party from Illinois was approached by some Lakota along the Platte:

> They are all a begging set of Lazy scamps and will bear
> watching but no signs of any fight. We had part of a kettle of
> some *beans* last night left so the Boys got two Indians at
> them. They pitched in pretty steep for a while but finally got
> as much as they wanted, but the boys would not let them
> stop eating until they were all gone. Toward the last they
> could not eat but one bean at a time—full for once.[72]

Tactics sometimes got rough. When a train refused to stop for a group of Pawnees, the warriors pricked the oxen with their lances, spooking the teams and overturning a few wagons. The captain handed over some shirts, coffee, sugar, and fourteen hundred pounds of flour. Along the Arkansas an uneasy wagonmaster first parlayed with leaders of two large Kiowa and Comanche villages near Fort Atkinson, then provided several sides of bacon, sacks of sugar, and six hundred pounds of flour. The Indians, he thought, "regarded the things we were giving them, as a sort of tribute."[73] According to news reports in 1856, trains to Santa Fe each were each forced to give two or three hundred dollars' worth of goods in order to pass safely.[74] Dozens of thefts were reported, a few substantial. Arapahoes acknowledged taking twenty-two hundred sheep from one drove in 1855. They were starving; trade had stopped in the wake of the Grattan massacre; smallpox had kept their hunters in camp. They agreed to pay damages out of annuities.[75]

The government naturally tried to keep the situation from getting out of hand. A special allowance of a thousand dollars in gifts was distributed in 1849 and another five times as great was provided the next year in an effort to placate Indians along the roads.[76] This suggested a give-and-take maneuvering already under way. In November 1848 Thomas Fitzpatrick returned from Missouri to find a huge gathering of Indians awaiting him at Bent's Fort. There followed a remarkable exchange. Besides the usual gifts presented at a "Big Talk," Fitzpatrick's guests asked for more. The council was occasioned partly

> by the numerous travelers passing on the different
> thoroughfares of the country, and coming in contact with
> the Indians. In many cases those travelers found themselves in
> a very weak and unprotected state and in order to extricate
> themselves out of the dangers which they imagined
> themselves in, [they] promised the Indians, that I, the United
> States Agent, would reward them [the Indians] well for any
> kindness or good treatment shown American citizens. . . .
> [M]any of the chiefs and warriors [had] . . . documents in
> their possession showing and explaining acts of kindness and
> good treatment extended by them to the writers of those
> various documents.

Vouchers, in other words, were presented, in expectation that these "heretofore hostile hordes of savages" would be given supplies for helping the emigrants, or at least for not harming travelers or pressing them for food. Fitzpatrick paid up.[77]

Indians drew on the government more directly by simply taking supplies and stock from officials and those close to them. William Bent billed Washington for eighty-three animals seized by Cheyennes, Arapahoes, Kiowas, and Plains Apaches during the winters of 1854 and 1855. Agent Robert Miller reported that Kiowas had stolen four cattle from his contractor, first shooting arrows at the animals and cutting the tails off a few to stampede them, then threatening the teamsters—all this, he wrote indignantly, as the contractor was returning to Bent's Fort after distributing the Kiowas' annuities.[78]

No image of Native Americans was more common than that of begger and thief. Indians were a "filthy, lazy, thieving, worthless set of beings," a forty-niner wrote in a typical comment on the ones he met along the trail.[79] The perception fit well the parallel often drawn between plains peoples and North African bedouins—shifty sorts, both of them, dangerous when they had an edge and liable to take anything within reach. However, the Indians were acting sensibly enough, especially when we remember the setting where whites and Indians met, a limited habitat that was the Indians' only source of needful things. Vital resources of the river valleys were vanishing. Indians could go nowhere else, nor could they command resources from the outside to match their losses. But the valleys were, in a sense, being replenished. Enormous amounts of food and livery were moving along the rivers, more every year, virtually none of it offered to them and, in fact, all of it helping to destroy what they had to have.

What whites saw as begging and thieving can just as well be seen as Indians working within a delicate nexus of limited possibilities. They had to balance the means of getting what they needed. Pushing too hard against emigrants threatened annuities and other inducements; that support would continue, in turn, while the government believed the Indians ready to prey on the travelers. In any case, the friction along the trails is best understood in the context of the Indians' deteriorating situation. The elements of life were dwindling, hostile pressures were growing, the weather was worsening, and their options were narrowing.

After that, things really got bad. In the summer of 1858 white prospectors discovered gold in Cherry Creek, a tributary of the South Platte at the site of present day Denver. The subsequent rush to the Rockies accelerated the changes already under way on the central plains and deepened the Indian's difficulties. Within a couple of years, the condition of the Cheyennes and others in the region was desperate.

The discovery of gold in Colorado had five lamentable consequences for plains tribes. First, it sent an enormous surge of new traffic across the already overtraveled trails. As many as a hundred thousand persons headed for the diggings in the spring and summer of 1859, a flood far heavier than the busiest years of the California hysteria. Thousands of these travelers were "go-backs," easily discouraged men who turned around before or just after arrival. Thus, the land felt a double burden, optimistic flow and disgruntled ebb.

Second, the goldseekers pre-empted one of the pastoralists' prime wintering areas. Denver, Auraria, and more than a half dozen smaller gold camps sprang up along the upper South Platte valley. Oxen soon were grazing the area's good grassbeds, while the excellent stands of pine and cedar at the foot of the Rockies were harvested to build cabins, hotels, dry goods stores, and saloons. The Cheyennes and Arapahoes "are very uneasy and restless about their country, the whites coming into it, making large and extensive settlements and laying off and building Towns all over the best part," William Bent warned in December of 1858.[80]

Third, that new settlement in turn depended on a continuous flow of people and goods between it and urban centers in Missouri and eastern Kansas. Mining equipment, clothing, hardware, and tools and materials for town-building, as well as massive shipments of food were taken up the Platte and Arkansas. By 1866 more than fifty thousand tons of freight a year were being carried to Denver.[81] The number of freight wagons plying the Santa Fe trail grew from eighteen hundred in 1858 to more than three thousand in 1862.[82] This trade, with the continuous human traffic to and from the mines, spawned new businesses along the roads, especially "road ranches" providing meals, provisions, fodder, and services for travelers and freighters. By 1861 these enterprises lined the great valley of the Platte, no more than twenty miles apart, from east of Fort Kearney to the outskirts of Denver. Customers could buy flour and wheel rims, pickles, brooms and chamber pots, panes of glass and rifles, sweet oil, gate hinges, bar iron, narcotics and neckties. Among the most popular items were firewood brought from high on the creeks feeding into the Platte and hay cut from bottom grasses surviving away from the trail.[83]

Fourth, Colorado-bound whites intruded for the first time in significant numbers into the country between the Platte and Arkansas valleys. To the uninformed argonaut, the quickest way to the mines seemed to be directly westward from Kansas City, up the Smoky Hill or Republican Rivers. Travelers soon discovered that this central route, while indeed the shortest, was also the most dangerous, especially over its final arid stretch, and after 1860 most travelers stuck to the older roads. Nonetheless, traffic along these central routes never stopped entirely, and promoters' interests soon were aroused. Denver's first stage service, the Leavenworth and Pike's Peak Express, initially followed the Republican River; two dozen stations were established along the route.[84] This country had been left almost wholly to the Indians, but now the white invasion struck directly into these river systems, with their rich grasses and stands of trees, including the Big Timbers of the Smoky Hill and Republican. The new traffic quickly took a toll, as hinted by the Kiowa calendar. In it the summer of 1859 was called the "timber-clearing sun dance" because when the bands assembled where Timber Creek flowed into the Smoky Hill, east of the big timbers near modern Hays City, the Kiowas found that the dense grove they had expected had been entirely felled.[85]

All these troubling changes heightened tension between Indians and whites, which in turn led to the fifth development: a greatly increased military presence. Within a few years several new army posts had appeared on the plains. Plains soldiers faced the same difficulties and lived with the same limitations as the Indians bands; cavalry troopers, after all, were essentially pastoralists in uniform. It was hardly surprising, then, that the government established posts at some of the pastoralists' favorite wintering spots. Fort Wise was at the Big Timbers of the Arkansas, Fort Wallace at the Big Timbers of the Smoky Hill, Fort Larned at the Pawnee Fork's junction with the Arkansas, Fort McPherson at the forks of the Platte, and Plum Creek station at one of the few heavily wooded canyons in the Platte valley. Indians bitterly resented the posts, not only because of the new military threat, but also, as Thomas Fitzpatrick had predicted in the early 1850s, because they realized the troops would quickly deplete what was left of their essential resources.[86] Especially galling was Fort Wallace, built near the grassbeds of Pond Creek and the Smoky Hill's prime timberlands. The Arapahoes reportedly pledged to kill one white man for every tree cut down.[87]

In short, the rush to the Rockies speeded up the changes eroding the Indians' position. Soon the Platte and Arkansas valleys were supporting cattle—not emigrant oxen this time but ranch stock, year-round chewers of the grass. The Union Pacific Railroad was snaking up the Platte by 1867, supplied by "wood and tie" camps using trees cut from high up the feeder canyons. One such business had thirty thousand cords of wood standing at once for use by construction crews and nearby army posts.[88] The last of the famous river groves was finally stripped away. In 1869 and 1871 government linesmen surveyed the the Arkansas and Smoky Hill bottoms, where

thick forests of cottonwoods had once sheltered thousands of Indians. Now surveyors dismissed the area in their field notes: "Land
level, Soil 1st rate. No timber."[89]

After 1860 relations between Indians and whites degenerated rapidly, and by 1864 full-scale conflict was under way, precipitated by
the bloodletting at Sand Creek in November of that year. Four years
later, after a second assault on Indian winter camps, this time on the
Washita River, the military power of the Cheyennes and Arapahoes
on the central plains was broken for good. Historians have usually
traced these wars of the 1860s to the discovery of gold in 1858.
The stampede to the Rockies, the story goes, suddenly challenged
Indian independence and the supremacy of their economy and
lifeways.

The Colorado gold rush did indeed have a profound impact on
plains peoples, but it was not a sudden alarm that awakened the
Cheyennes to a new and unforeseen assault. The years after 1859
saw a culmination of changes that had been building for nearly forty
years, a complex of problems that the Indians themselves had a
hand in making. Those changes stemmed from the twin invasions of
Indians and whites, an interactive ecological assault with a concentrated, cumulative wear on vital, limited habitats. Ultimately, this
was a story of competition for the wherewithal of plains life—and,
beyond that, a rivalry for cultural control of the interior steppes of
North America. Both the nature and the outcome of this contest
were suggested in a moment along the Platte road in March of 1859.
A party of goldseekers, caught by a spring snowstorm, had spent a
miserable evening far from shelter. The next day one of them wrote
in his diary:

> Last night Rogers cut down a lone cottonwood tree, high up
> in the branches of which was tied a dead Indian. On my
> protesting that such sacrilege would bring down the whole
> Sioux nation upon us, he replied that he was going to have a
> fire if he had to fight every Indian on the South Platte. As
> the tree struck the ground, bones, blankets, red ochre and
> trinkets flew in all directions.[90]

The environmental crisis of the 1850s rivalled the more famous calamities that have inspired dozens of books and hundreds of scientific investigations—the ranching collapse of the 1880s, the Dust Bowl of the 1930s, and the drought and agricultural collapse of the 1950s. Like those others, this one resulted from a combination of natural and historical factors, the coming of drought and human misuse and miscalculation. The Cheyennes were caught by a hard lesson learned painfully over and over in the West. They came to the central plains pursuing opportunities. Like so many others, they were drawn by what must have seemed most obvious—the extraordinary abundance of space and animals and the grass to feed them. They discovered, however, that what was abundant was not nearly as important as what was scarce.

On this point we can turn for a last time to the natural sciences. In 1840, at the same moment that the Cheyennes were settling onto the central plains and High Back Wolf and Little Old Man were making their peace with the Comanches Little Mountain and Shavehead, and just as farmers were starting to gather in Missouri for their trip across the plains, a book was published in Europe: *Organic Chemistry and its Application to Agriculture and Physiology*, by Justus von Liebig.[91] In this study Liebig proposed what has been called the "law of the minimum." It goes roughly like this: an organism's growth, reproduction, and maintenance are conditioned not by the abundance of essential resources but by their minimum availability.

Liebig's Law should have been printed on cards and handed out to everybody who has ever been drawn by the dream of the West. Optimism and ambition are fine, Liebig tells us, but take along some skepticism and humility. Pay attention to what you see, but look just as hard for what you do not. For Liebig's Law is really a first cousin to Murphy's: if you want to know what is going to happen to something, look for what will hurt it the quickest and the most.

For the Cheyennes, that meant looking past the millions of bison, past the shortgrass pasture the size of western Europe, to the rivers and their fragile, limited bounty. The same hard lesson—the tyranny of scarcity over abundance—has been taught time and again with different actors, each with a particular gleam in his eye: farmers and ranchers, traders and merchants, a host of dreamchasers. The way to the West in many ways has been the story of people who have learned the wisdom of Leopold and of Solomon. You can live out West, but if you do, and if you hope to keep your gains ahead of your losses, you'll have to live fast and die often, and you better understand something of the structure of the world, the cycles of the year, the natures of animals, and the virtues of roots.

Central High Plains As Seen
from the Colorado Front Range
(Photograph by L. McClure
courtesy Denver Public Library,
Colorado, McC176.)

Old Stories Beneath the New
*Just beneath the surface is evidence that
the plains hold some of the continent's
oldest stories. Here, in central Kansas,
is the floor of a dwelling where families
lived long before Europeans stumbled into
what they called their "new world."
(Photograph courtesy Kansas State
Historical Society, Topeka.)*

Rivers of Life
Cottonwoods, shallow streams,
and grassy river valleys, like this stretch
of the South Platte, blended to create
distinctive environments that offered vital
resources missing elswhere on the high plains.
(Photograph courtesy Colorado Historical
Society, Denver, Colorado, F37,373.)

Sanctuary
Native pastoralists moved into these
precious refuges to find the essentials of
winter survival for themselves and their
animals—wood, water, grass, and shelter.
(Photograph courtesy Denver
Public Library, Colorado, F9521.)

Plains Pastoralists
Cheyenne camps, typically holding
forty or so people and a few hundred horses,
consumed considerable pasturage and fuel.
Destruction of those resources, far more
than military campaigns, undermined their
independence. (Photograph courtesy Denver
Public Library, Colorado, F15643.)

The Freezing Time
*In winter, the high plains became
one of the continent's most treacherous
environments. Blizzards threatened all who
ventured from the protective creases of rivers
and streams. (Photograph courtesy Denver
Public Library, Colorado, F17757.)*

March of the Grass-Gobblers
Overland migrants, who enjoyed the plains
during the safest and most generous seasons,
destroyed and consumed voraciously the
valley resources that Plains Indians needed
in the stingier winter months. (Photograph
courtesy Colorado Historical Society,
Denver, F490.)

American Icon
*The bison, the largest life form in the
Americas, was an irreplaceable asset of
Plains Indians, a vital trade commodity,
a food source for white settlers, and,
to millions of outsiders, a symbol of
the great West. (Photograph courtesy
Colorado Historical Society,
Denver, F36,279.)*

Looking for Lunch
*Just as was true of Indians and their horses,
the bison could survive their annual cycle
only if they had some access to the varied
habitats and different resources of the plains.
They became both priceless assets and
formidable competitors to Indian pastoralists.
(Photograph courtesy Denver Public Library,
Colorado, F18015.)*

2
Animals

In the study of the ways in which animals manage to do the things that
are so obviously useful to them, all failures *are of great interest.*
Niko Tinbergen, *Curious Naturalists*

The Cheyennes came to the plains looking for opportunity, but
they found catastrophe. Their troubles arose not from any one cause
but from the confluence of several. Some of these changes were the
result of human will, some were responses of plants and creatures to
historical events, and some were part of old, recurring cycles. But
that was only part of what was happening. The developments sketched
out in the first essay were wound up with others, which had their
own consequences, including some that were affecting and were affected by changes of the first sort. It's a complex business best visu-
alized not as a chain of events but as a web.

Among the strands of change, one was particularly devastating to
plains Indians. Between 1840 and 1880 the American bison was
driven almost to extinction within its primary habitat, the Great
Plains. The near disappearance of this animal, the largest life form in
North and South America, is one of the best known and intensely
studied episodes in American environmental history. It has inspired
a large technical and historical literature.[1] For many scholars and
laymen alike, the bison's decimation was the quintessential expression of human greed and its potential to gobble up nature's bounty.
Except for the Dust Bowl of the 1930s, another eco-drama in the
same setting, no event stands more starkly in the popular mind as a
case of environmental misconduct.

The bison's story is indeed a cautionary tale—although not in the sense in which it is usually told. This famous American calamity shows the dangers of easy answers, the necessity of consulting the insights of many disciplines, and the imperative to consider events from the viewpoints of all actors—human and otherwise. For western historians it is an especially persuasive reminder of their field's tangled nature. The story of the buffalo, like that of its homeland, is one of seemingly unconnected parts that turn out to be inextricably bound together: wagon trains and blizzards, native hunters and blooming sequences of grasses, diplomacy and the weather. Exploring such connections, in turn, can reveal larger patterns of the region's historical dynamics.

Bison had inhabited the central plains on and off, and perhaps continuously, for thousands of years. They had provided a crucial source of subsistence for whatever humans had lived there; and it was on the central plains that the buffaloes first were pushed to the verge of extinction.

Trying to explain their destruction is complicated by the fact that no one knows how many buffaloes were alive when the mass dying started. Calculating animal populations is a complex and difficult task, even when done by specialists in the field.[2] Comments from early observers are nearly worthless. Suddenly confronted by vast numbers of animals in the unfamiliar openness of the plains, white emigrants fell back on vague, if memorable, metaphors. They wrote of distant herds blackening the country like dense woodlands and moving over the land like the shadows of scudding clouds. When observers tried to set numbers to what they saw, the results varied wildly; one party's guesses for a day's sightings ranged from ten thousand to a hundred million. In most accounts there is a mix of bafflement and giddiness, a feeling of children counting fireflies.

Even among scholars the range of opinion is distressingly large. The best recent estimates are from Dan Flores and Tom McHugh, who approach the problem by asking what can be more reliably known—the numbers of cattle, horses, and other modern grazers that can survive on the various parts of the plains grasslands. Then they apply those figures retroactively, adjusting for certain variables, to come up with educated guesses of the maximum population of bison. McHugh suggests about thirty million buffaloes were living on the entire Great Plains in the early nineteenth century; Flores estimates 24 to 26 million.[3] Given those figures, the bison's peak population in the area considered here was probably between three and five million.

Everyone agrees on one point, however: there were millions of bison south of the Platte River as late as the 1820s and 1830s and virtually none by the mid-1870s. In explaining this destruction, most attention—and so most of the blame—usually goes to the period of the great hunt, from the late 1860s to the 1880s, when meat suppliers for railroad construction crews, sportsmen, and above all commercial hunters who catered to an expanding industrial market for hides focussed their sights on the plains buffaloes. This slaughter did account for the deaths of several million animals throughout the Great Plains; but the bison were in serious decline well before then; their population on the central plains may have dropped by as much as half before the great hunt got under way. Concentrating on the final bloodletting distorts the chronology, and doing that it avoids perplexing questions with illuminating, if ambiguous, answers. The bison's brush with extinction had deeper roots and more complex lessons than in the story as typically told.

As early as the 1840s, in fact, discouraging words already were heard. In 1842 John Charles Fremont wrote that Lakota on the upper Platte River were distressed over diminishing numbers of their favorite game, and a year earlier the overlander John Bidwell had learned that buffaloes were fast disappearing from that area: "If they continue to decrease in the same ratio that they have for the past 15 or 20 years, they will ere long become totally extinct."[4] That sort of remark was increasingly common by the end of the decade. Where their guides had once seen enormous herds, soldiers and engineers now told of areas scarcely sprinkled or entirely emptied of the animals.[5]

By then Indian agents were unanimous that bison populations were collapsing. Often quoting native leaders, they reported the situation steadily deteriorating during the 1850s until tribes were on the brink of starvation. "The bands of Indians on the plains suffer greatly, at particular seasons, by cold and hunger," Thomas Twiss, agent on the upper Platte, wrote in 1855. "The buffalo is becoming scarce, and it is more difficult from year to year for the Indians to kill a sufficient number to supply them with food and clothing. The old and the very young Indians are the greatest sufferers." Two years earlier Thomas Fitzpatrick had warned that the Cheyennes, Arapahoes, and many Lakota "are actually in a *starving state*. They are in abject want of food half the year . . . [due to] the rapid decrease of the buffalo." Some Indian traditions suggest a crisis brewing by the end of the 1840s. In the winter of 1848—49, Kiowas along the Arkansas made "antelope medicine" for a great hunt of the pronghorns, an extreme measure taken only when bison provisions had failed badly, and for the next four years the Kiowas' calendar had notations for "few or no bison."[6]

To observers of the day, the main cause was obvious. Overland travelers were to blame. Emigrants supposedly had a twofold effect: they were killing the bison outright, and their hunting plus the general clamor of the columns of wagons were disrupting the animals' lives and frightening them away. "We see the white men everywere," a Lakota spokesman told his agent. "Their Rifles kill some of the game, & the smoke of their Camp fires scares the rest away . . . ; our little children are crying for food. We are obliged to travel many days before we can find Buffalo."[7] This complaint, from 1859, summed up a recurring lament nearly twenty years old. By the mid-1840s Cheyennes and Sioux were grumbling that emigrants were frightening bison away and forcing their hunters into the country of hostile neighbors.[8] The army engineer Howard Stansbury concluded the same a few years later: "Driven from their ancient and long-loved haunts [along the Platte], these aboriginal herds . . . seem destined to final extirpation at the hand of man."[9] The Indian agent Thomas Fitzpatrick agreed with Indians who attributed the scarcity of game entirely to white emigration: "The travel upon the roads drives [the bison] off. . . . [Indian] women are pinched with want and their children constantly cry out with hunger." If the situation continued, he warned, a general famine was imminent.[10]

This explanation is remarkable on two counts. First, it was one of those highly unusual occasions in frontier history when everyone seemed to agree. Indians and whites, Pacific-bound farmers and nomadic hunters, agents and native leaders—all said that overland travelers were slaughtering and scattering the bison. Second, this universal opinion, seemingly so self-evident at the time, does not make any sense.

For one thing, the emigrants were appallingly poor bison-killers. To be sure, they looked forward to bagging some of these near-mythic creatures, and at the shaggies' first appearance men grabbed their rifles and sprinted for their horses; but accounts of impromptu buffalo chases have more pratfalls than heroics. Galloping off after their prey, men often ended up losing their way and sometimes their horses, chasing each other, shooting at trees and sagebrush, and returning frustrated and unburdened by meat or trophies. Their exhausted, stumbling horses looked, as one man put it, "like the tail end of a hard winter."[11] This should not be so surprising. Its clumsy appearance aside, a bison was a fast and agile quarry that could be brought down only by a well-placed shot.[12] If overlanders had any experience with hunting, it was with quite different sorts of game, and even practiced riders discovered that pursuing bison was a specialized skill demanding practice and luck; George Armstrong Custer once killed his own horse (his wife's favorite, Custis Lee) during a chase. Most would-be nimrods quickly tired of the sport and soon returned to the grind of travel.

Emigrants rarely saw more than a few buffaloes killed at one time.[13] Instead, many cited as proof of the slaughter the abundance of "blanched skulls and bones" that Richard Burton, traveling the Platte in 1860, recommended as fuel in the treeless basin.[14] The problem with these observations, so graphic and convincing on their face, is that travelers had been writing of thousands of skeletons since the earliest crossings. The "evidence" of the travelers' butchery, in other words, was there before the travelers.[15] Besides that, there is the problem of the arithmetic of slaughter. Based on the most conservative guesses at the number of buffaloes, travelers in one of the busiest years of traffic—1850—would have had to slay at least three or four or six animals for every man, woman, and child among them to reduce the herds on the central plains by even five percent.[16] Nothing close to that was happening, as a superficial scanning of overland diaries will quickly show. Many parties either reported no bison or saw only a few at a great distance. Of those who encountered the herds, many made no effort to hunt. Of those who hunted, many failed, and those who succeeded usually killed five or fewer for parties of twenty or so persons. Even this speculation, furthermore, derives from the time that emigration was at its peak. The impression that overlanders were killing off the bison, however, was commonplace well before then, at a time when travelers numbered not thirty thousand or fifty thousand in a year but two thousand or three thousand. To diminish appreciably the herds in 1845 or 1846, each man, woman, adolescent, child, and infant would have had to kill a buffalo every ten miles or so, from Fort Kearny to Independence Rock.[17]

The other belief, that emigrants "frightened away" the bison, is even more outlandish, at least if taken literally. When in large herds and on the move, buffaloes were not known for their shyness; in later years locomotives, some with passengers shooting from car windows, would be forced to stop as thousands of beasts surged over the tracks and around the cars. Another question is more to the point: where were the bison frightened *to*? Buffaloes might have learned to avoid the immediate vicinity of the roads, as will be discussed below; but Indians and agents were not complaining that game was being driven back a modest distance, just out of molesting range. They were saying that it was increasingly difficult to find any animals at all. Sometimes they seemed to argue, as some writers still do, that columns of wagons were disrupting well-established patterns of movement and so complicating greatly the Indians' efforts to find the herds. The best sources today, however, agree that bison had never moved so predictably. Their shifting about seems to have been, in the words of a leading authority, "inscrutable fluctuations in their comings and goings."[18] In short, there were no recurring patterns for the emigrants to disrupt.

This testimony may tell us something about the witnesses, particularly their quick assumption that white Americans were the main agents of all significant changes unfolding on the western frontier; but as explanations of the bison's fate, these opinions are dead ends.

What was going on here? *Something* was happening to the buffaloes; but what? An important clue lies in the geographical pattern of their decline. The bison were not just disappearing. They were disappearing far more in one area—the westernmost portion of the central plains—than in others.

This change seems to date from the 1840s. When the Stephen Long expedition toured the western edge of this region in 1820, along the South Platte and Front Range, Edwin James told of herds so dense that his men could stand on a hill and watch their own scent as it blew across the carpeting of animals. In the same area in 1835, Henry Dodge wrote day after day of "innumerable" and "immense" herds of buffaloes that "surrounded us . . . making the prairie almost black."[19] F. A. Wislizenus found much the same thing in 1839, Rufus Sage in the winter of 1842–43, and John Charles Fremont the following summer. Traveling down the Arkansas from the mountains in 1842, the preacher Joseph Williams saw bison in large bands that grew into a vastness, many separate herds that filled his view of the country for two weeks.[20]

Within a few years, the picture was changing dramatically. Dragoons bound for New Mexico in 1846 saw virtually no buffaloes along the Arkansas west of the present Kansas-Colorado border, and by the early 1850s travelers rarely saw any past the Cimarron cutoff. Along the South Platte, where Long, Fremont, and others had gawked at thousands of acres furry with animals, buffaloes were rarely spotted by the 1850s. Testimony was unanimous, rather, that the greatest swarmings were east of there and north of the Arkansas.[21] The situation on the Platte was similar. Bison, it is true, were an increasingly unusual sight along river's main valley after 1850, but within that overall scarcity, they were rarer still the farther west one went. At the eastern end of the river, on the other hand, bison were sometimes so numerous that they were considered a menace to the farmers rapidly filling the country. In the Nebraska town of Wood River Center, in 1859 shaggies laid waste to a prominent citizen's garden and threatened worse. "Our beautiful town site has been rudely trampled upon by those ugly-looking beasts . . . ," the local editor wrote. "We intend to keep some weapons handy, so that, should they kick up too much dust around our office, or rob the porkers of their accustomed slop, we shall not be responsible for their safety."[22] As for the country between the Platte and Arkansas, reports from the few whites who ventured there made it clear that the the buffalo's range was shrinking eastward. By 1857 it extended not much farther west than the 101st meridian, about 150 miles east of the Rockies.[23]

This seems improbable at first glance. Then and now, the general impression has been that an advancing white settlement was pushing bison and Indians before it, always westward, farther away. In this part of the plains, however, just the opposite was true. A man riding west from Topeka would have seen his first buffaloes after a hundred miles or so, and found them at their thickest for another two hundred miles before the herds started to thin. For the last hundred miles and more, from his first hazy hint of the Rockies until they loomed above him, any glimpse of a buffalo would have been unusual. Far from being pushed ever westward, the buffaloes were pulling back from the mountains, *toward* the white settlements.

Here is a double puzzle. Bison were disappearing, although not for the reasons everyone gave; and they were disappearing mostly where they seemed to be the least threatened. However, this situation appears peculiar only if we look for explanations among the usual suspects, the white pioneers typically seen as the authors of all grand and sweeping changes. If instead we consider Indians at least as significant in shaping events of the day, if we allow them equal billing as historical actors, other answers begin to emerge, ones more reasonable in face of the evidence.

Native hunters are the obvious place to begin looking for answers, first of all, because bison were vanishing where Indians were and whites were not. As discussed in the first essay, the native population on the central plains was booming during these years. The region's resources were being used by from fifteen thousand to twenty thousand persons by the 1850s, a lot of them recently arrived in a westward drift from the Missouri valley. The new Indian arrivals had emigrated in part because they were lured by the apparently limitless bounty of the plains bison. By the same terms, however, this move brought with it a growing dependence on that single resource.

This is not to say that the Cheyennes and other plains peoples relied on buffaloes for all their material needs. They hunted other animals. As late as their sojourn in the Black Hills, women planted corn. More important was the gathering of wild plants. A recent study catalogued 121 edible forbs, woody shrubs, and grasses on the plains. Some, like lambsquarters, sarvisberries and haws, were familiar to white settlers; but the native menu was far greater, including prairie turnip, beebalm, and buffalo gourd, ricegrass, pussy toes, and much more. The long and slender bulbs of *Calocortus gunisonii* (what the Cheyennes called "war bonnet") were gathered and dried, then ground into meal and boiled for sweet winter mush. Pounded and dried into small round cakes, one type of red currant, *Ribes inebrians*, was sometimes eaten straight and sometimes stewed with inner scrapings from buffalo hides. Dozens of plants were used to cure ailments from dyspepsia to lung hemorrhages. If pounded into a powder, the leaves and stem of *Lithospermum linearifolium* (or "goldie") were said to revive a paralyzed limb; when brewed into tea and rubbed on the face and head, it relieved temporary irrationality. Plants were used as well in the making of shelter and weapons and for a variety of other purposes. Young men chewed the leaves of

Monarda menthoefolia ("bitter perfume") and blew them onto their favorite horses to give a pleasant scent to the manes and tails.[24]

That said, the Cheyennes certainly became increasingly reliant on bison when they shifted onto the plains. Buffaloes provided a considerable part of their subsistence, not only food but shelter, clothing, saddles and other equestrian equipment, weapons, religious objects, toys, and many of their life's details. Men and women combed their hair with the rough side of a dried bison tongue and swatted flies with a stiffened tail. Besides filling these immediate needs, buffaloes supported plains Indians indirectly. No matter how imaginatively they used the natural bounty of the plains, natives could not find everything they wanted there. They had to reach outward. To import what they had to have, Indians traded the most desired items available around them—robes made from bison skins and, to a lesser degree, bison meat.

Cheyennes and other plains peoples were hunting bison for trade at the time of their first contact with whites. That trade grew over time and shifted increasingly to white traders. The nature of that exchange by the mid-1850s is suggested in the accounts of Elbridge Gerry, whose post near Fort Laramie was an important gathering place for trade among the tribes between the Platte and Arkansas. In December 1857 two traders, Jonathan Smith and Nicholas Janis, took from Gerry a large load of goods on credit—dozens of blankets, hundreds of bundles of beads, much tobacco, several dozen "cocoa" and "ebony" knives, hundreds of yards of cloth, including muslin and bed ticking, coffee mills, combs, a gross of awls, teakettles, and a few hundred hair pipes. Six months later they were back with 213 buffalo robes, "parflesh," and miscellaneous skins of bears, wolves, badgers, wildcats, antelopes, and deer.[25] Plains tribes carried on a similar business with New Mexicans, who brought the Indians many of the same articles as well as crucial foodstuffs, especially cornmeal and *piloncillos*, cylindrical cones of unrefined sugar imported from Mexico. These were swapped for bison robes, horses, mules, meat, buckskins, and a few native products, such as moccasins.[26]

Indians were using bison robes and other animal skins to provide indirectly for food they could not produce (corn), for manufactures helpful in a highly mobile life (lightweight blankets and material for durable clothes), for satisfaction of habits and traditions (tobacco, coffee, sugar, beads, and vermillion), and for tools (knives and awls) to help in the hunt that supplied hides for further exchange. This exchange was a critically important part of the commitment Cheyennes made when they moved from the Missouri valley into the open country. Besides relying on resources essential to keeping their horses alive and moving, as discussed in the first essay, they were accepting a life that left them doubly reliant on the bison that seemed so extraordinarily abundant. That game had to satisfy more of their immediate needs; it also had to pay for many other things they no longer could provide for themselves.

Given the Indians' reliance on bison for such a remarkable range of needs and given the growth in native population, it would not be surprising if hunters were taking a growing toll on the herds. Indeed, the trade in buffalo robes, one measure of the Indians' impact, apparently was substantial during these years. Several posts appeared between the Arkansas and Platte—Bent's Fort on the Arkansas and Pueblo upriver from it, Gerry's on the North Platte, a business run by Geminien Beauvais near the Platte forks, and four posts on the South Platte, one a branch of Bent, St. Vrain and Co. Except for Bent's Fort, they were not impressive to outsiders; Richard Kern described Pueblo in 1848 as "a miserable looking place . . . a compound of Spaniards, horses mules dogs chickens and bad stench."[27] Nonetheless, they were the funnels through which moved a considerable commerce. By the mid-1840s large shipments of robes were moving down the Arkansas and Platte.[28] In fact, the same overland travelers who blamed their fellow emigrants for wiping out the herds (without actually seeing any mass butchery) also described heavy wagons passing them on the way eastward with many thousands of robes bound for market.[29] Those cargoes, the results of vigorous hunting by newly arrived Indians who were killing many thousands of other bison for their own immediate uses, were evidence of one obvious possible reason for the bison's declining numbers.

When we look to the Indians as one likely cause of the bison's troubles, another question immediately arises. Natives were hunting throughout the central plains. Why, then, were buffaloes dying off in one place (to the west) and not in another? Trying to answer that question emphasizes another crucial point. Just recognizing Indians as agents of change is not enough. We cannot hope to get the story right without some effort at sorting out the relationships among Indian groups in these years—their migrations, their territorial rivalries, their accommodations, their political tensions. This native history of the plains is as intricate and often as troubling as that of the whites who have crowded Native Americans largely off the pages of our texts.

A key to understanding this story is the phenomenon of buffer zones. Also called neutral grounds, contested zones, and "debatable sectors," these were areas that lay between territories of competing native groups, land that both groups wanted and tried to use, but that neither could control outright. They were in a way the Indians' frontiers, both in the sense of boundaries between peoples and of areas of shifting influences and realms of power. Students have long recognized that buffer zones played some role in relations among Indians; the nineteenth-century anthropologist Lewis Henry Morgan made them part of his basic definition of the tribe itself.[30]

More recent work, however, stresses the connections between those contested spaces and changing animal populations. Put simply, a buffer zone was something like an animal preserve. Such an area came into being partly because it was a prime habitat for a popular game animal. Different native groups naturally were drawn to such a space to exploit the bounty; but if no single tribe was strong enough to keep its neighbors out, a curious result followed. Animals found a degree of refuge, paradoxically, precisely because they were highly desired by competing groups. That sounds odd to anyone used to the modern marketplace, where desirable resources fare as well as a couple of mice in a roomful of cats. But in a neutral ground native hunters were restrained by fear for their own safety. They could not occupy the area year-round; they entered it always alert to the presence of enemies; they could not hunt at will. Thus, game enjoyed a measure of protection. In fact, animals often left more vigorously hunted areas and headed like refugees into these safer zones, boosting the faunal population still more.[31]

There were two neutral zones on the central plains during the 1820s and 1830s (see map, p. 64). One lay to the far west, between the forks of the Platte and extending somewhat below the river's southern branch toward the Arkansas. "This section of country is what is called the neutral ground . . . ," Colonel Henry Dodge wrote during his visit in 1835. "It will not admit of the permanent residence of any Indians, and is only frequented by the war parties of different nations."[32] Contesting tribes included the Cheyennes, Arapahoes, and Lakota—

who, recall, were pushing into the country from the north—and the Comanches, Kiowas, and Plains Apaches to the south. The other neutral area was to the east, covering much of the Republican River basin and most of the great valley of the Platte. The same western tribes fighting among themselves in the first zone vied for this territory with the Pawnees and other groups from the Missouri valley, such as the Sac and Fox, Delawares, and Otoes.

These buffers, the contested seams among Indian groups, are crucial to understanding what was happening on the plains. They tell us a lot about the changing dynamic among various peoples jostling for control of vital resources. As hunters and warriors strained against one another, those resources, including bison, were spared the full devotion of native consumers. The buffalo, in short, got a break. As long as no winner emerged, or as long as rival tribes came to no reckoning, the herds would find some sanctuary. If, on the other hand, a buffer were eliminated, hunters would be able to proceed with few restraints, and bison would be left far more vulnerable.

In 1840 the western neutral zone suddenly vanished with the famous peace between Comanches and Kiowas and their Cheyenne and Arapaho rivals, the event described at the opening of the first essay (see map, p. 65). A general peace then spread from those tribes to the Plains Apaches and the Lakota. Dan Flores has recently suggested that the Comanches sued for peace so they might gain allies against Texas frontiersmen and yet another wave of displaced natives, the tribes from the southeastern United States recently removed to Indian Territory. Pushed from the south, Comanches also would have unthreatened sanctuary in wintering spots along the Arkansas watershed. The Cheyennes and Arapahoes, for their part, would have access to horses, bison, and forage that had brought them to the west central plains in the first place. In the context of the changing power relationships of the plains, the Great Peace of 1840 made perfect sense.[33]

For the same reasons, it was bad news for the bison. This *detente* allowed former competitors to live and hunt in reasonable safety throughout the western half of the central plains, from the Arkansas to the North Platte and from the mountains eastward to the other buffer, where these new allies still had to worry about the Pawnees and other enemies. Soon bands were wintering in woodlands close to the mountains, and in summer visitors found large gatherings—women and children as well as hunters—a sign of some security. Along the South Platte, an area Henry Dodge had said would "not admit of the permanent residence of any Indians" in 1835, Fremont in 1843 found an "extremely populous" Arapahoe village of 160 lodges seemingly well provided by "a regular supply of the means of subsistence."[34]

The results were soon apparent. William Byers, founder of the Denver *Rocky Mountain News* and an early Colorado booster, wrote in the 1870s of conversations with traders who had operated posts along the South Platte forty years earlier. During the 1830s, one told him, "he never looked out over the walls of the fort without seeing buffalo, and sometimes they covered the plain. At that time their moving columns surged up against the mountain foot." After about 1840, he recalled, business began quickly to decline, and the forts were successively abandoned, starting with those farthest west, "owing to the decrease of the buffalo in their vicinity." Although shaggies might still be seen occasionally at the site of modern Denver as late as 1846, there were fewer and fewer during the 1840s and 1850s. Eventually, by Byers's own observations, bison were first encountered more than a hundred miles east of the mountains: "The herds are thin on the edge, thickening to the eastward. Small bands occasionally wander ten or twenty miles farther west, but the line is quite distinctly marked."[35]

So, peace, in a sense, was killing the bison. The *detente* among western plains tribes loosed their hunters more freely onto the herds, which soon began shrinking alarmingly. To say that, however, only turns the puzzle another way and, alas, raises more questions. What economic dynamic was at work here? If Cheyennes, Comanches, and other Indians were a significant force in killing the buffaloes, what were the circumstances and motives? Hypothetically they could have been setting out to slaughter as many as they could to generate the greatest possible trade and convert these animals into the maximum material wealth, just as white professional hunters would do twenty years later; but that seems unlikely. These animals, after all, were also supplying much of their daily needs, and Indians presumably would want to have large numbers of them around indefinitely. They certainly said as much. What situation, then, would leave them apparently destroying the mainstay of their way of life?

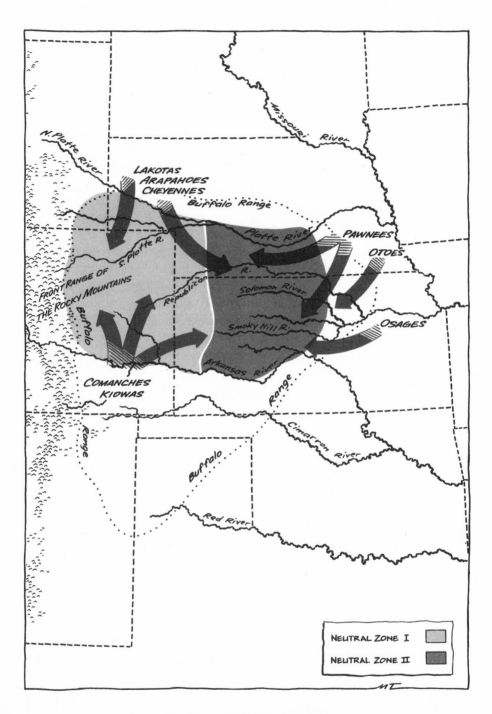

Bison Range and Neutral Ground, 1830s

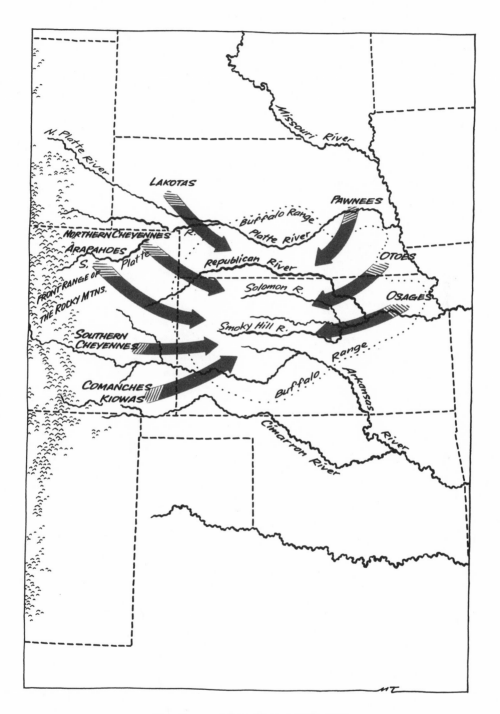

Bison Range and Neutral Ground, 1840s–1860s

These questions, which are among the most important we can ask, are also some of the most difficult to answer. Luckily, however, there are a few hints in the record. In 1855 the agent of the upper Arkansas, J. W. Whitfield, estimated that the 11,470 Indians under his charge were killing roughly 112,000 bison annually, or about ten animals per person. Among the southern Cheyennes and Arapahoes, the ratio was higher, about thirteen-to-one.[36] Those numbers are for the population as a whole. The men actually doing the hunting were each killing an average of nearly forty-three bison per year, or about one every eight days, year-round, sick and well, storm and shine.

The Cheyennes presumably were harvesting these animals for their twin purposes—filling their subsistence needs and trading for outside goods with robes and meat. They seem to have been killing more bison than necessary for the first purpose alone. According to a recent close analysis, plains peoples had to harvest six buffaloes a year per person to provide food, clothing, and shelter.[37] Indians on the upper Arkansas were killing buffaloes at twice that rate, if Whitfield's estimates are close to accurate, so a good part of their harvest probably was going to the second purpose of the hunt— trade. The six-a-year subsistence estimate, furthermore, assumes that hunters were relying primarily on bison for food, yet the Cheyennes and Arapahoes, Whitfield reported, were also killing forty thousand deer each year (about eight for every man, woman, and child) as well as seven thousand bears and more than three thousand elk.[38]

All this raises some puzzling questions. The Cheyennes were hunting bison and other game with considerable success; and yet they were still periodically suffering from shortages of food and vital items acquired through trade. In 1855, the year of Whitfield's estimates of the hunt, the agent of the upper Platte reported that in the wake of the Grattan massacre and the subsequent turmoil, virtually all trade had stopped on the central plains. This interruption left Indians in a crisis, he wrote. They were in desperate need of trade goods, and he used the occasion to add once again that because of the bisons' steady decline, Indians found it increasingly difficult to feed and clothe themselves. With winter approaching—his letter was dated 10 October, so snow could come any time—interruption of trade made it "a matter of great moment" that relief be sent right away. He called for an immediate increase in annuities of corn and other provisions.[39]

It would be of great help to know in detail just what was going on in that trade. How, specifically, were these bands using the buffaloes they were killing, especially those swapped for outside goods? How did that exchange proceed? How much of what kind of goods were the Cheyennes obtaining, and what did they consider most important? Unfortunately, questions like those are unanswerable, at least at present. Unlike the fur trade in Canada and other parts of the West, that of the central plains was not conducted through huge enterprises, like the Hudson's Bay Company, with distant headquarters bulging with records and correspondence from the field. Documents from the largest firm, Bent, St. Vrain and Co., and from smaller businesses suggest a little about the extent of trade and some of what was bartered, but there is virtually nothing about evolving native demand, how trade jibed with the Indians' changing needs and desires and how the Cheyennes and others might have become increasingly reliant on what merchants were offering.

There is one intriguing possibility—alcohol. All observers agreed that plains natives were inordinantly fond of stong drink. "[The] passion for intoxication amounts almost to madness," one wrote, and Henry Dodge agreed: "[Indians] will sell their horses, blankets, and every thing else they possess for a drink of [whiskey]. In arranging the good things of this world in the order of rank, they say that whiskey should stand first, then tobacco, third, guns, fourth, horses, and fifth, women." In 1842 John Charles Fremont found that along the South Platte buffalo robes were exchanged for a variety of goods, but principally for alcohol diluted with water. "A keg of it will purchase from an Indian every thing he possesses—his furs, his lodge, his horses, and even his wife and children," he wrote.[40]

The drug trade, in other words, may help explain the apparent vigor of the Indians' commercial hunting, even in the face of shrinking herds. In any case there were other essential items available only from the outside world in exchange for bison products. Lakota leaders told Thomas Fitzpatrick that they would welcome suppression of the whiskey trade, because their people's robes then would go to buy flour, corn, sugar, and coffee, "which would be much more beneficial to their families."[41] Between liquor and those other necessities, there must have been a substantial pressure to hunt for the hides that were the stuff of trade. Still, a lot of questions await answers. The internal dynamic of the native robe trade remains one of the most important understudied subjects of plains Indian history.

Certain points, however, are perfectly clear. Indians on the far western parts of the central plains were killing a lot of buffaloes. The huge herds there were beginning to shrink. That shrinkage was bringing some severe economic difficulties; and the decline of the bison, furthermore, whatever the cause, was also affecting profoundly Indian politics and diplomacy.

As mentioned in the first essay, the Cheyennes' move to the plains put a terrible stress on their social structures and political cohesion. The land's insistence that for long periods every year they break up into bands and into smaller camps to find adequate pasture and protection for their horse herds naturally eroded their sense of common identity. The bison's demise aggravated this crisis. As the Cheyennes pursued a resource that was both irreplaceable and disappearing, the strain on the bonds among kinsmen and allies increased considerably.

In the Cheyennes' own accounts of these years, the persistent theme of fragmentation is often tied to growing difficulties in the hunt. By 1854 the People had divided into three groups that came together only for such great ceremonies as the sun dance and renewal of the Sacred Arrows. The Northern Cheyenne hunted mainly north of the Platte in the Black Hills and on the Powder River. Among the Southern Cheyenne, the Hair Rope People, Southern Eaters, and Scabby Band stayed close to the Arkansas, while the Ridge Men and Dog Soldiers lived partly along the South Platte and hunted especially near the headwaters of the Republican and Smoky Hill, "for here the prairies were darkened by great herds of buffalo, untouched by the slaughter caused elsewhere by the Ve?ho?e's [white men's] continuing to push westward."[42]

At this stressful time came the shocking murder of White Horse, head chief of the Kit Foxes warrior society, by Walking Coyote, a member of the rival Bowstrings society. Walking Coyote had been angered by White Horses's theft of his young wife. Such a breach of etiquette, however, was never an excuse to kill a fellow Cheyenne. Murder was an unspeakable breach of custom. More important, it was a direct threat to the People's livelihood because, tribal accounts make clear, murder left the Sacred Arrows, the Cheyenne's holiest possessions, stained with drops of blood until they were cleansed through the appropriate ceremony. Bloodstaining in turn let off a terrible stench that hovered about the lodge and the camps along the Arkansas that were the Arrows' home. The bison, which hated the smell of death, then vanished. After White Horses's murder, Southern Cheyennes were forced to move south for a while to hunt with the Kiowas along the Cimarron, where two of their men were killed by the "Hairy Nostrilled White Men" (Mexican hunters). In the summer of 1855 the Sacred Arrows were cleansed, but soon afterwards Walking Coyote, in another dispute over the same wife, was murdered by a man named Winnebago. Once again the stench drove the bison out of the country.[43]

Troubled accounts like these suggest the close interplay of politics, social change, and the gathering economic crisis. Regardless of how one might trace causes and effects in such a story, there is an implicit recognition that the alarming loss of a precious resource was intimately connected with an erosion of unity and, with that, a loss of respect for codes of behavior so crucial to the People's sense of themselves. Things were coming unstuck, and the bison's disappearance was fundamental to the Cheyennes' problems.

The natural response was to look for more buffaloes. The bands that had hunted so energetically close to the mountains, in the newly opened neutral zone, shifted their attention to areas where bison still were plentiful—eastward, into the remaining neutral ground also desired by Pawnees and other tribes close to the Missouri valley. Ten years after the peace of 1840, Southern Cheyennes and Arapahoes apparently had developed a distinctive annual pattern of movement. After wintering along streams to the west, they headed east to hunt among the receding herds. Thomas Fitzpatrick reported that in March of 1850 virtually all among the Arkansas tribes gathered in the spring at Big Timbers before slowly moving downriver to the Cimarron cutoff and dispersing at the start of the hunting season.[44]

Over the next decade summer travelers on the Santa Fe trail consistently told of meeting natives on the lower Arkansas but seeing few, if any, farther west. By 1858 agent Robert Miller distributed annuities for the upper Arkansas tribes at the Pawnee Fork, rather than at Bent's Fort, because all recipients, even the Cheyennes and Arapahoes formerly found farther upriver, were on hand in early summer and ready to hunt in that area. Goldhunters that year found large villages a week or ten days downstream from Bent's Fort but were surprised at what followed: "One remarkable fact is that . . . we had not seen an Indian since we left the Pawnee Fork." When they reached the foot of the Front Range and the South Platte valley, where fifteen years earlier Fremont and others had seen crowds of Indians (and plenty of bison), they saw virtually no other humans until late summer and early fall, when Indians arrived for winter camping.[45]

That, the Cheyennes realized, would sharpen the already in-tense competition for the remaining neutral zone. The point was made dramatically in autumn of 1851, when a Sioux and Chey-enne delegation headed for Washington, D.C. met with Pawnee leaders. At this conference, the Loup Pawnee chief Big Fatty of-fered to smoke with Alights on a Cloud, a prominent Cheyenne; but Alights on a Cloud would not put his lips to the pipe. Peace with the Pawnees, he said, was the last thing he expected or wanted.[46] As western hunting grounds were cleared of bison, he seems to have been saying, a quickening conflict with tribes on the east central plains was inevitable.

The following decade was, indeed, anything but peaceful. Sources from all sides, including reports from white agents and Indian oral traditions, tell of ever more brutal clashes for control of the eastern neutral zone. The weakening Pawnees suffered terribly, but so did the Cheyennes, Kiowas, and Lakota, as suggested by the names the Cheyennes gave to these years: "The Summer of Much Weeping" (1853), "Bull's Son is Killed by the Wolf People" [the Pawnees] (1854), "The Dog Soldiers Celebrate, But the Kit Foxes Mourn" (1855), "Ice Leads a Starvation Journey, But Lives to Scalp a Pawnee" (1857).[47]

Part of their difficulty came because tribes to the east had far better access to firearms. When a large party of Northern Chey-ennes and Lakotas caught a group of Pawnees along the Republican River in the summer of 1853, several Potawatomies showed up with large-bore rifles with ranges far greater than attackers' bows and ar-rows. They killed twenty-three men, mostly Cheyennes, then taunted the others by shouting insults and stuffing their victims' hearts into their bullet pouches.[48] The next spring a huge force of Kiowas, Comanches, some Southern Cheyennes and Arapahoes, and a few Osages set off into central Kansas to wipe out all enemies they could find; but this foray, too, ended disastrously. Near the Kansas River a much smaller party of Sac and Fox stunned them with heavy losses—about a hundred wounded and sixteen killed. Once again their bows and arrows had been no match for the enemies' firearms. During the three-hour battle, an agent told of the story he heard, "the rifle told [on] almost every shot, either on rider or horse."[49]

The lesson was not lost on the humiliated westerners. Thereafter they pressed the government to pay annuities in rifles and ammunition, not food; the year after the calamitous battle of 1854, their agent could persuade tribes along the Arkansas to take flour and rice only by promising weapons the next year.[50] This insistence probably spoke partly of the paltriness of the annual food ration. More than that, however, Indians were probably demanding firearms as the means to press an increasingly desperate and costly effort to control the eastern plains and to gain full access to the herds there. Somewhere, in any case, Indian men were falling in alarming numbers. An agent estimated in 1855 that the adult female population of the Cheyennes, Arapahoes, and Comanches (but, strangely, not the Kiowas) was half again that of adult men—a sure sign of bloody and endemic warfare.[51]

Looking back, the pattern is clear enough. When the western neutral zone vanished, so did the bison. Unfettered hunting was followed by growing hunger, and peace led to war more bitter than ever. The larger point is that buffaloes' dying and the Indians' statecraft and politics cannot be understood apart from one another. The fate of the bison was intimately and complexly bound up with Indian emigrations, with their evolving patterns of power, and with the maneuverings of native diplomacy during one of the most dynamic periods of change the plains would ever see.

But saying that once again slides past the question raised in the first place. Indians were hunting buffaloes, and buffaloes were dying off, and Indians were killing Indians to control what was left; but did the hunting alone bring about the great dying? More precisely, was the rise in native population and the intensified hunt enough to push the bison so quickly toward extinction? The answer, almost certainly, is "No."

Indian overhunting, whatever the natives' needs and no matter how great their effort, cannot alone explain what was happening. The numbers just don't add up. Even with normal attrition, the herds could replenish from six to nine percent of their numbers every year.[52] That would go a long way toward putting back the animals that Indians had taken away. To be sure, the methods and strategies of native hunters probably made their impact worse than it might have been. Until a way was found to put bison hides to industrial uses, trade was mostly in robes. For these, the more pliable hides of females were much preferred, especially those taken in the fall and winter when the fur was thickest. When hunters gave their most dedicated attention to cows in autumn, they were culling many females newly impregnated during the summer rut, thus compounding the demographic cost.

Nonetheless, the native trade cannot have been the sole cause of the disaster. For one thing, the same point that proved especially threatening to bison cows in autumn—that the market demand was for *robes*, not hides—was also a highly effective protection for the herds. Unlike the later slaughter by professional white hunters, who simply stripped the carcasses and sold the hides, stiff and green, the Indians had to process the skins laboriously to turn them into marketable robes. That work, done by women, was a slow business. It took several days to flay the animals and prepare the skins that one man could provide in one good hunt. Preparation of robes, in other words, was a bottleneck in the sequence of trade. With only so many female workers available, men had no reason to kill more than a certain number of bison. This placed an effective cap on how many animals were hunted.

Thus, on the one hand, Indian hunters must have been part of the problem—where there was a recent surge in hunting, to the west, the bison were disappearing—but on the other hand, that could not have been enough. The full explanation must lie in some *combination* of factors, some especially dangerous interaction of events. As native horsemen were chewing at the herds, something else must have been trimming the numbers as well.

Part of the cause was likely a series of new diseases carried in by horses, mules, cattle, and sheep that were living in or crossing the plains. Anthrax apparently had appeared by around 1800, and brucellosis, tuberculosis, and a variety of parasites likely were acquired from Pacific-bound animals. Some of these maladies, brucellosis in particular, both killed directly and crippled the survivors' capacity to reproduce. Direct proof of these scourges is virtually impossible to come by, but the after-the-fact evidence is suspicious. Bison gathered into refuges later in the century, for instance, were shot through with these diseases.[53]

Those afflictions, however, were only hints of something much more important. Anthrax and brucellosis were part of a wide-ranging biotic onslaught. The main historical events of this assault were the overland migration of hundreds of thousands of people and animals and the occupation of the country by new Indian societies and their tens of thousands of horses.

These events set in motion several chains of changes. Among these were the Indians' vigorous hunting and their diplomatic shifts just discussed—developments, in turn, bound up with the environmental transformations that were the focus of the preceding essay. Those events redefined the terms of survival on the plains and redrew the limits of living there. If we could look closely enough, we likely would see that virtually all life forms, from antelopes to face flies and voles to jackrabbits, were in some ways affected. For one animal, however, the results are clear. Whatever else was killing them, the bison were also dying because their world was changing.

Over the centuries the bison had worked out elaborate accommodations and arrangements with the plains terrain and its life forms, both fauna and flora. To outlanders they seemed to drift freely over the land, seemingly without reference to anything but whim; but in fact they were meshed tightly within a complex environment. Modern researchers are only beginning to understand the bison's intricate connections with the plains biota. Their feeding styles, for example, supplemented those of prairie dogs; together the two species stimulated vital nitrogen content in grasses on the edges of the rodent villages. With their own urination, bison created patches of invigorated grasses that greened early, died late, and produced more biomass in between. (On the other hand, there were limits to such interaction. Saliva dripping from a buffalo's maw apparently did nothing to encourage growth of forage.)[54]

The best illustration of just how beautifully the bison fit their environment was their annual pattern of movement. The most basic points on this subject, however, have been muddled by one of the most stubborn misconceptions about this much misunderstood animal—the myth of migration. Throughout the nineteenth century and well into the twentieth, the belief persisted that as autumn waned buffaloes migrated, more or less *en masse,* to somewhere on the far southern plains, then returned northward in the spring. The purpose, of course, was supposedly to escape the harsh winters. A variation held that all bison shifted southward a few hundred miles from their respective summering spots, with herds in the Dakotas moving near the Platte, for instance, as those along the Platte drifted to north Texas.

All recent studies reject these notions, however. Besides certain logical difficulties, the evidence of the animals' whereabouts at various times of the year simply did not jibe with any such patterns of mass shifting from north to south. Sightings from around the plains were so inconsistent and jumbled that, as Frank Gilbert Roe put it, advocates of the migration theory have been forced to argue that buffaloes invariably migrated, except when they didn't.[55]

The current opinion is that buffaloes remained throughout their lives in large, somewhat vaguely defined home ranges. Within those ranges their movements were in one sense random. They followed no precise annual routes. No one could have predicted to what exact spot any one animal or herd would move from day to day and from season to season. Rather, they drifted in a "fickle wandering" and with "an utterly incalculable irregularity."[56] That did not mean, however, that they moved without intent or pattern. Bison did not migrate within their home ranges in the sense of returning by established paths to the same *places*, but they did select certain *habitats* over others. A buffalo might be in any particular spot by chance, but the type of setting and terrain was chosen purposefully.

The plains are composed of a series of microenvironments with unique ecologies. Each of these offered the buffaloes its own peculiar opportunities and difficulties, and over time the animals had learned to use these different habitats to maximum advantage. By a subtle and complex arrangement, bison moved to one or another of the microenvironments in response to "a variety of natural and cultural stimuli."[57] Cultural stimuli might be short-term intensive hunting or the burning of grass to control movements of the bands of animals. Of the natural factors, the most important were seasonal changes in climate and weather.

The latter explains best why and how bison moved with the calendar.[58] Early spring found buffaloes in the low grassy valleys of rivers and creeks. Hungry and thin from the winter's demands, they concentrated there to graze on the midgrasses and tallgrasses that were the earliest to sprout and mature. Forage here was thicker and more diverse than on higher ground, and each bison spent time walking and choosing among the many sorts of grasses, shrubs, and forbs. This browsing and heavy grazing continued for a couple of months. In late spring the herds began shifting out of the valleys to the uplands. By then the early-sprouting riverine plants were flowering and starting to lose nutritional value. As tallgrasses reached about to a bull's knees, furthermore, their ratio of protein to carbohydrates became much less compatible with the bison's digestion. Just then the highlands began greening with the late-sprouting shortgrasses.[59]

By June the bison were grazing mostly across the millions of acres of grama and buffalo grass on the broad, rolling divides between the rivers. In one sense millions of animals were converging in the summer onto a great common gathering ground, but as they came out of the confining valleys they also fragmented into small groups of a hundred or so that roamed independently over the highlands. Forage here was much less dense, but except in drought there was plenty of it, as long as the clusters of animals kept moving. Shortgrasses reached their peak growth in mid-summer, just in time for the scattered herds to congregate in huge numbers for their mating season. At that point these grasslands took on another, subtler appeal. The animals' rut involved a variety of activities besides copulation— specialized play, grooming, aggression, defense, and the tending of cows after mating. This "social time investment" robbed bison of the hours they had used earlier in the spring to move around and select the varied menu along the rivers. Such browsing time was unnecessary now, however, since they could find enough nourishment in the shortgrasses that grew almost anywhere they stood.[60] Courtship and mating lasted a month or so, after which the animals broke up once again into smaller herds, then wandered over the uplands for several more weeks.

By summer's end, buffaloes had started to drift off the highlands in a gradual process consuming several weeks. They headed once again toward the riverine bottoms. This dispersal was also a concentration, as the scattered herds all sought out the valleys that offered far less room to roam than they had enjoyed in the summer. In a rare description by a trapper of long experience, James Clyman wrote that "in the fore part of winter . . . they colect in the lower valies and most Sheltered parts of the vast plains . . . Whare they remain all winter if not interrupted."[61]

It's important to understand why the bison were crowding toward the lowlands. They were not looking for forage. The midgrasses and tallgrasses, so succulent in spring, were practically useless by this time of year. In the months ahead buffaloes would rely mostly on shortgrasses, which cured naturally and kept much more of their value. Shortgrass could be found just about anywhere, on the high ground the animals were leaving as well as along the streams. The rivers did offer much more reliable water supplies during the driest part of the year, from October to March. During those months the bison grazed close to the rivers, trying to find what they needed within that smaller range.

The main reason for staying so close to the valleys, however, had to do with the weather. When blizzards and "northers" roared onto the plains, bison crowded into the woods along the streams. Wintering along the South Platte and Cherry Creek in 1842–43, Rufus Sage observed that frequent snows and arctic air "had driven [buffaloes] from the open prairie into the creek bottoms" that now "were completely blackened with their countless thousands." Maximilian of Wied told of the same seasonal retreat along the Missouri. When the animals take refuge in the river forests, he wrote, "it is often almost impossible to drive them out of the wood. . . ."[62] Alexander Toponce, a freighter, saw why. His train was caught by a blizzard along Montana's Quaking Asp River in January of 1866. In cold so deep his oxens' horns burst and peeled away from the pith, Toponce watched hundreds of bison drift off the tableland and crowd into the river's thick timber. Those unable to find room froze where they stood. The next spring their bones made a whitened border along the open plain just outside the trees.[63]

Bison met winter's threat, in other words, not by hoofing it toward Mexico, as the migration myth had it, but by moving into a particular kind of terrain and habitat, by selecting one part of the varied plains environment over others. River valleys offered shelter and usually adequate food when the plains were most treacherous. Then, as the weather mellowed and the taller grasses began to green out along the bottoms, the buffaloes would be close to the nourishment they needed so badly to rebound from winter's deprivations. With that, their annual cycle continued its roll.

Two points should be made about the bison's yearly cycle. First, the pattern of convergence and dispersal between the different environments was a splendidly choreographed adaptation. For reasons just explained, it fit the bison's needs; but the grasses also benefitted. As noted in the first essay, grazing actually stimulated the above-ground growth of the newly risen river forage—as long as such grazing was not continued too long. That problem was avoided when the buffaloes vacated the valleys in early summer. Tallgrasses, an essential source of food in the spring, were left largely alone to flower, reproduce, expand their root systems, and reach their full height. Meanwhile the far larger shortgrass territory could support the foraging bands and rutting crowds until the rivers, with the next generation of taller grasses now assured, drew back the millions of grazers. This "two-field rotation system," the complexities of which are barely suggested here, was a delicately tuned and balanced mechanism.[64]

Second, this mechanism, like all finely calibrated systems, was easily disrupted. The mid-century invasion of people and animals had a devastating effect. Early on, overlanders like Joel Palmer complained that "the grass is very poor in the Platte bottoms, having been devoured by the buffalo herds. . . ."[65] Quickly, however, that situation was reversed. As the overland migration grew from a trickle to a flood in the late 1840s, emigrant animals controlled the Platte and Arkansas valleys from the first weeks of spring, denying buffaloes access to these grasslands when they needed them badly. The thick columns of oxen, cattle, and sheep, furthermore, did not stop devouring the forage in June, as the bison did, but continued to forage ravenously until late summer. Cattle ate heavily from all kinds of grasses, but they wore especially hard at the tallgrasses, since their tastes were adapted to the more humid ecologies to the east.[66] The beds of big and little bluestem had little chance to renew and mature.

After that came winter foraging by Indian horses. Natives and their herds also sought protection by crowding into the same dense woodlands favored by bison. A young army officer wrote in 1845 that the Big Timbers of the Arkansas were

> a thinly scattered growth of large cotton-woods not more
> than three-quarters of a mile wide, and three or four miles
> long. It is here the Cheyennes, Arapahoes, and the Kioways
> sometimes winter, to avail themselves of the scanty supply of
> wood for fuel, and to let their animals browse on the twigs

and bark of the cotton-wood. The buffaloes are sometimes driven by the severity of the winter, which is here intense for the latitude, to the same place to feed upon the cotton-wood.[67]

The various year-round nomadic residents of the plains—buffaloes, horses, people—faced the same limited set of options, and not surprisingly they found themselves using the same tactics and depending on the same limited resources.

The implications for the bison are not hard to imagine. In the spring the emigrant stock denied them access to vital resuscitory feeding. When the buffaloes returned to the valleys in the fall, the wagons and oxen were gone, but the grasses were mostly stripped away and more and more of the timber was gone, leaving them vulnerable to the demanding months just ahead, even as they faced the competition of Indian horses and native wood-choppers. Year by year, the overall extent and quality of the riverine ecologies crucial to the bison's annual renewal was worn down.

Here, to return to the point raised at the start of this essay, is probably the true cause behind the persistent impression that white travelers were solely to blame for the bison's troubles. Emigrants did have a hand in the crisis, but not as they saw it at the time. They were not hunting buffaloes to extinction. Nor were they dispersing terrified animals to distant ranges. A close look at the evidence, in fact, shows that as the spring migration got under way, buffaloes simply withdrew a relatively short distance from the main Platte road, probably to the nearest pasture as yet unshorn by hungry oxen.[68] Emigrants struck their killing blow by pre-empting a critical environment and by devouring its vital resources. Travelers saw fewer and fewer bison along the river roads because those bison had less and less reason to go there.

Buffaloes were dying, then, partly for the same reasons that Indians and overlanders were facing their own troubles. These animals, after all, lived by the iron rule of Liebig's Law, just as their predators did. Events after 1820 lowered dramatically the minimum availability of some of the bison's irreplaceable necessities. White and Indian newcomers were breaking into the buffaloes' annual cycle at its most vulnerable point, and the changes they brought destroyed the animals' most limited resource that supported them at the chanciest time of year. The result was dramatic. Suddenly, over a couple of decades, the plains lost their ability to support a huge portion of one of their most successful and prolific forms of life.

The bison's ecological problems posed no dangers for white emigrants, but for plains Indians they were catastrophic. The Cheyennes had first moved onto the plains partly in pursuit of bison. They committed to a way of life that made them increasingly dependent on that seemingly abundant game. That commitment also required that Indians rely closely on one particular part of the plains— its rivers and their valleys. That, in turn, meant that they, along with the overland travelers, were undercutting the means of life of the animal resource that had brought them onto the plains in the first place.

Indians, in short, were in a bizarre fix. Their chief resource had become their competitor. By controlling for themselves what bison needed, Indians were hastening the demise of something they themselves had to have. Eventually all might have settled into a lasting arrangement, perhaps with fewer Indians hunting less vigorously and allowing more room for the bison's needs; but the point is wholly speculative. Too many developments beyond the Indians' control were moving far too quickly to give natives and animals the time to work things out. The reality was a perverse and unbalanced situation that was nothing close to self-sustaining.

Then came the drought. Animal populations were subject to natural environmental changes as well as to evolving human circumstance. As discussed in the previous essay, these years fell into two starkly different climatic parts. The first was an extraordinarily wet period from the mid-1820s to the late 1840s, with the most bountiful sustained rainfall between 1600 and 1950. Following that "monsoon" was a brutal drought that lasted through the 1850s and struck especially hard in 1849, in 1855, and from 1859 to 1861. The dry spell, thus, coincided with the precipitous sag in the bison population. It is only common sense to look for some connection between the two.

Drought threatens the buffaloes in several obvious ways. Springs and creeks on the highlands dry up and even major rivers occasionally go to sand. Shortgrasses, the summer staple of the bison, develop poorly, with the upper, leafy portions giving off thinned and stunted growth. These plants are conserving their root systems, their most important assets for long-term survival, but in the process many weaker plants die. In effect, the shortgrass community is sacrificing a large part of its members to insure that some will be there to expand when the rains return. The immediate result, however, is a calamitous shrinkage of forage available for grazers. When the rains go away, they take much of the material basis of bison life.[69]

Not surprisingly, the animal community has shrunk dramatically during past droughts. On the region's long timeline are extreme cases when lingering droughts apparently devastated buffalo populations. On the southern plains and southwest, bison bones largely disappear from the archeological record twice during the past seven thousand years, between 5000 B.C. and 2500 B.C. and between A.D. 500 and A.D. 1300 Both periods apparently were ones of long-term drought. When wetter times returned after 1300, the numbers of bison in those areas rebounded dramatically. The Neo-Boreal period, or "Little Ice Age," from about 1570 to 1850, was substantially cooler and, according to some, a good bit wetter on the plains. It may have brought a further rise in bison population.[70] The overall impression is of long spans of organic, cyclical change, a swell and contraction like slow breathing, with numbers of bison rising and falling with rain and its absence. Within these longer trends were many smaller variations. Since 1300 the plains climate has fluctuated among generous rains, average precipitation, and drought, with severe dry spells of five to thirteen years coming on the average of two or three times each century. Presumably the bison population grew and declined in response to those short-term punctuations, replaying on a smaller scale the more dramatic swings of earlier times.

When we think of buffaloes not as millions of individual animals but as a species, dying during drought appears as an effective survival strategy. Like the grasses buffaloes ate, the biomass of bison had adapted to the erratic plains climate by reducing its size when the rains stopped, conserving a smaller part of its full potential during a time of deprivation. From this perspective, the dwindling of buffaloes in the 1850s might be seen as an ecological phenomenon with no relation to the human events of the time. Here, perhaps, was simply the most recent of dozens of adjustments, greater and lesser, that stretched back over millenia. Once again drought required a culling, just as wet years would later allow the herds to flourish.

From another view, however, the situation was uniquely threatening. This natural turn of an ancient story came when the bison were under exceptional stress from other events—the mass invasion of two-legs and four-legs, the occupation and overworking of the river basins—that had nothing to do with natural cycles. Those changes were threatening enough under the best conditions. Already, in fact, bison were dying during the 1840s, at the end of what were the wettest years on the plains between the time of Elizabeth the Great and Dwight Eisenhower. The drought aggravated—and its impact in turn was aggravated by—those human events. The coincidence of the two developments, the natural and the historical, made each of them more—much more—dangerous than it would have been alone.

When the rains slowed, and the highland ponds went dry and its grass curled up, the bison's answer, predictably, was to head for the rivers. There buffaloes would find the best chances for forage and water, or at least that had been the case in the past. Now, however, they found that lifestuff mostly controlled by others, and besides that going to where they could eat and drink brought them close to native hunters. During the driest years, as noted in the first essay, Indians stayed close to the rivers, partly for the same reasons the buffaloes were drawn there. And by bleak fortune, those were also some of the seasons of heaviest overland traffic, when the toll was heaviest on those sustaining sanctuaries. In short, bison found a crucial ecological niche fatally crowded.

Zoologists have a term for what was happening: "species packing." This concept, first coined about twenty years ago and applied since then in other contexts, is useful to understand what was going on here. The idea is simple: if any particular environment allows the slightest room, new life forms will enter to compete for resources. What's surprising is how many species can squeeze in, with the result a dazzling diversity of creatures. One biologist has compared this to a popular nightclub where more and more people crowd onto the dance floor, all adjusting to the others, always with room for another couple or two. But there's a catch. Closely packed species can thrive only if their environment is constant and stable. Changes bring trouble quickly, and the more new species that crowd in, the less change it takes to cause trouble. Where species are "loosely" arranged, things must change dramatically before any one of them is threatened, but "with closely packed species, only a small environmental fluctuation is tolerated. . . ."[71]

To put it mildly, "small fluctuations" is *not* a phrase that anyone would ever use to describe the plains. The weather and climate, from season to season and year to year, are extraordinarily unstable. Within that instability, several historical changes at mid-century—mass invasions, war, tumultuous native politics, and shifting diplomacy—packed all sorts of new dancers onto floor, new tenants into those precious life niches that too many creatures, human and otherwise, had to have. The result was disastrous both for the bison and for those who relied on them.

What killed the bison? Change killed them—a complex of natural and historical events that, working upon one another, were transforming life on the central plains. This explanation, of course, runs against the familiar portrait of that day. Lewis Garrard, visiting a Cheyenne camp on his way up the Arkansas in 1846, was moved by the sight of some young mounted warriors:

> I thought, with envy, of the free and happy life they were leading on the untamed plains, with fat buffalo for food, fine horses to ride, living and dying in a state of blissful ignorance. To them, who know no other joys than those of the untaught savage, *such* a life must be the acme of happiness; for what more invigorating, enlivening pleasure is there than traversing the grand prairies, admiring the beauties of unkempt, wild, and lovely nature, and chasing the fleet-footed buffalo. . . .[72]

This romantic vision—of people and animals living in statis, of Indians innocent of change and passing their days freely and at ease, of a wild and lovely West filled with limitless bounty on the hoof—has proved remarkably persistent. Just as resilient has been its corollary—that the bison died in their millions almost wholly at the bloody hands of greedy, mindlessly wasteful pioneer invaders.

Over time, in fact, those perceptions and the buffaloes have proved equally hardy. Today the animals' population has rebounded enough to make them once again an economic asset, this time as the makings of steaks, chili, burgers, and "buffalo dogs" in western eateries. It's a typically ironic and complicated lesson in the story of western resources. In our day, when we have put buffaloes on our nickels and flags as symbols of the sad loss of a vanished age, they turn out to be as prolific as rabbits. In the last century, when bison stood for the West's fecundity and generosity, they offered our best case lesson in how easily plenty can disappear.

In the end this story should warn us away from easy answers. The way to the West is to remember the connectedness of life there. The West's history is often one of patterns within apparently disparate elements. Those patterns, in turn, often teach us how the land beyond the Missouri is a country of both expansive opportunities and rigid limits, and how the West is utterly intolerant of whatever pushes it too far. There is a lot to learn about living in the West by studying how the buffaloes have died there.

The Historically Silent
*No actors in the drama of emigration to the
plains have been more neglected than these
—Native American women and children.
How their lives changed reveals much about
larger patterns of cultural and environmental
history. (Photograph by David F. Barry
courtesy Denver Public Library,
Colorado, B937.)*

Plains Labor
Moving to the plains meant less status and
more work for Indian women. Scraping bison
hides to turn them into robes consumed an
enormous amount of their time and energy.
(Photograph courtesy Kansas State
Historical Society, Topeka.)

Changing the Land
*In one of the most rapid
environmental transformations in our
history, the cooperative effort of men,
women, and children created the basis for a
new economic order—and destroyed the last
hopes of Native American pastoralists.
(Photograph courtesy Kansas Collection,
University of Kansas Libraries, Lawrence.)*

The Harvest as Conquest
The family was the most effective machine
of pioneer conquest. Women and children
worked alongside men at even the heaviest
land-altering labors, like harvesting.
(Photograph courtesy Kansas Collection,
University of Kansas Libraries.)

Fiddler on the Roof
Music was among the most common ways
that families carried their mother culture with
them onto the plains. Lively melodies were
often played inside the earliest houses,
and sometimes on top of them.
(Photograph courtesy Kansas State
Historical Society, Topeka.)

The Town as Family
Everyone—adults and children, males
and females—acted out familial roles not
only in their homes but also in the civic world
of communities that sprang up across the
central plains. (Photograph courtesy
Colorado Historical Society,
Denver, F41082.)

The Victorian West
The trappings of Victorian America were
available almost right away from drummers
and at stores like this one found in most
towns within a few months of their creation.
(Photograph courtesy Colorado Historical
Society, Denver, F35,099.)

Cultural Instruction
A classroom was a seedbed of values
transplanted onto the plains. With the help
of flags and aphorisms hung on the walls,
children learned the basic values of Victorian
American culture along with reading,
writing, and arithmetic. (Photograph
courtesy Kansas Collection, University
of Kansas Libraries, Lawrence.)

3
Families

The root of the kingdom is in the state.
The root of the state is in the family.
Mencius

God gives the solitary a home . . .
But the rebellious shall live in a parched land.
Psalms, 68:6

People, land, and animals are bound in a common history as they use and change each other. Another force, that of social and cultural institutions, has also played a part in making the story of the central plains—and of anywhere else. This force is peculiar to humans, although it is tangled with the rest. How people treat the land and its creatures depends partly on the structures of human societies and the values embedded in them; the physical world, in turn, affects the collective lives of its human inhabitants.

Of all human institutions, the family is the most thoroughly studied. Anthropologists, sociologists, psychologists, and historians have written hundreds of books and thousands of articles to puzzle out the family's role in human culture and in individual lives.[1] There are no firm conclusions; nobody seems to agree, in fact, on what a family is. Everybody, however, would affirm its significance. The family is a person's earliest and most important continuing influence. It is the innermost circle of a society's arrangement, and it has the prime responsibility for performing essential functions. The family reveals a lot about what people believe, about who controls whom, and about how they cope with change.

Given that, we have paid remarkably little attention to the family's part in western history. This essay considers a few ways families can be studied to illuminate the workings and developments of plains peoples, both Native Americans and westering pioneers, and how these peoples have influenced one another. The focus is on five definitions of families in these, and in most other, societies: a procreative mechanism, a unit of economic production, a cultivator of cultural values, a relationship of power, and a means of social adaptation.

▭▯▮▬

The family, first, was a reproductive force. Unless a society is increased by masses of immigrants or captives, it will survive only if, year after year, its babies outnumber its newly dead. A people's ability to compete for control of a place—or, once conquered, to maintain some cultural integrity—also depends partly on the ability to keep numbers up. Demography is destiny, at least to some degree. When a society's families fail to give it the children it needs, that society will pay a price.

As everyone living outside a cave now surely knows, the European invasion brought a catastrophic decline in the Native American population. Students argue over just how calamitous the impact was. During the four hundred years after 1500, some say, the aboriginal population of North America dropped by more than ninety-five percent, while others say sixty or seventy percent. Whichever is accurate, this was the greatest die-off in the human record. In a way the conquest of native peoples begins and ends here. Facing aggressive, land-gobbling invaders, Indians, over those four centuries, could keep at most only two or three of their own people for every twenty they lost.[2]

The most obvious causes of this disaster were old-world contact diseases that decimated new-world peoples whose isolation had left them vulnerable to contagion. Tribes of the central plains and neighboring areas, like natives everywhere in the western hemisphere, suffered appalling losses. The greatest killer, smallpox, hammered them over and over. The Lakota reported outbreaks in two successive winters, 1779–81, then again in 1810, 1818, 1837, 1850 and 1861.[3] When Pawnee raiders brought the disease back from New Mexico in 1801, it quickly spread up the Missouri and southward as far as the Texas coast, ravaging the Ponca, Oto, Iowa, Omaha, and Wichita.[4] By Comanche tradition, smallpox along the Red River and Rio Grande in 1815–16 reduced their population from ten thousand to six thousand; the Kiowas also suffered considerably.[5] Other diseases washed over them: measles (Lakota called 1844 "The Rash Breaks Out on Babies Winter"), cholera, influenza, whooping cough, pneumonia, bronchitis, catarrhal fever, gonorrhea, syphilis and several diarrheal disorders.[6] Maladies already present may have worsened; the Omaha referred to malaria as "white man's sickness."[7]

Initially diseases were actually an advantage to central plains tribes. Before 1849 plains peoples were relatively less ravaged than their eastern enemies, the Pawnees and others whose villages along the Missouri were far more accessible to whites and thus more vulnerable to contagion. The Cheyennes' and Lakotas' comparative isolation gave them an edge in their struggle to dominate the central plains; but that advantage turned against them, in yet another variation of the dynamic described in the first two essays. The Cheyennes at first had enjoyed expanded opportunities offered by the spacious and abundant plains, but then had found themselves constrained by their reliance on the rivers and on their limited, dwindling resources. Similarly, as they faced the threat of imported contagion, their nomadic, pastoral lifeways initially kept them more out of harm's way. In time, however, their need for the rivers drew them close to what was, after 1848, one of the most biologically treacherous areas in North America. It was one more twist of the knife.

The overland trails were like gigantic linear petri dishes, environments superbly suited for cultivation and transmission of diseases. Motley crowds converged there with dippings from microbial reservoirs throughout the world. As they moved along the trails, members of a typical emigrant party made brief exchanges among hundreds of persons, drinking from the same water sources and eating and sleeping close to the rot of one another's garbage, offal, and excrement. When the dying began, they often buried their corpses in shallow graves that were easy marks for wolves. Travelers told of body parts strewn about, half-eaten legs and arms reaching from the ground. Passing through in 1849, one woman called the plains "this boundless city of the dead."[8]

The Indians, pulled to the trails by their deepening needs, were squarely in the path of migrating diseases. For white Americans, the year 1849 has a wondrous ring to it, smacking of adventure and daring and infinite possibilities; we've even named a professional football team after it. Among Southern Cheyennes, 1849 is called

"The Winter When the Big Cramps Take Place." According to tribal tradition they lost close to half their people to cholera. The Kiowas, whose pictograph for the summer of 1849 shows a man screaming in pain with his knees drawn up to his chest, recalled this epidemic as the most terrible event in their history.[9] Emigrants testified of the carnage. A family stopping by a stream for a noon meal suddenly noticed the hand of an Indian corpse reaching ghoulishly from its hastily dug grave beside them; when a young girl ran in panic from the sight, she fell over another body hidden in the tall river grass. Others reported decomposing bodies stacked in tipis along the road.[10] The natives' "simple remedies" were useless against cholera, smallpox, measles, and other new diseases, the head of the central superintendency wrote of the area in 1855, and the resulting losses were horrendous.[11]

In effect, plains peoples were caught in a crossfire along newer and older lines of contact. As some contagions surged westward with the overlanders, others seeped in along traditional routes from the southwest. In the Kiowas' "Smallpox Winter" of 1861–62 a blanket brought from New Mexico infected a village along the Arkansas, from which the scourge spread among the Cheyennes, Arapahoes, Sioux, and eventually the Arikaras.[12] By then the growing mercantile enterprise along the roads and the military posts, built to protect all the rest, increased the odds of disaster. In 1866 and 1867 back-to-back cholera epidemics burned through the region, hopping among army posts and fledgling towns. "I do hope that the Indians will get the Cholera!" an officer wrote his wife from Fort Wallace. "One of our Delawares died of it–so it appears that Indians are not exempt." He may have gotten his wish. After a patrol two weeks later, he wrote of coming across a large encampment, recently abandoned: "We found some Indian graves in the trees and on platforms of poles–the dead were mostly children–very little fellows most of them!"[13]

Trees full of dead babies: it is an arresting image, and it reminds us that these epidemics were inseparable from the migration of many species, from people and horses to oxen and anthrax, and from the ecological shuffling and environmental degradation that brought a steady worsening of the Indians' lot. Their living standards sagged; they were drawn more to rely on travelers and agents; that contact, in turn, brought more disease. The cumulative effects were suggested by the report of a special medical agent sent to the Arkansas in September of 1863. Of the many illnesses he identified, some posed an immediate threat to life (pneumonia and influenza), and several were chronically debilitating (bronchitis, catarrhal fever, gonorrhea, syphilis, and several disorders resulting in diarrhea). There were also twenty-five cases of a mysterious malady, perhaps a bacterial invasion through insect bites, that left victims grotesquely swollen and often dead within two days. Such an illness, and several of the others, indicated a dangerously low threshold of infection because of insufficient diet and generally poor health, a point emphasized by the report. The sick were nearly destitute of clothing and close to starvation, the doctor wrote. After waiting weeks for annuities, they were now eating mostly unripe fruit and the putrid flesh of sick animals.[14]

The immediate impact of disease was so terrible that it is easy to miss other results, indirect but almost as deadly. Any society's economic life will be temporarily crippled when so many people die so quickly. The result is not hard to imagine, with animals not hunted, fields untilled, and babies not suckled. Malnourished people naturally invited further diseases.

Other effects are even easier to overlook, because to understand them we have to ask and look for what did *not* happen. In mathematical terms, the Indians' demographic disaster stemmed both from mass subtraction and an equally terrible lack of addition. Not only were North American Indians dying by the scores of thousands; survivors were also less capable of putting more Indians into the world. The calamity came both from rising mortality and dropping fertility.

Diseases normally strike hardest at the youngest and oldest—those persons who are least able to produce children—but the new epidemics, generationally speaking, were great democrats. They bit savagely into all age groups. As wave after wave of diseases struck Indian peoples, huge numbers of potential mothers and fathers died, with a cumulative result of many more infants never conceived. This effect was compounded when the same disease invaded more than once over a relatively short span of time. The result was a heartbreaking demographic rhythm. Those who survived the first assault, now immune, began making and rearing children, only to see their unprotected sons and daughters taken away when the plague once again swooped down. In 1832 smallpox reportedly killed half the residents of four Pawnee villages, including, their missionary said, most persons under thirty. Six years later the great smallpox outbreak of 1837–38 took almost everyone under fourteen.[15]

Making matters even worse, several diseases crippled the ability of surviving couples to produce children. Smallpox left many men sterile and many women less able to carry fetuses to term. Tuberculosis (which, if not introduced by Europeans, apparently became more common and virulent after their arrival) clogged genital tracts, made intercourse painful, and often led to spontaneous abortions. Venereal diseases produced genital lesions in women and sterility in men. Women with malaria were more likely to deliver prematurely. Among men, malaria brought lethargy, malaise, and decreased desire.

Alcoholism had a similar effect. This last disease, both physical and social in its etiology, should encourage us to ask other questions about the psychological impact of these pandemics. If depression is the most common psychological cause of individual male impotence, what is the result of collective despair on a society's husbands, wives, and lovers? At that level of inspiration where the physical and emotional blend, the act of sex is partly an act of hope. Many Native American couples, otherwise ready and able to make love and babies, surely looked at the nightmare around them and wondered, "What's the point?" The effect of malaise on fertility is unproveable, but the record hints occasionally of a mass hopelessness. By Omaha tradition, for example, a twin epidemic of cholera and smallpox just after 1800 reduced this once-powerful group to barely three hundred persons, down from perhaps three thousand several years before. Seeing little ahead to attract them, and supposedly horrified by their own pocked faces and believing their children would inherit the scars, the Omahas marched *en masse* against the Cheyennes, Pawnees, and Otos, intending to fight to their collective death. A few survivors eventually returned to their villages (where later diseases would ravage them again).[16]

The raw census numbers tell a lot of what was happening. Already noted was the imbalance of the sexes resulting from endemic warfare–three women for every two men among the Southern Cheyennes and Arapahoes. That suggests, at the least, a mass uncoupling of conjugal units and a general marital instability. Even more revealing was the ratio of children to their elders. In a reproductively robust society the number of children will far surpass that of adults.

Among the Cheyennes of the Arkansas valley, by contrast, sons and daughters made up barely a third of their population.[17] Struggling to stay alive in the present, these Indians, as families, found it increasingly difficult to send babies into the future. Their numbers were figured not by multiplication but division—or, as an official put it matter-of-factly, "the Indian tribes on this frontier are fast passing away, with the . . . number of deaths exceed[ing] that of births."[18]

To put it mildly, the families pressing against these natives were more successful in reproducing themselves. Euro-American plains pioneers were something like a generational juggernaut. The fertility index among white settlers on the Kansas frontier in 1860, measuring the number of children under ten per women of child-bearing age, was greater than anywhere in the world today. It would exceed that of Ethiopia (the current leader), double that of Columbia, and more than triple that of the United States.[19]

White families were also far more likely to keep people in the world once they had put them there. Frontier oral history is full of pioneer tribulations, but there is little to indicate that life in most of the West was more treacherous than elsewhere. It may have been a good bit safer, and folk myths to the contrary, there is not the slightest hint that hostile Indians posed any significant threat to the westering population. (The plains residents who had by far the most reason to fear death from hostile attack were Indians, primarily from other Indians fighting for control of vital areas and resources.) The mortality in Cloud County, Kansas, is a case in point. Recently settled by whites, it had a population of 2,323 in 1870. That year it recorded a single death from Indian attack, that of an eleven-year-old boy. There were twenty-three other fatalities. None suggested any threat peculiar to the frontier. Besides two drownings and a man shot while duck hunting, all were from disease. Adults died mostly from consumption, which they had probably had brought with them. Fourteen of the year's dead, nearly sixty percent, were children—an appalling percentage today but one normal for that time. As on the overland trails, the frontier's promiscuous mix of emigrants occasionally posed unusual dangers, but such situations were pretty rare.[20] Most child deaths, as in Cloud County, were from illnesses like scarlet fever and whooping cough as common in Pennsylvania and Georgia as in Kansas or Montana.

All in all, the plains frontier was not a particularly dangerous place to live—unless, of course, you were an Indian. Among white pioneers there was nothing resembling the murderous scythings of disease, nor the grinding malnutrition and deterioration of living standards that ate away at Indian numbers. The white population profile— low mortality and high fertility—was the mirror image to that of the natives. When the two are seen as competing systems of creating and maintaining people, the advantage could hardly be clearer. Regenerative weakness versus demographic clout: it was not an even matchup.

□□□□□

The pioneers' heroic baby-making gladdened the hearts of many national spokesmen, who warned white, old-stock parents that they were in a breeding contest for control of the new country. The competition, however, was not from the Indians but from elsewhere. The winner of an essay competition sponsored by the American Medical Association at the end of the Civil War caught the point:

> [T]he great territories of the far West, just opening to
> civilization, and the fertile South, now disinthralled and first
> made habitable by freemen, offer homes for countless millions
> yet unborn. Shall they be filled by our own children or by those
> of aliens? This is a question that our own women must answer;
> upon their loins depends the future destiny of the nation.[21]

In one frontier history's many bits of black humor, pioneers were warned, even as they overran and outbirthed western natives, that they had to keep up, spawn for spawn, with another wave of fertile invaders flooding in behind *them* from the east.

Not that they needed the encouragement. Frontier parents produced a lot of children because in many ways it suited their interests. Husbands and wives were not equally eager for new babies. Mothers bore the brunt of child care, an exhausting set of tasks heaped on top of their usual load of work. Bearing and birthing infants was also dangerous; as everywhere in America, a western woman was most likely to lose her life through the process of giving life to someone else. Nonetheless, the frontier birth rate was prodigious and for several reasons. Dispossession of Indians opened vast sweeps of land at a time when eastern farm acreage was increasingly crowded and expensive. That drew a disproportionate number of young couples just beginning their prime child-producing years. Parents also may have been less concerned with birth control because they felt more confident than their eastern cousins that their children would grow up to find plenty of cheap farmland of their own. Most fundamentally, a large family was an economic asset; if children were more a burden and threat to women than to men, they also offered enormous advantages to both.

As its second definition, a family—not its men, or women, or any particular members, but the family as a whole—was a productive unit. Its members did not exercise the same power, or control equally the results of their labors, but the family was nonetheless a mutually reinforcing group of workers who relied on their own collective efforts for their economic survival and hopes of prosperity.

The common impression of the frontier is that of a place where solitary men, with eyes steeled and muscles flexed, confronted and changed the new land largely through their own efforts. The real story would be clear if we could follow a household of plains homesteaders on their daily rounds. Assuming a family dwelling was already built, the father might work the fields—breaking sod, planting and harrowing in the spring or harvesting in the fall—or he might build fences, plant an orchard, or tend to business in town. During high summer he might be gone altogether, searching for work until the crops fully ripened. Besides her many household duties, the mother would care for the large garden, milk several cows, churn butter and prepare eggs for sale at market, and see to miscellaneous chores within a thirty-yard radius of the soddie's threshold. Girls and boys would range among most of the adults' work, while also doing their own. As young as two or three they helped in cleaning, bringing in fuel, and caring for pigs and chickens. By five or six they were milking, gathering eggs, and hauling barrels of water from as far as three or four miles away. At eight or nine they were helping in the fields, caring for young siblings, and herding cattle, sometimes as hired hands for childless neighbors.[22]

These children also provided much of the day-to-day subsistence. Until crops began to yield an income, this family had to find its food from its immediate vicinity. Children from three or four upwards spent considerable time searching out and gathering a remarkable variety of wild plants—pigweed, purslane, sourdock and other greens, edible weeds, roots for tea, berries, wild plums, and many fruits that grew thickly along the streams. Older boys and girls shot and snared rabbits, squirrels, deer, prairie chickens, and other game. Adults brought in some meat by hunting bison, but even here children often helped. While riding with his daughter, Luna, and other young relatives, Walter Warner came across a small herd of buffaloes pursued by hunters. Luna Warner described in her diary how the family quickly moved into action as a team. After her cousin killed one bison, they spotted another about a mile away:

> Pa took Arabella's [her young cousin's] horse and went after it. I went afoot, got there long before Pa did. . . . As soon as the horse saw the buffalo she snorted and stopped. Pa got off. He handed me the bridle while he went for the buffalo, revolver in hand. The buffalo saw him and went up the ravine out of sight. Pa went to the top of the hill and back on the other side, but saw nothing of him till at last he happened to spy him. He fired and then they came right toward us. The horse sprang and snorted and whirled around me, but I kept fast hold and talked to her and she arched her neck. Patty [a young friend] had just come from chasing the other buffaloes, then she went for him and worried him until Pa had shot four times. Then he [no relative, just the buffalo] fell dead in the ravine. . . . [We] hitched the oxen to the buffalo and dragged him up where they could skin him . . . [and] they all went to skinning the buffalo with pocket knives. After it was dressed I went and drove up the oxen.[23]

Here was the frontier's domestic economy cut down to a scale we can understand. What normally is described as the job of manly nimrods is done by a man in cooperation with girls and boys of varied ages, down to the skinning with pocket knives.

No wonder, then, that most who headed west, at least those coming to the farming frontier, preferred living as part of a family. In Buffalo Township, a freshly settled section of the recently formed Cloud County, Kansas, about nine out of every ten persons lived as related members of a family household. Many of the rest boarded with families. There were plenty of youngsters crawling and toddling around the newly cut soddies. Households with children averaged nearly three apiece; seven out of forty-seven had five or more.

For the same reasons families liked to settle close to relatives. The popular image of pioneers breaking bonds with their relatives as they moved west is easily exaggerated. Especially on the farming and stockraising frontiers, families often tried to transplant or quickly reweave those webs of relations so important to rural life. The Oklahoma land rushes are a case in point. These frantic scramblings for some of the last unclaimed land on the plains are normally pictured as the ultimate examples of hell-bent individualism and the frontier's fierce, atomizing competitive spirit. A recent study of one of the last and largest rushes, however, shows that related families among the boomers commonly devised elaborate strategies to seize neighboring pieces of land. Others quickly swapped claims to nuzzle closer to relatives. The dust had barely settled before much of country had resolved itself into interconnected holdings among parents, children, grandparents, siblings, cousins and in-laws.[24]

Buffalo Township once again is a case in point. Although settled only a few years, thirty-seven of its hundred dwellings held people with the same names and origins as neighbors. Among these were many single men living alone; at first glance they might have seemed solitaires, but in fact they were baching it next to kin. Besides these obvious relatives, there were several suspicious cases of foreign-born settlers from the same homelands—Danes, Swedes, Norwegians—who clustered together. This was the pattern throughout the central plains. Surprisingly often interlocking family networks moved westward intact, or a single household would lure out relatives, who in turn would entice their own kin until a matrix of relations spread over whole counties and more. The teenage diarist Luna Warner, she of the family buffalo hunt just described, came to Kansas as part of group with connections so complicated that one needs a roster to keep them straight. Her father and two of his brothers were married to three sisters. These three households had nine children among them, including two from one brother's deceased first wife, who had also been a sister to the three current wives. A widowed brother to the four sisters came along with his daughter, as well as his deceased wife's brother. Alpheus Cleveland, a "distant relative," was also in the neighborhood.[25]

These were not extended families in the strictest sense. Parents and children typically did not share their roof with aunts, grandparents, or cousins. The nuclear arrangement persisted and remained the focal point of settlers' labor and emotional lives, but their work and leisure also meshed into housefuls of kin nearby. The advantages of such clan settlement were enormous. Many labors of rooting into a place—house-building, breaking ground, harvesting, fighting prairie fires, some hunting of larger game—were far easier done collectively. Although strangers could help one another, and did, families obviously were better off arriving with tested relationships intact and ready to use. There were, besides, dozens of ways that intimacy, a depth of shared knowledge, and a seasoned intuition allowed neighboring relatives to respond to each other's crises and daily needs. Luna Warner's relatives stepped in to do heavier tasks around her homestead, for instance, while her handicapped father, Walter, worked at what he could, including clock-making in town, and when her alcoholic "Uncle Howard" (actually her uncle's brother-in-law) suffered *delirium tremens*, a collection of relatives took turns nursing him through.[26]

For many, family support came from much farther afield. A Nebraska homesteader was asked by his sister if she could send anything to help. He provided a list: "Here it is. a yoke of cattle, a wagon, a cow, a well, an orchard full of fruit, a good house & barn, a crib full of corn, 6 big hogs, and a house full of Furniture. put em in bbl & send by express C.O.D."[27] His joke acknowledged that settlers often relied heavily on necessities, from medicine and clothes to seed and money, pumped onto the plains via mail and rail from relatives back east or in Europe. Families themselves moved back and forth along those lines of communication and support. Parched or eaten out by drought or grasshoppers, parents and children returned to live briefly with relatives, gathering resources and strength for another try. A pregnant wife might shuttle to her parents in Missouri or Indiana in time for birthing in a safer setting.[28]

Thus, a plains settler often lived within three concentric rings of support. At the center was a nuclear family, itself composed of complementary, mutually supportive parts. Next was a familial community of separate households, all within a day's ride of one another. Beyond that was a family network ranging outward over regions and even continents.

We are used to thinking of the frontier as a splintering, fragmenting influence on national life; and so it was, but working against that tendency was the family. Because their vast productive and sustaining power made them hugely valuable, families rooted and quickly spread, and as they did they pulled against the centrifugal force of westering emigration, knitting together rural settlements and connecting them with societies that had sent them forth. Families were the most powerful influence counteracting the frontier's isolating, exclusivist inclinations.

That binding, unifying tendency contributed to another important consequence. As they supported one another, families were finally and absolutely undermining any last glimmering hopes of native autonomy. A homesteading family, as a productive unit, also ought to be seen as an extraordinarily efficient machine of environmental change. Its several parts worked together to transform the land. The father's strength was needed to break the sod, but with new steel-tipped plows boys and girls as young as eight or nine could handle subsequent plowing while their father broke more land or saw to other tasks. Children harrowed the turned soil, sometimes using sticks and kitchen knives to bust the thick clods, and once crops were up they spent hundreds of hours pulling native weeds. The same children tended cattle and sheep. Those hoofed invaders were, in effect, given protected possession of pasture and water essential to the survival of indigenous grazers. As they promoted hayfields, furthermore, children, mothers, and fathers were altering plant ecologies by favoring some grasses over others—forage that was, of course, also denied to wild ungulates. As they progressively constricted native animals' food supplies, pioneers were also killing outright thousands of bison, antelope, deer, elk, and other creatures, which then were slaughtered and cooked by mothers and fed to fathers and children who, newly refueled, would get on with the work of changing the land.

This is not to say these families were in control, any more than the Indians had been. As with the natives, many of their changes were wholly unintended. Seeds of eastern grasses and weeds, including Kentucky bluegrass, arrived in the cracks of wagon beds and the guts of cattle. (Life was transformed beneath the ground, too, when emigrants inadvertently carried in eggs of new species of earthworms and other invertebrates. Quantitatively, in fact, this invasion was arguably the most significant; on the eastern plains today the biomass just below the surface, including many subterranean hitch-hikers that had come with the homesteaders, is greater than that up top.)[29] The farmers' intentional changes, furthermore, had consequences far beyond their understanding. Busting the soil, slaughtering most large indigenous ungulates and disrupting foraging arrangements among the survivors, cutting trees and undergrowth along the streams, extinguishing prairie fires, and crowding cattle, sheep and horses into spaces incapable of feeding them—these and other workings had results that were sweeping, complicated and totally unforeseen: elimination of natural root systems, erosion of stream sides and silting of creeks and rivers, destruction of diverse communities of complementary grasses, shrubs and forbs, denial of fire's regenerative functions, loosening and leaching of the topsoil, raising its temperature and revising its chemistry.

Pioneer farmers wrote of their labors as beneficent gifts to future generations. In fact, these families were undermining their own future. They set in motion intricate patterns of biotic and material change that eventually would drive thousands of families, many of them their own descendants, back out of this country. However, in the short run farmers and stockraisers completed the process, begun partly by the Indians themselves, of removing the basis of Native American material life. As already seen, by the 1850s pastoral hunters, overlanders, and their animals had destroyed much of the forage and groves along rivers, and by the 1860s bison populations were badly decimated. Now, in the 1870s, new intruders brought changes of far greater magnitude. For the first time the century's invasions were profoundly altering land away from the heavily traveled Arkansas and Platte Rivers—the valleys of the Republican, Solomon, and Smoky Hill Rivers, the hundreds of smaller streams, and the giant sweeps of highlands between the many watercourses. These had been the Indians' hunting and grazing ranges, as vital as the bottomlands of the Platte and Arkansas. The legion of farmers was transforming these huge expanses into something that natives could never again use in the older ways.

Boosters and politicians were fond of marking their society's triumphal advance with maps of newly surveyed land.[30] A better measure would have shown country taken up, year by year, by homesteaders. Between 1870 and 1880 sixteen new counties were formed in west central Kansas. Virtually no farms were there at the decade's start, but at its end an area nearly as large as Massachusetts, about 4,220,000 acres, had been claimed. Of that, 1,228,000 acres, roughly equal to Connecticut and Delaware combined, was being cultivated. Land broken to the plow increased by 1,139 percent during the second five years alone.[31] Far more than the geometric march of range and township, the invasion of the soil-rippers measured the rapidly expanding grip of white possession. This ecological conquest was more lasting than all military campaigns and any government policy; and its chief agent, the most effective enemy of the Indians' pastoral economy and lifeways, was the pioneer family.

Families laid claim to the country in another way. Besides making over the land physically, they carried in heavy loads of cultural baggage. As they planted crops and inadvertently sowed new weeds, they were also creating a social environment, a valuescape, establishing schools and churches, broadcasting seeds of ideals and intolerances.

As its third meaning, a family is a conveyor of traditions and social form. Its role in transplanting values and institutions is not easily described. At the simplest level, a single family doggedly tried to carry its past into the new country. The most cramped sod house was often jammed with articles heavy with cultural meanings—books, photographs and lithographs, knick-knacks, musical instruments or a music box, pieces of fine clothing and delicate porcelain. These items were worthless to the economic tasks at hand. Set among everyday tools and simple furniture, they were reminders of the pioneers' dual obsessions: making the land pay and transplanting what they considered the essentials of their mother culture. Books represented an explicitly recognized heritage. Teacups and a silver spoon recalled distant relations and reinforced respect for manners. Memories of childhood lessons were embroidered into tablecloths. An idealized photograph of parents strengthened a generational order and summoned up dozens of encouragements and injunctions. Music combined all these. With a guitar or parlor organ came songs expressing a body of public sentiment and tradition, while singing itself was a sensual conjuring of past moments, absent relatives, and implied responsibilities.

These connections do not begin to describe the subtle interactions between family and the transmission of values. So snarled together were the two that the very absence of families had an effect, as shown most clearly among the all-male parties that passed over the plains on their way to the Pacific coast. The sudden change of landscape made men realize how much of a break they had made.

The immediate response for many was to pine for wives and children left behind. Some wrote with drippy melodrama. One Sunday morning on the trail Solomon Gorgas imagined his children going to church (his "rosy cheeked tribe of happy urchens racing on to the House of God"); then there was a dramatic end to his letter: ". . . but I must stop—my heart—oh dear!"[32] We can almost see him press his wrist to his forehead. More often the words show genuine pain, and through that, how important families were in these men's lives:

> I drempt last night I was home. I thought I was mighty
> happy. I thought little Sis was standing by the door. I thought
> she had grown tremendous but I knew her. . . . To tell you
> the truth Tilda I have been homesick several times & if I get
> home I am sure I never will leave it again for along time.
> This trip will do for a single [man] but I firmly believe a
> married man had better stay at home. . . . When little Sis
> begins to talk, learn her to call me, wont you?[33]

Some travelers observed that men, when separated from families, soon lived like the animals they drove; but when a female appeared, things changed. "How strange! Our whole camp is quieter, obscene and improper language not heard just because a woman is in camp," a diarist wrote when a wife and husband joined his party more than a month down the road: "Without society men almost become desperadoes, *men are not for men.*"[34] It was not women *per se* that made the difference, he was saying, but "society," which here meant the complementary, mutually reinforcing ideals of wife and husband. If a child showed up, with its implied need for safekeeping and instruction, single men felt other powerful expectations, unspoken and unquestioned. It was a kind of cultural chemistry. Floating alone, any one of the family's parts, a man or woman or child, was an inert element; but if two or three were brought together, they were transformed by spontaneous creation, individuals into roles and obligations. Men instantly were protectors, women civilizers, boys and girls receptors and bearers of traditions. Five unrelated persons were a bunch of travelers or settlers. A family of five was a cultural imperative.

On arrival in an area of new settlement, families, as social and cultural institutions, were quickly tangled in the making of communities. The relationship was complicated. A community is usually made up of families; but that's not *all* a community is, and a bunch of families does not necessarily transform into one. On the frontier, in fact, the family could retard the formation of communities in their fullest sense.

A true community requires that its members associate their interests with it and with its survival and its full development. In a sense, its people must surrender part of their individual identity and their commitment to their most intimate institutions, the family in particular. On the frontier, that shifting of commitment came slowly or not at all. For reasons described earlier, the needs of the day tightened family bonds. People looked more to their immediate kin, not less, and as a result they were more likely to place the interests of family above, and often in opposition to, any larger collective whole. This tendency was naturally aggravated by the rapid, even frenzied, movement of people.[35]

Historian John Mack Faragher has suggested that the frontier's vaunted individualism was often something else—a kind of "familialism." It was not a case, that is, of lone men and women standing against the world, but of families and kin groups protecting their own and posing their interests against larger, broader collections of people outside the familial perimeter. This naturally retarded the flourishing of society in its fullest sense. A community, according to sociologist Conrad Arensberg, is "the minimal group capable of reenacting in the present and transmitting into the future" a society's "cultural and institutional inventory." By those terms, most new western communities were not doing their job fully. Weakened and undermined by their people's mobility and by self-protective families, they often suffered from arrested development.[36] There was a parallel here to the fragmentation of Native American communities moving onto the plains just prior to white pioneers. In both cases the challenge of a new life broke down wider identities and threw people back on the support of their closest relations. Family and community were, in this sense, opposed.

That said, it is just as clear that communities and families cannot be understood apart from each other. The family might indeed have limited the scope of communities and their maturation; but in the communal life that *did* develop, the family's stamp was obvious. Family and community ultimately bled into one another.

The earliest public life on the plains frontier, for instance, is best understood as a projection of impulses at work inside its homes. The first political action often was the formation of a school district. Laws usually promised, even required, the founding of a school once a certain number of children were living more than a prescribed distance from an operating schoolhouse, but in reality it was almost always up to local residents to take the initiative. Sometimes that meant recruiting enough students to reach the critical mass that would bring in public funds. When the Tripp family passed through Jewell County, Kansas, excited locals looked at their wagon bulging with children and tried to bribe them to stay with the best available land.[37]

The founding of a school, then, was not a case of government imposing an obligation for the social good; rather, settlers were pressing government to help in extending their domestic lives into the public sphere. Cash-strapped farmers pooled funds to hire teachers and build schoolhouses, an outlay that said a lot about their determination. While paying to get their own farms started, Kansans and Nebraskans were establishing more schools per thousand children than could be found in Michigan or Massachusetts.[38] Schoolhouses became the earliest gathering places and school programs some of the first collective entertainments. These performances, idealized in pioneer reminiscent literature, ought to be seen as complex expressions of a drive to implant outside values. Watching and listening to children recite and declaim, the audience was seeing common ground established among (and imposed upon) varied peoples, and not just in the specifics of history lessons and verses memorized. Education always had far broader functions. In a boy's reading of Shakespeare and a girl's posing in tableau, plenty could be learned about sex roles, moral nuance, and definitions of character. On stage was a wide range of social givens, the shoulds and ought nots that parents were expected to pass generationally in the home.

This garbling of the familial, the social, and the political was even clearer in early urban centers, including the cattle towns that we usually remember as the holy cities of the masculine, bowlegged, rootin' tootin' frontier. Historians lately have made this point in the context of western women's history. Earlier writers usually ignored women's shaping influence because women rarely held positions of formal political power.[39] Nevertheless, in many areas—charitable work and relief for the poor, temperance reforms, suffrage, education, campaigns against prostitution, and more—women shaped urban life virtually from the time the first boards were nailed together.[40]

Recent work on these topics has driven home the lesson that the "doctrine of the two spheres," the Victorian injunction that women were to keep to the home while men saw to all aspects of business and government, tell us little about what was happening in western towns.

These points are healthy antidotes to the older, male-dominated story of town-building; but they tend to obscure a larger lesson. In local politics generally, not merely in women's lives, the line between home and community was always blurry. Many influential adults, males as well as females, held a particular vision of what their towns should be, and that ideal was a Victorian family writ large. Elected leaders were to be good fathers, benevolent but strong; women were to set a moral tone and keep this collective home, figuratively speaking, swept and tidy; community vices, if not suppressed, should at least be kept out of sight, like a whiskey bottle behind a hat box on the top shelf of a closet. This ideal was imperfectly realized in public life, of course, just as in individual homes. Town fathers were guilty of abuse and neglect of their civic families, mothers of moral brow-beating. Schools were short of money, just as housewives never had enough time to teach at home. The community, as family, seemed always to have some scapegrace brother-in-law living uneasily under its roof, stumbling in at teatime and smelling of beer.

Still, as a means of understanding what was going on, this familial patterning tells us a lot. Cowtown conflicts often were expressed in the rhetoric of the proper family, and some political fights sounded like battles over parenting strategies. Bordellos first were tolerated because their fines and taxes fed the town's coffers, and, besides, the cathouses were irrepressible. "Where the carrion is there you will find the buzzard," a Dodge City editor wrote.[41] When opposition nonetheless developed in Abilene, Mayor Joseph G. McCoy, "father of the cattle trade," exiled prostitutes to a plot of land just outside town. Income from the houses would keep the urban household solvent, he argued, while upright homes would be doubly protected; corrupting influences would remain out of sight while providing an outlet for depraved desires.[42] Reformers would have none of it. Calling the sprawl of bagnios and whiskey holes a "vile ulcer," they waved away the pretense that vice could be segregated, especially in such close quarters. (They had a point. A couple of years later Wichita citizens objected to prostitutes' nude bathing in the Arkansas close to downtown and their "reckless riding and ex-posure on the thoroughfares.")[43] Unless this "devil's addition" was closed, the editor of Abilene's *Chronicle* warned, "almost the entire community may become debauched—including little school chil-dren." No income was worth that price. Above all, he argued, indi-vidual morality was inseparable from a town's collective character. Families and community were of a piece: "Personal virtue and pu-rity are necessary to the real happiness and growth of a community. The fountain cannot rise above its source—if the people are im-pure, the town must be so likewise."[44] The next year the cattle trade shifted to other termini, higher fines were imposed on harlotry, and the flesh trade, while not eliminated, was drastically reduced.

The same impulse could be seen in dozens of less dramatic ways. Public entertainments were compelled to meet standards of civic parents. There were, it is true, freak shows and sidewalk grostesqueries, such as an armless veteran who loaded, primed, and fired guns with his feet and another man who could "swallow longer things" than could an African ostrich.[45] However, more formal acts were careful to present their credentials. One of Dodge City's most popular per-formers was the former school mistress Louie Lord, who promised that her performances "exclude every low epithet or immoral idea." The summer months brought "Old John Robinson's . . . STRICTLY MORAL CIRCUS" and that of Dan Costello, advertised as the "best regulated, best managed and most respectable" in the nation.[46]

This line of analysis can obviously be pushed too hard. Towns were not familial commonwealths. Settlers' loyalty and identity stayed mainly with their immediate kin and household. Policy was set according to business interests at least as much as to hearthside values, and politicians often piously invoked images of family to maneuver for factional and private gain. The very vehemence of morality campaigns testified that there was vice enough to go around, and then some.

Nevertheless, the fact that politicians and editors appealed as they did, playing to their public through a rhetoric of domesticity, tells us something basic about popular sentiment and prevailing at-titudes. Hypocrites or not, townspeople felt a powerful need to act out publicly the virtues of the Victorian home. Even those who thumbed their noses at the moral order, on a closer look, could show how strong the family's hold could be.

Take, for instance, the cattle town's most famous wild things—cowboys and whores. Teddy Blue Abbott was a cowpuncher, rounder, and the most famous memoirist of the cattle trail. He recalled proudly that "we wasn't respectable and we sure didn't pretend to be;" but two paragraphs earlier, remembering cowtown prostitutes, he wrote that "we all had our favorites once we got acquainted. We'd go in town and marry a girl for a week, take her to breakfast and dinner and supper, be with her all the time."[47] Those prostitutes, as Anne Butler has shown, often married legally, but not to nice fellows like Teddy Blue and only very rarely, in contrast to romantic tradition, to lovestruck deacons who took them away from it all. Usually they found husbands among the pimps, saloonmen, and the bottom-scrapings of the western *demi-monde*.

Cowboys and prostitutes cannot have believed that their actions would bring them the slightest respectability. Whores might have hoped their husbands would give them some stability and protection, although almost always they found more exploitation and abuse in marriages that, in Butler's words, "failed miserably in the area of domestic tranquility."[48] Perhaps a subtler impulse was at work. Familial form and structure were so fundamental that just about everyone followed them. "Soiled doves" and rambling cowboys were ordering their worlds in ways basically akin to the guardians of morality who condemned them. Whatever their backgrounds, and regardless of how differently their present days were turning, these new westerners instinctively tried to give their lives context and meaning by replication of family, however tenuous its form.

Everything written so far could easily leave a reader with two misconceptions. I have written of families monolithically, as if each were an organic whole. Family members played different roles, as they changed the land and made babies, but as pictured here the parts have meshed as one. Families also have appeared rather static and stable. They have seemed fixed and unchanging within a world in flux.

In fact, these families were as contentious, flexible and sometimes as unstable as ours are today. By its fourth definition, a family is a relationship of power. Authority and control are never equally distributed; neither are the benefits and the fruits of family labors. That disposition of power, furthermore, could shift with circumstances. As families moved onto the central plains and faced new opportunities and difficulties, the changes worked differently on their various members, giving to some and taking away from others.

For quite a while now historians have developed these themes in telling the story of Euro-American pioneer women. Heading west had quite different meanings and implications for emigrants, depending on their gender. Women perceived the new country differently from men, saw different possibilities and threats in it. They generally made the move more grudgingly, and for good reasons. They would be expected to do more with less. They faced the tasks of making a proper Victorian home and rearing children under trying, even brutal conditions and often without the help of kinsfolk and trusted neighbors. Their lives were relatively more isolated. Prospects of widowhood were in some ways more daunting than back home. Egalitarian frontier myths to the contrary, women were unlikely to gain much more influence in their new homes, and the decision to stay or to bail out and head back east usually rested far more with husbands than wives. Children, in turn, had perspectives fundamentally different from their parents, and although they had considerable control over their own lives, within the family their power was certainly less than that of either parent.

The different perspectives and imbalanced power naturally made for plenty of conflict and estrangement. Tensions were aggravated by frontier conditions—the stress of relocation, confinement in a dank house smaller than a modern garage, the blister and freeze of erratic weather, the relentless wind, the weight of work, the nagging tension from gambles taken with all possessions in the pot. Domestic abuse may have been further fed by what one writer called a "subculture of violence" among plains settlers.[49] Practiced bullies found encouragement (and excuses) to do as they wished, and in isolated households there was little to stop them. As today, most violence in homes remained hidden, but the record includes enough cases, including some genuine horror stories. A Nebraskan reportedly broke his wife's arms, left her outside overnight with a broken leg, and roasted her pet dog alive in the oven.[50]

This is not to say that most homes were dens of abuse. Many letters and diaries are full of affection, loyalty, mutual support, and love. Frontier life could draw husbands, wives, and children together as well as set them at one another's throats. The lesson, rather, is that the move west unsettled familial relations. It pulled more on the resources and energies of some than of others; it left some more vulnerable and some in firmer command.

For most plains pioneers, the family was the inescapable emotional arena of daily life and the setting that most determined their limits of the possible. We cannot begin to understand the social history of this part of the West until we take into account the cross currents inside these frontier households. The meaning of the westward movement, as personal experience, varied according to many factors, none more consistent and revealing that a participant's place within his or her family and how that place changed in the new country.

This holds true, furthermore, as much for Native American emigrants as for whites. These themes—the shifts of power inside families, the responsive changes to new conditions, and the very different experiences that resulted—in fact were more clearly shown among Indians, because in many ways their move onto the plains involved much greater modifications in lifeways.

It is difficult to overstate the importance of family in Native American society and life. Cosmology is expressed as familial connections. The Kiowa sacred cycle concerns Grandmother Spider and the War Twins, two boys created from one who was the Son of the Sun. The tribe's spiritual guardians are sacred bundles called the Ten Grandmothers, each of whom was originally watched over by a brother and sister. Plains peoples conceive of natural forces as living in households and having family squabbles. Human relations with, and obligations to, other life forms are pictured and explained through kinship. The Cheyennes' right to hunt bison and other animals, for instance, derives from a series of tests and a race between beasts and a man who was aided by a bison cow and calf who came to him as humans and formed a household with him. Bears, the plains animals most closely resembling men, have been considered especially close cousins; an enthnologist recently wrote of being awakened in a camp in Yellowstone National Park by the cries of an elderly Cheyenne woman: "Come quickly! The ancestors are eating the garbage!"[51]

To say that family is a metaphor for the world misses the point. The world is not *like* a family; existence *is* an intricate knitting of familial bonds. Family is both the mechanism that best explains how the world works and the structure on which each of its parts—people, muskrats, the whirl of stars—is hung. Not surprisingly, it has also been the basis of human social organization. Other associations, notably warrior and religious societies, cut across lines of kinship, but the family has been the fundamental unit from which an Indian community has been made.

It was quite important, therefore, for each person to be able to plot his or her place in the mental map of kinship. The Cheyenne language has twenty-eight basic terms for familial relationships. These can be modified and extended, however, to express about twenty thousand variations.[52] The various emphases of lineages and group-ings implied through language were part of the social geometry in which an individual acted. That structure went a long way toward de-termining one's duties and prerogatives, one's closest allegiances, and the limits of permissible behavior. Power and favors and things flowed through those family linkages. Within them, a person found a measure of protection and access to necessities. Anyone outside, by contrast, was severely disadvantaged in seeking the fruits of human converse.

When Indians like the Cheyennes moved out of the Missouri val-ley onto the plains, their family arrangements changed, conforming partly to conditions and demands of the new setting. As Fred Eggan argued nearly forty years ago, natives who came from quite different backgrounds adopted similar kinship systems and social structures.[53] A couple of trends stand out. The family in its broadest definition— a kinship network that bound individuals into broad, extended groupings—fragmented. Cheyennes no longer lived in large com-munities, as they had in horticultural villages along the Missouri. For most of the year they lived instead in "camps," each of which was essentially a matrilineal and matrilocal extended family made up of a couple, their unmarried daughters and sons, their married daughters with their respective husbands and children, and any other adopted relatives. Within a camp, or *vestoz*, each "elementary fam-ily" of parents and children had its own lodge, but all cooperated in acquiring and preparing food, caring for children, and other tasks. As already noted, this splintering was in part a response to an envi-ronment that could support sizable concentrations of people for only a small part of each year. These smaller groups were also much more efficient for people relying on hunting within a limited range, re-gardless of ecological particulars.[54]

The family changed also at a more basic level. Polygyny, a man's taking of more than one wife, became far more common. There were

two incentives. So many warriors died in the bitter warfare for control of hunting territory that, as already noted, women outnumbered
men, often by as many as three-to-two. Widows were absorbed as
additional wives in other households, usually that of one of the
widow's married sisters. Surviving husbands, furthermore, needed
more family workers, since, as will be described shortly, a mounted
hunter could kill more animals than one wife could process. The
need for more hands to prepare hides also drew women into marriage at an earlier age, at least among some groups. By the 1880s
most Blackfoot women (or girls) were marrying at twelve, four or
five years younger than in the 1780s.[55]

Every student of plains Indians is familiar with these developments. Rarely, however, are they set in the larger context of western
history. When they are, they encourage us to think of the family as
the basic adaptive mechanism of all emigrants, native and white, as
they tried to make their way in the new setting of the central plains.
All reached toward the most practical family size and groupings of
kin; all sought a balance between the household and wider circles of
relatives. Their solutions could be quite similar. A Cheyenne
vestoz, with its mutually supportive lodges of intermarried nuclear
families, was not so unlike the clustering of Luna Warner's clan in
Osborne County.

Just as with whites, these changes and the move west had varied
meanings and implications for different members of Native American families. The point is made best by looking at the experiences
of Indian women. Moving onto the plains offered them some advantages. The hide trade brought manufactures that eased some
domestic tasks: metal sewing awls, hide scrapers, brass kettles, bed
ticking, heavy cloth to line the inside of lodges, curve-bladed butcher
knives, and skeins of thread.[56] With trade goods women developed
more varied and utilitarian clothing styles; the older costume of the
central and south plains, a skin skirt and poncho that was removed
in warm weather to reveal tattooed breasts, was giving way by the
1850s to a long dress of trade cloth, with kimono sleeves and inset
gores.[57] Horses with travois lessened the burden of carrying goods
from camp to camp. In at least one case the horse and trading culture led to a ceremonial change that women must have welcomed.
Traditionally a Comanche man's death was followed by the ritual
killing of his wife (or wives) and horse (or horses). By the early

nineteenth century, however, tribal herds were proliferating, and women were becoming more valuable in preparing animal skins for trade. In 1816 these developments ran head-on into another consequence of the coming of Euro-Americans. When smallpox ravaged the Comanches that year, mourning relatives reportedly slaughtered five thousand horses and, presumably, hundreds of women. By the 1820s, only a horse or two were slain at a man's death. Women were spared.[58]

On balance, however, women's position worsened. Something similar seems to have happened in many other parts of the world, as native societies participated with growing enthusiasm in European trade. The decline of women's status was partly from the commercial involvement itself, but it apparently was especially acute when trade encouraged the abandonment of an agricultural for a hunting economy. Anthropologist Peggy Sanday has categorized various economies according to the relative status of women. In horticultural societies, she concludes, women are likely to exercise the greatest influence; among pastoral hunters, their status is the lowest. When they switched economies, then, Cheyenne women moved also precipitously down the scale of feminine prestige and power. Within a generation or two, they suffered a major downward slide of status.[59]

That slippage can be understood best by answering two questions about native economic life and how it was changing. First, who was in control? Among the communities of the Missouri valley, presumably similar to Cheyenne society before the move west, both men and women had significant authority over production. Men were in charge of the hunt and the game it brought in. Women controlled the gardens and their produce as well as dogs and all household furnishings.[60] Especially among matrilineal groups like the Pawnees, Arikaras, and Mandans, ceremonies reflected this economic influence; the Mandan's Okipa ritual ended with the theme of "the Female Principle [as] the locus of power."[61] We should be careful about falling into a "golden age" syndrome. Women's lives within these gardening economies may or may not have been their "finest hour," as Margot Liberty suggests, but women certainly seem to have had significant influence and control over economic life, and therefore considerable social clout.[62]

Emigration to the plains quickly upset the ratio of sexual power. Gardening virtually ceased. All other economic functions were overshadowed by hunting and the acquisition of horses—activities that were meant to provide, directly or through trade, most of a group's needs. Everything brought home from the chase belonged to the male hunter or to the man who had provided the horses. Control of the most important tools and most valued products, in other words, shifted rapidly to one of the two sexes. Women left behind their proprietorship, and with it much of their cultural heft, at the gardens and villages along the rivers.[63]

The second question is who was doing the work? It is useful here to use an "energetics" approach, assessing the relative energy spent by men and women in native economic life. Both sexes labored, of course, and the heightened emphasis on hunting and warfare demanded considerable efforts by men. As already seen, this new life also exacted an awful toll in warriors and hunters. However, it seems clear that women's expenditure of energy, compared to men's, grew considerably greater with the move onto the plains. Women kept most of their older domestic duties. They still gathered wild plants and fuel, prepared food, made and repaired clothing, constructed and maintained lodges and many of their furnishings, and cared for children, the elderly, and the infirm. They did those jobs in a new quasi-nomadic lifestyle that required them to break and make camp several times a year. Horses, it's true, eased somewhat the labor of trekking about, but it is easy to overstress the advantage. Trade and horses also brought larger tipis and more things to put in them, and thus more work in setting up lodges and greater loads to carry around. Some tribes, furthermore, learned relatively late how to make full use of the animals; the Cheyennes were still adapting horses to warfare and nomadism well after 1840. If women had more help in moving, they also moved more often and had more to transport when they did. For most, it was at best a wash.

Women were also freed from almost all horticultural work, but that gain, too, was more than offset by another development. Use of the horse brought a startling imbalance in the two steps of the plains hunting economy—killing animals and processing them. Astride a horse, one person could slay animals far faster than another person could flay and butcher them, prepare and preserve the meat, and convert the skins into goods. Because the first step was done by males and the second by females, the total effort demanded of women in removing, scraping, pegging, and rubbing animal hides increased vastly with emigration onto the plains, especially as the Indians' position deteriorated and their hunting of bison grew more frantic. By the figures of an Indian agent in the mid-1850s, Cheyenne women on the average were each skinning and processing the meat and hide of a bison every couple of weeks, not to mention helping with some of the deer, elk, and bear brought to camp.[64]

Another factor, "reproductive ecology," has to be included.[65] Of all jobs in any economy, bearing and nurturing babies are arguably the most important. This work provides the people who make and do everything else. Lactation, in fact, ought to be classed as an essential part of subsistence production, an effort as important as planting or hunting or fishing; in a study of a New Guinea tribe, an agricultural economist estimated that breast milk accounted for 2.4 percent of all food consumed. It follows that any fair reckoning of energy spent in maintaining an economy must include that used for childbearing and infant care. That expense, of course, comes almost entirely from females; and it is considerable. To meet the extra energy requirements for pregnancy and a year of breast feeding, by one estimate, a woman would have to eat the equivalent of forty kilograms of mongongo nuts, seventy-five kilograms of rice, or five hundred Big Mac hamburgers.[66]

As described at the start of this essay, plains Indians were not reproducing their numbers successfully. That did not mean, however, that women's energy costs were correspondingly reduced. Sterility and impaired conception—problems that would have saved women the bodily expenses of childbearing—were only part of the reason for low fertility rates. Stillbirths and child mortality were probably more significant. Studies in other cultures, in fact, show that when infant mortality is high, families typically compensate with higher birth rates.[67] Thus, women were probably still carrying, bearing, and nursing a lot of babies—mothers, that is, were paying the high costs of motherhood—but the fruits of their efforts, the children they had paid for, were being destroyed before society could reap the benefits.

The move to the plains, then, reduced Indian women's control within their economic and material life even as it increased the demands on their efforts and energy. It was hardly an even swap. This redistribution of effort, with women expected to spend more of their inner resources, ought to be seen against the backdrop of the first two essays—the deepening crisis that left Indians with dwindling food supplies, a deteriorating environment, and a heightened competition with both people and animals. Women had to do more with less, and to do it under harsher conditions than those their grandmothers knew. If the calamities of the 1850s and 1860s were exhausting and debilitating for Indian men, how much worse they must have been for their wives, mothers, and sisters.

In a larger sense the women's plight brings home a basic point. Besides being a productive unit, a family was a changing relationship of power and a group of individuals who experienced the same events differently. Seen that way, families have a lot to tell us about the diverse, and often disturbing, history of the plains.

The family, in its fifth and final definition, is a social bond; it is a means by which whole communities are continuously reshaped to adapt to new circumstances. Just as individual families adjusted internally to survive through changing times and surroundings, so did families, as webs of related households, respond to the rapidly evolving conditions of the plains frontier.

Once again some of the best illustrations come from the Native American experience. For a hint of possibilities, take an incident that occurred along the Platte in 1854. An Indian agent, Jonathan Whitfield, still spanking new to the job, met with several Cheyenne leaders to discuss their grievances. Although the Treaty of Fort Laramie (1851) had provided for protected passage of white emigrants along the Platte road, the Indians had changed their minds. Now they presented four demands. They insisted, first, that all white traffic along the Platte cease. Next they called for annuity payments to be made partly in cash. Third, they wanted the rest paid as guns and ammunition. Finally, they made a demand that must have rocked Whitfield back on his heels: a thousand white women should be provided as wives for Cheyenne men.[68]

It is a wonderful vignette, partly because it allows so many meanings. Were the chiefs tweaking the nose of their fresh new agent? Were they commenting pointedly on the one-way marital congress, in which virtually all unions (except those following capture) were of native women and white men? It is hard to say, but what is perhaps most intriguing is how that last demand is set with others that were so shrewdly practical. Looking back, no one would deny that emigrant traffic threatened the Cheyennes, or that annuities in cash and arms would have given them greater flexibility in facing their difficulties. Given that, the demand of white wives, however outrageously improbable it might seem to us now, was likely considered by Indian spokesmen an immanently practical move.

Actually, the chiefs' demand is not surprising. The family, as sexual union, always had played a crucial role in the Indians' reaching out toward the world beyond their immediate communities. Marital and sexual bonds created practical and symbolic connections with purposes far beyond human procreation. Sacred stories were full of copulations between heaven and earth, women and bears, bison cows and men, all of which were not just injunctions to be fruitful but reminders that the world's disparate parts had a rightful association to one another. Ceremonial intercourse recognized the creative and unifying potential of sexuality. Among most Missouri valley and plains tribes, for instance, a younger man received spiritual power or membership in a male society, or both, by providing his wife for sexual intercourse with a distinguished and respected older man, often a kinsman of his father. A woman became a copulatory link, joining her husband to other associations and drawing into her family valuable abilities and assurances against ill fortune. Among the Hidatsa and other groups, a similar ritual recalled the rutting of a primal bison with a human female, thus renewing a vital cycle and attracting bison herds to return and be hunted. The women involved were expected to be of exemplary character and faithful to their husbands, and being chosen for these ceremonies was a high civic and familial honor. Thus, rituals expressed and used sex's socially integrative power while reinforcing stern rules of sexual conduct.[69]

When tribes moved out of the Missouri valley onto the plains, they brought along these ceremonies—but with some revealing variations. Among the Cheyennes, Arapahoes, and Atsinas (or Gros Ventres), ritual intercourse apparently was often kept symbolic; the actual coital deed remained undone. When an Arapaho elder passed to a younger man the spiritual authority to sponsor a sun dance, for instance, the older man went around midnight with the sponsor's naked wife to a spot between the sacred Rabbit-tipi and the camp. In a ritual closely resembling ceremonial copulations of the riverine groups, he prayed to the Man-Above and offered the woman to him and to lesser gods, while all village residents remained quiet and closed in their lodges. Then, according to the anthropologist George

A. Dorsey, who peeked, the elder passed a medicinal root (symbolic enough, to be sure) from his mouth to the woman's, a gift she then gave to her husband. Beyond that she remained untouched, although, an informant assured Dorsey, "the temptation is great."[70]

Why the restraint? As mentioned several times so far, moving to the plains forced Indians to live in small groups most of the year. It wore away at a tribes's common identity. In the face of such fragmenting forces, a high premium was placed on close bonds among male hunters and warriors, both within a camp and among members of different bands. The modified ritual retained a belief in the sexual passage of spiritual strength and authority; but by eliminating coital contact it presumably reduced the possibility of jealousy among men. At the same time, by requiring husbands to accept on faith that intercourse remained symbolic, it reinforced self-discipline and mutual trust.[71]

Just as sex was used to establish connections with sustaining spiritual power, so too it could forge a link with useful humans outside a family or group; and as with the ritual preliminaries to the Cheyenne sun dance, these intimate reachings were marvelously flexible and adaptive. In early contact with tribes of the upper Missouri, white men were frequently given women as bedmates. Most visitors saw this as whoring, pure and simple.[72] Some prostitution did occur, but the women bartered were captives from other tribes. When an Indian man provided a white visitor with a member of his family, on the other hand, the purpose was quite different. A Euro-American man, especially one bearing exotic goods and with obvious connections to faraway seats of influence, appeared to offer various sorts of potency. "The Indians believed that these traders were the most powerful persons in the nation," Meriwether Lewis wrote during his visit among the Mandans. Intercourse with such a man was a means of siphoning away precious power. White visitors who thought they were buying sex on the cheap got the situation exactly backwards, at least from the native perspective. They were not taking but giving, not using but being used.

The Indians' sexual and marital contact with whites has to be understood within this continuum of meanings and functions. The intimate bond of women and men bound individuals into couples; through their offspring, it wove nuclear families into webs of kin who helped feed and protect one another; it linked those groups to others and to sources of spiritual and secular power. It is in this context that we can best appreciate one of the most significant roles of sex and marriage among plains Indians—that of facilitator of trade.

Trade had been an essential part of native life for centuries before European contact, and earlier peoples may well have used marriages to make and maintain economic alliances. The archaeologist Margaret Hanna, using a sophisticated analysis of earthenware from part of the south Canadian plains, has argued that late prehistoric bands contracted a small number of marriages with otherwise unrelated groups, some close by and others distant, to encourage peace and to obtain resources unavailable locally. The larger lesson, Hanna writes, is that "the intermeshing of political, economic, and 'social' aspects within any one activity [marriage, in this case]" was a common and beneficial feature of these cultures.[73]

That statement could serve as a guiding principle for understanding families through their later history on the plains. As trade quickened and networks expanded with European contact, familial connections with outside sources of goods became increasingly important. Besides a marital link between groups, a man of one tribe might be adopted by a prominent figure in another.[74] By marrying or adopting out one of its own to the right member of another band or tribe, or to a white trader, a family could create a mutually gratifying economic relationship. These unions brought greater predictability and security in a time of growing conflict and unrest. Economic exchange was assured; goods and furs, with their consequent profits and status, moved where both sides wanted them to go; disputes could be smoothed over through tested methods woven into traditions of family and kin.

This is not to say that all benefitted equally from trade marriages. As usual Indian women stand mostly mute in the record, so we do not know how they felt about these arrangements. As key links in a commercial exchange, they had greater access to goods that doubtless made their lives somewhat easier.[75] However, they also seem to have lost some command of an important part of their personal lives. Although unmarried women had never been fully free to choose their mates, among the Cheyennes there had been a relative degree of autonomy, and divorce was remarkably simple. During this period, however, fathers and brothers may have exerted increasingly rigid authority over marriage decisions of daughters and sisters. Just as the switch to a hunting economy left women with shrinking influence in economic life, so women may have lost control as well of their own sexuality.

Marriages were also a key element in the fragmentation, divisions, and growing tensions within the social order of bands and tribes. Economic gaps within a band grew wider, a change to which matrimony contributed in two ways. By marrying his sister or other female relative to the right outsider, a man could control the flow of trade and reap its maximum benefits. For some plains families, marrying outward became a calculated strategy to expand their wealth and strengthen their standing; anthropologist John Moore has found that exogamous unions, partly to facilitate trade, were far more common among families of Cheyenne chiefs and headmen than among the general population.[76] Taking more wives, a man could also expand his production of bison robes; increased trade in turn brought in more goods and horses with which to support and buy more wives. Polygyny was an especially good investment because women working together achieved a kind of economy of scale. A Blackfoot chief explained to the Earl of Southesk that one wife could dress one hide every thirty-five days, while eight wives, working together, could process about one hide each every nineteen days.[77] Relative changes in wealth in turn affected families' status, power, political influence, even their spiritual standing. So marriage-enhanced trade helped a man and his relatives pay the fare to a higher social station, and once there, by the rich-get-richer principle, they could solidify and build on their position and increase their distance from those beneath them.[78]

Marriage-enhanced trade also aggravated deeper stresses and divisions among larger social units. The Kiowas split into two factions, one seeking trade with whites and following Kicking Bird, the other attracted to the impetuous bully Baitalyi (Sunboy), a well-known fighter with many warrior-kinsmen who was an outspoken opponent of accommodations with whites, economic or otherwise.[79] The Southern Cheyennes were rent by a similar division. Those opposed to economic and social exchange with whites looked to the Dog Soldiers, a warrior society that emerged as a band in the 1850s. Other bands, which usually remained closer to the posts and white travelers along the Arkansas River, cultivated trade and favored peaceful relations with whites. These latter groups were known for their large lodges, abundance of horses and other goods, and sometimes for their reluctance to share the bounty; a subgroup of the relatively affluent Wotapio band was known as "the Stingies."[80]

Both factions used marital strategies to pursue larger goals. Under the traditional matrilocal practices, exogamy threatened to take away the best warriors of the Dog Soldiers. That was unacceptable, so male leaders among the Dog Soldiers encouraged their men to marry endogamously and tried to persuade women from other bands to marry and bring their families into theirs.[81] John Moore suggests that men also turned to the practice of "putting a woman on the prairie," the gang rape of a woman by a soldier society with permission of her brothers, to force resisting sisters into marriages that best suited the group's military needs.[82] Among the other bands, those oriented toward trade and peaceful relations with whites, prominent families heartily supported exogamy. Interband marriages created and sustained economic and political alliances among powerful lineages, while sexual unions of native women with white traders and middlemen kept open the lanes of commerce.

It was among that latter group, those who did reach out for trading contacts, that fundamental changes took place that were full of implications for plains history. Marriages between natives and whites stirred the pot of plains peoples and created new cultural amalgams. The point was made well during John Charles Fremont's trip to the central plains in 1842. As Fremont headed for the Front Range of the Rockies, making his way up the South Platte, he first found a camp of traders, former New Englanders, with their Indian wives and "a number of little fat buffalo-fed boys" who amused him by turning somersaults. Two miles farther he found Jean Baptiste Charbonneau, son of Sacagawea and Toussaint Charbonneau, in camp with several Mexican-Indian families, including the wife of Jim Beckworth, the famous mulatto mountain man and scout originally from Virginia, whom Fremont had met a little earlier.[83]

Here, on one of those expeditions portrayed at the time as a bold foray into territory largely untouched by civilization to the east, Fremont, the Great Pathfinder, arrived to find that the family frontier had beaten him cold. This blond ideal, symbolically staking claim to this country for Anglo-America, found himself in the plains equivalent of a lower east side neighborhood—an ethnic slumgullion stew with elements of various Indians, French, Mexicans, whites, and blacks. Liaisons between trappers and Indian women have al-

ways been part of popular tradition, of course; but typically the cou-
plings of mountain men and Indian maidens have been portrayed as
either romantic unions of great souls or the brief ruttings of priapic
bear-men. In fact, these marriages, and the resulting "little buffalo-fed boys," were integral parts of the region's economic life and
evolving society.

Indian-white marriages had long been common among
"residenters," employees or independent middlemen working with
British companies, and among agents for larger American firms.[84]
The American Fur Company's Robert Meldrum, who first married
among the Crows about 1830, kept as many as six wives at once
and produced at least twelve children during his thirty years as trader
and diplomatic liaison. In his classic *Systems of Consanguinity and
Affinity of the Human Family*, the ethnologist Lewis Henry Morgan
found Meldrum an invaluable source on Indian kinship patterns and
marriage customs.[85] Unions became much more common, however,
after around 1840, as the beaver trade declined the nature of the fur
trade changed. In the past mountain men had done their own trap-
ping, then funneled the pelts to fur companies. Now most became
middlemen, relying on native hunters to supply skins of bison, bears,
deer, and raccoons, which then were sold to agents. The previous
economic chain had been white-white; now it was Indian-white-
white. With that, marital and familial connections became far more
valuable, both for natives and whites. Again and again in the biog-
raphies of mountain men the pattern appears: bachelorhood in the
"free trapper" days of the beaver trade, then a shift to the job of
trader, and with that marriage to a Cheyenne, Arapahoe, or Lakota.
Prominent examples from the central plains include William Guerrier,
Bill New, John Simpson Smith, Elbridge Gerry, Chat Dubray, and
Seth Ward.

The result was a growing mixed-blood population that increasingly influenced the contours of central plains society. This cultural
meld was most apparent in those areas that have emerged as the
focus of these essays—the Arkansas and Platte valleys: the corridors
of invasion, the region's most vital living space, the ground of conflict and exchange, and the life lines of commerce. If John Charles
Fremont had moved southward from those South Platte camps of
Yankees, Indians, French and Mexicans, he would have found an
extraordinarily diverse familial web along the upper Arkansas. Tho-

mas Fitzpatrick reported about 150 persons living at the trading and
farming outposts of Hardscrabble and Greenhorn in 1847. About
sixty were "old trappers and hunters," mostly Anglo-Americans,
French Canadians, and Mexicans, but there were a few Scots and
English, "nearly all having wives, and some have two." Besides some
Mexican and Anglo-American spouses, most came from a remark-
able spread of tribes: Blackfoot, Assiniboin, Arikara, Lakota,
Arapaho, Cheyenne, Pawnee, Snake, Sinpach (from west of the Great
Salt Lake), and Chinook (from the Pacific Northwest).[86]

The same could be found along the Platte. For five hundred miles
or so, its valley became a community of families of former trappers
and their native spouses. The best known of these businessmen was
James Bordeaux, at one time chief factor at Fort Laramie, but there
were many like him. Elbridge Gerry, who had trapped in the Rockies
since the 1830s, married the daughter of a prominent Oglalla, Swift
Bird, and began trading out of Fort Laramie and later at his own
post downstream. Seth Ward, having scoured the Colorado Rockies
for beaver, opened a post on the Platte at Sand Point in 1851, by
which time he had a Brule wife "given him by her brothers." With
his partner William Guerrier, a former trader with the Bents married
to a Cheyenne, Ward developed a vigorous trade stretching from
the Arkansas to the Niobrara in Nebraska.[87] Geminien (or Jim)
Beauvais took at least a few Lakota wives while a trapper for the
American Fur Company. Later, on his own, he used those relations
to develop an enormous trade in bison robes at his posts near Fort
Laramie and on the South Platte.[88]

In stark contrast to the Jeremiah Johnson stereotype of the mountain man as misanthrope and romantic solitaire, many of these men
were hip-deep in developmental enterprises. They became officers
in the first town companies, speculators in city lots, cattlemen, and
agricultural promoters. They helped open wide the gates for scores
of thousands of other Euro-Americans—farmers, ranchers, merchants, railroaders, town-builders, well-diggers and irrigators, bull-
whackers and freighting kingpins—the whole crew of new possessors
who would finish the process of making the plains untenable for
both the natives' pastoral lifeways and the trapping-trading economy
that brought these men out west in the first place. The changes they
ushered in came with astonishing speed. An eighteen-year-old Southern Cheyenne woman who married a white trader in 1845 would

have seen the bloody disaster of Sand Creek before she was forty. The bison would have been long gone before she was fifty. By her early middle age, a camping ground where she had cared for her young children might hold a county courthouse or a Methodist church with its sermons, lyceums, and temperance meetings. Another familial system quickly took root, projecting its radically different, exclusionist values through the culture spreading over the land. Individual and social intercourse on the central plains was redefined as a variation of the Victorian family.

In that new social household, Cheyenne wives and swarthy children were at best an embarrassment. A woman's diary entry along the Platte road in 1863 summed up a common feeling. "Almost every house that we come to are [sic] occupied by a Frenchman with their [sic] Indian wives," she wrote. "What a shame and disgrace to our country."[89] Historian John Mack Faragher has suggested that this attitudinal tide was a crucial turning point in western—and American—cultural life. The era when fur-trade marriages flourished, he writes, was a "frontier of inclusion," a time wracked with conflict, to be sure, but also a period of interpenetration and cross-fertilization of many cultures. The rapid invasion of Euro-American families at mid-century, however, was a "frontier of exclusion." Native peoples, defined out of hand as backward and unassimilable, were pushed to the fringes of the newly dominant society.[90]

His point is a good one. The first period was a rich and complex ethnic exchange, and the second a time of ascendant intolerance. It has to be emphasized, however, that in one way the earlier "inclusiveness" had always been severely limited, as the Cheyenne chiefs perhaps were saying to agent Whitfield. White men were quite willing to mingle cultures by marrying Indian women. They showed not the slightest interest, on the other hand, in white women bridging the gap by taking Indian husbands. The plains pattern was no different from anywhere else in the orbit of European colonialism. By mutual consent white men and native women moved out of their own cultures and into the familial circles of the other. Native men and white women stayed put.

A few practical effects of this lopsided marital exchange were obvious. As tensions mounted, harsh treatment of Indians came more easily because there were few white women in native communities. In patriarchal white societies, on the other hand, there were no Indians to act as authoritative spokesmen, since all natives living in white families were women, and thus outside circles of formal power. Those Native American wives and mothers, of course, were exceptionally vulnerable to the changes in power and values sweeping the plains.

Predictably, mixed marriages often did not survive. In yet another maneuver for advantage, many husbands withdrew from these unions, *conjugus interruptus*, in favor of others more prudent and profitable. Seth Ward settled in with a new white wife at a Kansas City estate and became a booster of Platte valley ranching.[91] Jim Beauvais made a modest fortune selling supplies to Colorado goldseekers, then turned the business over to his son and moved to St. Louis, a wealthy retired broker between white and native economies. The domestic shufflings could be poignant. The army guide Percival Lowe told of a colleague, Slim Routh, taking a young Lakota wife at Fort Laramie, then marrying a white woman in Denver four years later. At the wedding Lowe glanced up and saw Routh's Indian wife on the porch, watching the ceremony through a window.[92] Like her, many native women found themselves, quite literally, shut out.

Nevertheless, a surprising number of marriages proved remarkably resilient. Among the best known was that of William Bent to two daughters of Grey Thunder, the Cheyennes' keeper of the Sacred Arrows. Owl Woman, called by another trader "a most estimable woman of good influence," died in childbirth; Yellow Woman was killed by Pawnees in 1865.[93] There were many other such marriages, enough that by the mid-1860s anybody trying to draw up a simple ethnic roster of the central plains would have had a tough time of it.

As a good case study, consider one of the best known events of that time, the Sand Creek massacre. Like so much plains history, the story of that bloodbath has almost always been told as a clash of starkly distinct cultures. The nature of the lesson has varied, sometimes with savage raiders getting their just dues and, more often, with the militia slaughtering native innocents. Whatever the moral tone, the ethnic lines are clear: whites here, Indians there.

Look closer.[94] The night before the attack, the militia commander, John Chivington, arrested a local rancher, John Prowers, and seven of his cowboys. Chivington was worried that Prowers would warn the Indians, since he was married to a Cheyenne, Amache, whose father the subchief Ochinee, called One Eye by whites, in fact would be killed the next day. Also at Sand Creek were George and Charles Bent, sons of William Bent and Owl Woman, as well as Edward Guerrier, the mixed-blood son of William Guerrier, Seth Ward's partner, whose mixed-blood son had married one of several mixed-blood daughters of the trader Elbridge Gerry. Ed Guerrier later would marry another of William Bent's children, Julia, whose half-sister Mary, another of Owl Woman's daughters, was at a nearby ranch at the time of the massacre, living as the wife of R. M. Moore, a prominent landholder as well as Bent County's first school superintendent. Camped east of Sand Creek was Making Out Road, who may have been Owl Woman's sister, with her daughter Cheyenne White Girl, child of the trader and future Dodge City businessman Charles Rath. A generation later Cheyenne White Girl's son by a white father would become a football star at Carlisle Institute. His half-uncle, Morris Rath, Charles's son by a second wife, was full-blood white but spent his childhood close to his mixed-blood relatives before going on to play second base and shortstop for (who else?) the Cleveland Indians and Cincinnati Reds. (Morrie Rath played against Boston in the 1919 World Series. His lifetime batting average was .258).

Back at Sand Creek, the village also held an Arapaho woman, Ma-hom, or Snake Woman, and her daughter Mary. Ma-hom was the widow of the Kentuckian John Poisal, a trapper who had lived with his family in early Denver. She was also the sister of the famous Arapaho chief Left Hand, who died at Sand Creek. Besides Mary Poisal, who was married to a local rancher, Ma-hom bore four other children, including a daughter who had married Thomas Fitzpatrick and a son who would be an army contractor at the Battle of the Washita four years later. (Following that second disaster, according to one story, his Cheyenne wife attempted suicide). The sutler at nearby Fort Lyon, Charlie Windsor, had a Cheyenne wife at Sand Creek. She survived by finding refuge in the lodge of another white trader who was there, John Simpson Smith. He, like Poisal, had lived with his Indian wife in early Denver and in fact had been an officer in the first town company. Now, five years later, Smith was with his wife, their young child and an older son, Jack Smith, about twenty. Jack survived the attack but was murdered the next day by militiamen who apparently had not had enough.

Of all the lessons we have taken from Sand Creek, this is perhaps the clearest—and the least recognized. Even in the 1860s, when the mining, ranching, and farming frontiers were just nudging into the central plains, the peoples and cultures there were snarled into a knot almost beyond tracing. As Chivington's men rode and shot and slashed into Black Kettle's village, they were, in some sense, butchering their own, just as, in so many ways since then, westerners have insisted on drawing clear lines of the us-and-them variety, lines that have a way of dissolving when we get close and try to follow them with our fingers. The result has added to the troubles and conflicts of westerners who deny the obvious when it has been all around them, even in their homes, and sometimes in their beds.

As a case in point, I offer E. B. Sopris. Sopris was with the militia at Sand Creek, and he took pride in the assault even into his dotage, long after he had become a leading citizen of Trinidad and a prominent Republican politician. In an interview in 1930, sixty-six years after the bloodletting, the eighty-seven-year-old Sopris claimed a special accomplishment. "I killed Jack Smith," he told LeRoy Hafen. "He started to run from the tent. I said, 'There goes a g--d half-breed.' Several of us shot. . . . At least I hope I got him. The half-breeds were much worse than the Indians." It was a common enough claim and sentiment, one we might read as a typical, if especially appalling, determination to keep those lines drawn firm and clear.

Take a closer look. In 1890, Sopris married Mary Skelley, a widow whose maiden name had been Mary St. Vrain. She was the daughter of Marcellin St. Vrain, brother of William Bent's partner, and Sioux Red, sister of the Lakota chief, Red Cloud. In the same interview in which Sopris boasted of his kill, he spoke warmly of his wife, but he said nothing of her being, to use his own term, "a god damned half-breed," and he spoke with special pride (and the same genealogical blackout) of his step-son, Will Sopris, great-nephew of Red Cloud, who after growing up the special pet of his Lakota grandmother was graduated from Denver University, where he pledged Phi Gamma Delta, and then from Columbia Law School, before going on to a successful career in the foreign service and in law.[95]

We can only guess at the sort of psychological skin-the-cat necessary for Sopris to live with the contradictions within his life, memories, and values; but it is worth asking whether his contortions were much stranger than the denials more generally of western society, which has not been especially eager to recognize the confluence of its peoples and their blood blending and has been even less willing to live with the implications. Nor, for that matter, have historians shown much enthusiasm for working within the complexities and cross currents of intermarriage and the convergence of peoples.

In a larger sense, the neglect is one of the family, broadly defined, and of the processes and issues that are unavoidable—that sometimes look at us across the dinner table—once we recognize that families were crucial to living and surviving in the West. One way to the West is through the study of this universal institution. No force in western history has been more neglected and none has been more important and revealing—as a weapon of conquest, as a vessel of culture, as a machine of change, and finally as a loom for new human weaves.

It was in those crossroads families, in fact, that Native Americans ultimately found the means of physical and cultural survival. After being overwhelmed and undercut by white invaders, and still facing a formidible array of difficulties, Indians have fashioned one of western history's great success stories, maintaining a sense of who they are and have been through webs of familial connections.

In 1954, ninety years after Sand Creek, George Bent's great-granddaughter, Lucille Lemmon, was living in Geary, Oklahoma (named for the massacre survivor Ed Guerrier). She wrote another Bent relative, carefully reconstructing her line back to William Bent and Owl Woman and bragging on her sons and daughters, giving both their Europeanized and Cheyenne and Lakota names. She told of marital difficulties and of hoping to visit Cooperstown, New York, with a Cheyenne dance group. Times were hard. In an echo from four generations earlier, she described bitter winters and difficulties finding fuel; there was some wood, she wrote, but others owned it. Still, she was getting along well and had made new dresses for her daughters to dance in at the Anadarko fair. She had no complaints and was looking forward to going to nursing school. "I believe," she wrote, "that God has been good to me."[96]

Lines on the Land
While roads and furrows partook of the
economic conquest of the central plains,
they told equally an imported story of pioneers
controlling and transforming wild country.
(Photograph courtesy Denver Public Library,
Colorado, F30712.)

Right-Angle America
*In dozens of towns like Ordway, Colorado,
settlers projected the illusion of rational order
on a diverse landscape: first a grid of streets
and then beyond it a checkerboard of cleanly
surveyed sections plowed into straight lines.
(Photograph courtesy Denver Public Library,
Colorado, F33122.)*

Cultural Beachhead
*Steeples rising beside new streets spoke of
the coming of another order, this one moral,
with its own lines and its own illusions of
transformation and control. (Photograph
courtesy Kansas Collection, University
of Kansas Libraries, Lawrence.)*

Respectability Transplanted
In a scene indistinguishable from one in societies back East, this couple sits proudly beside the proofs of their success: a sturdy midwestern house, imported trees, and respectable fashions of the day. (Photograph courtesy Kansas Collection, University of Kansas Libraries, Lawrence.)

Playing Indian
Once Indians were defeated and their
preferred way of life eliminated, white men
like these could rent Native American
costumes and act out fantasies of the
West's wild children. (Photograph courtesy
Kansas Collection, University of Kansas
Libraries, Lawrence.)

Ride on, Dude
For a modest fee, anyone could
live briefly in the imagined past of a rootin'
tootin' West. At night a hot bath and soft bed
awaited the twentieth-century adventurer.
(Photograph by Union Pacific Railroad
courtesy Denver Public
Library, F47329.)

Leaving the Past
A "True Girl of the West" is one of many expressions
of an enduring national fantasy of fleeing society and its
restraints into a land free of traditions and rules.
(Photograph courtesy Kansas Collection,
University of Kansas Libraries, Lawrence.)

The Orator
Just beneath the narrative
surface of the West, other stories, those of
native peoples, have always presented other
views of the country, its meanings, and the
place of westerners in it. (Photograph
courtesy Kansas Collection, University of
Kansas Libraries, Lawrence.)

4
Stories

Memory is made as a quilt is made. From the whole cloth of time, frayed scraps of sensation are pulled apart and pieced together in a pattern that has a name. . . .
Kim Stafford, "The Story That Saved Life"

And like other little children,
You want to dream a dream or two.
But be careful what you're dreaming,
Or soon your dreams will be dreaming you.
Willie Nelson, "It's Not Supposed to Be That Way"

Let us see, is this real,
Let us see, is this real,
This life I am living?
You, Gods, who dwell everywhere,
Let us see, is this real,
This life I am living?
Pawnee song

Stories have power. Western history has been shaped not only by exchanges among people, land, and animals and by evolving institutions like the family. Each part of the West is also what it is because of the stories people have told about it. I am referring in particular to narratives considered as specially associated with a particular place. Such narratives are woven through with assumptions—what a place is and is not, what can and cannot be done there, and how people are expected to behave. Stories of that kind

127

inevitably influence how inhabitants treat and respond to their immediate world. Those responses bring changes, which in turn can refashion the story as it runs inside the inhabitants' heads. Imagined narrative and human action fade into and feed one another.

That is true everywhere, but nowhere is the shaping force of stories more apparent than in the American West. For the past couple of hundred years, the land west of the Missouri has been the special playground of the mass imagination. The narratives spun off in the process have walked through the country, changing it profoundly. Since long before that, however, and throughout that time, other, quite different stories have been alive and working in the West.

All of these various stories, all carrying power, naturally have pushed and bumped against one another. We can think of western history as one of conflicting narratives. Just as its people have fought for control of resources and for dominance of institutions and values, so the West has been an arena where stories have contested to command that country's meaning, and thus to influence how the West is treated.

This essay considers a few of the ways in which these various stories have played roles in making western history. Compared with the preceding essays, the comments here are more speculative and the tone sometimes lighter. The perspective is also broader, drawing on experiences and writing from throughout the left-hand side of the nation's map. But the focus remains on the plains. In the molding energy of its stories, as in so much else, that country has a lot to teach us about the West at large.

Once again the West and westerns are "in." With *Dances With Wolves* and *Unforgiven*, movie versions are now two-for-three in the most recent academy award competition for best film. The predictable rush into new productions has triggered a brutal competition for prime "old western" sites and the best costumes and guns. One company's spokesman complained of a rival's monopoly of local props: "They'd have taken the sagebrush if they could have." At Old Tucson Studios "movies are stacked up like jets over O'Hare," according to *Entertainment Weekly*. "It's crazy," a director agreed. "There's a new Kevin Costner film that's booked practically the entire state of New Mexico."[1]

Three multipart television documentaries on the "old West" have appeared during the past two years, one of them accompanied by a hefty coffee-table book and a special issue of *Life* magazine.[2] *Architectural Digest* devoted an entire issue to palatial houses with plenty of bare timbers, adobe, cowhide, and native ceramics in Telluride, Jackson Hole, and several southwestern spots.[3] Western fashions have experienced such an upsurge in popularity that Cowles publications recently launched a new periodical, *Western Styles*. Denim manufacturers scramble to offer youthful and middle-aged customers an array of traditional, extra-tight, and baggy jeans in the usual blue as well as in rust, taupe, and a variety of earth tones. "There's a jean discourse going on," a California sociologist told a reporter from the *New York Times*.[4] The discourse apparently extends beyond jeans and fashion to their absence. A handsome model, buck naked except for his Stetson, sits atop a mechanical bull on the cover of a recent issue of *Naturally*, America's foremost nudist periodical.

The trend can be felt at the loftier levels of cultural life. The National Book Award for 1993 went to Cormac McCarthy's *All the Pretty Horses*, a bloody coming-of-age story that draws heavily on the western fictional tradition.[5] In fact, activities that recently were miles beneath the gaze of trend-watchers suddenly are marginally respectable. The London *Times Literary Supplement* devoted nearly two columns to this year's Cowboy Poetry Gathering in Elko, Nevada. The reporter provided examples from this "upsurge in cultural awareness," including this verse from the editor of the *Cowboy Poetry Review*:

He squatted on his boot heels,
His posterior was exposed and bare.
He did not see that rattler,
Lying coiled under there.[6]

As if to keep a gendered balance, a kind of cowgirl *chic* has emerged. Gail Gilchriest's basic advice book on style, *The Cowgirl Companion*, has received considerable media attention. Less known is Gladiola Montana's, *Never Ask a Man the Size of His Spread*.[7] This newest western renaissance also spans the generations. In cooperation with Hasbro, Inc., the nation's largest toy company, the promoter of the fabulously successful Teenage Mutant Ninja Turtles will soon market a new line of action figures, the "C.O.W. Boys of Moo Mesa," humanoid cattle that will "make the West a safer place to graze" by fighting villainous buzzards and other animals-gone-bad. Moo Mesa video games, a television series, books, songs, and shampoos are in the works.[8] To earn the cost of such playthings, parents can also look to the old West for inspiration and practical tips by reading a new approach to fiscal success: Emmett C. Murphy's *The Genius of Sitting Bull: Thirteen Heroic Strategies for Today's Business Leaders*.[9]

All this is a reflowering of an old national infatuation. The obsession has never been ours alone, of course. The western has appealed across a remarkable range of cultures and value systems. Its themes and images have been used by a broad array of European public figures, some fairly unexpected. The smooth boulevardier Yves Montand began his career in Marseilles music halls of the 1930s with a review, "Les Plaines du Far West," wearing a white hat and plaid shirt and belting out a frontiersman's hang-it-all refrain: "I don't give a damn, I don't give a damn/ 'Cause I'm gonna get through . . . Yeah!" ("Je m'en fous, je m'en fous/Moi je tiens le coup . . . Yeah!")[10] The western's spell is cast far beyond Paris, London, and Berlin, sometimes with deliciously ironic results. America's war in Vietnam was sometimes portrayed at home as a showdown with dark-hearted Asian sidewinders, and as the situation worsened in 1974, Richard Nixon encouraged Americans to leave the area on manly terms, "as a cowboy, with guns blazing, backing out of a saloon."[11] Today, nearly twenty years after we fled through those swinging doors, Vietnam is helping to revive its bombed-out economy with an unlikely product: "pa-weh," literally "far westerns," films starring their own folk in the John Wayne roles and with Indians played by Khmer tribesmen imported from Laos.

In some ways, however, westerns have always been uniquely American. Born and set here, they disclose in vague and general ways anxieties and aspirations peculiar to this nation. They may draw on universal mythic urges and replicate epic patterns found from China to Scandanavia, but out of those common makings they express our distinctive notions of violence and rebirth, authority and rebellion, honor and responsibility.[12] The American public can always find something there that speaks its mind, and academics can decipher it all in light of scholarly concerns of the moment.[13]

Today's upsurge in popularity is a typical case of enduring themes expressed through current particulars. The depth and inspiration of the craze was recently measured by a consumer research group. Thirty-one percent of our adult population consider themselves "western enthusiasts," according to this report, a figure that translates to roughly 57.4 million persons with a buying power of roughly

1.5 trillion dollars. These fans are young and affluent. Interestingly, women outnumber men two-to-one. The majority own some western clothes and jewelry, and more than a third have bought Native American crafts and western artwork.

Two points in the survey are especially intriguing. First, most of the new enthusiasts (eighty percent) live *outside* the West, and in fact many have only the fuzziest, contradictory notions about where the West actually is. At least as interesting are the sentiments and emotions that apparently feed this enthusiasm. A startling eighty-five percent of them think that their lives are much too stressful, compared to about half of the general adult population. These overwrought Americans are looking for "a simpler lifestyle, less stress, and a return to basic values." They long "for relaxation and escape—ways to simplify their lives and cut through the clutter."[14]

These would-be westerners want to go to that country that might be called our unofficial fifty-first state: the Western State of Mind. At first this state seems the shiftiest territory, now floating somewhere between Arizona and New Mexico, then near Montana, then sliding toward the Dakotas, its emotional terrain changing with the national mood and events and its surface features always evolving. However, when we look more closely, mapping its contours over time, this country, the perceived West, is also a remarkably enduring land. In its fundamentals, the imagined West is not so different today from a century and a half ago.

The persistence of that imagined West, furthermore, has had a profound, continuing influence on the West of reality. In the end, we cannot separate those two geographies—the Western State of Mind, and the western states of Kansas, Colorado, Nebraska, and the rest.

The modern western did not originate in the West. Its roots were in the experiences of the eastern frontier and in the cultural traditions of Europe and the parts of the United States dominated by Euro-Americans. It took its modern shape from the yearnings and stresses of late-nineteenth-century America east of the Missouri, those regions that would provide most of the demand and financial sustenance for the commercialized myth.

Westerns were, of course, set beyond the big river. Heroes and scoundrels did terrible battle on the grand stage of the far West, with its sweeping vistas of plains, mountains, and deserts. As a result it is easy to fall into the error of thinking of these stories as arising from the West and expressing the actual experience of living there. That notion is exactly backwards. Westerns did not arise in the West and go eastward to tell the world about that country and its people. They were born in the East, then marched beyond the Missouri and proceded to change things.

The attitudes and perceptions that gave the western birth were spread widely through eastern society, including the farmers and middling sorts, some of whom left their homes and moved into the "new" country. The pioneers, in other words, shared the expecations and illusions that were simultaneously shaping the modern western myth. In a sense these homesteaders and town-builders were the earliest actors in our first modern westerns. That does not mean, of course, that Kansas sodbusters pictured themselves as square-jawed scouts and disguised range detectives. It does mean, however, that as those pioneers were establishing their new lives, they were acting out fundamental perceptions of the West that were simultaneously creating the modern western elsewhere.

The most basic perception of the emigrants was that the West was radically, dramatically apart from the world they were leaving. The point is so obvious that it is easy to miss its implications, then and now. The West was fundamentally separate, the nation's geographical "other." Its landscapes, scale, and life forms seemed not just different; they were often startlingly alien. This remains true today. Outsiders on their first visit almost always feel the perceptual jolt. Take, for instance, the reaction of an eleven-year-old New Jersey schoolgirl, Nathalie Pagan, who recently won a trip to Yellowstone National Park. Afterwards she summed up her impressions in a report to her class:

> The waterfalls are taller than [our] school. Old Faithful is
> a geyser. Some lakes are hot, which keeps them ice-free so
> animals can get drinks in the winter. . . .The air is so clear
> you can see many miles. It doesn't smell like cars. The West
> seems to have more stars than New Jersey has people. . . .
> [We] saw many animals, including a deer, an elk, a wild
> coyote and a buffalo that blocked the road.

Concerning that last sight, she noticed something truly astonishing: "No vehicles tried to hit it [the buffalo]." "It seems like a dream," Nathalie concluded, and "Newark looks different now."[15]

Yellowstone is more strikingly apart than most of the West, but for centuries outlanders have responded much as Nathalie did. The reason, once again at the risk of stating the obvious, is not because the region is bizarre *per se*. The West is strange only in relation to what these viewers have considered normal. Every person's values and standards, whether of moral behavior or the definition of "big," are necessarily grounded in the immediate environment that he or she first knows. It can be no other way. That perceptual grounding becomes the measure of everything else. The French philosopher-geographer Eric Dardel makes the point:

> Before any choice, there is this place which we have not
> chosen, where the very foundation of our earthly existence
> and human condition establishes itself. We can change
> places, . . . look for [another] place, but for this we need . . .
> a base to set down Being—a *here* from which the world discloses
> itself, [before there can be] a *there* to which we can go.[16]

For everybody heading west, whether to visit or stay, the "here"— those deepest assumptions about what the world ought to be—was elsewhere. Their perceptions might evolve, they might learn much about their new home, they might grow to love it; but to a remarkable degree, their fundamental orientation never changed. A native of Indiana or Connecticut might move to Chase County, Kansas, or Greeley, Colorado, and he might live there for sixty years without ever leaving, walking his land every day, rearing children and growing old, but to some degree his perspective—his mental baseline from which he measured everything he saw and experienced—remains someplace else. His sense of the normal and expected had been formed in another world, and that is where it stayed. At some level, the landscape he saw every morning when he got up and looked out the window remained "there."

That sense of the West as fundamentally apart was the nearest thing to a common denominator among the varied writings of that generation who came into the country—the diaries and letters, novels and journalistic dispatches, doggerel and travel accounts. As a perspective it has great advantages. Many of our most vivid physical descriptions of the plains have been written by gawking aliens. These writers have set the West against mental landscapes of other places, then have written from the shock of differences. The forms and details of the land can appear fresh even to those who have never known anything else.

Few writers, for instance, have described the plains in more engaging detail than Richard Francis Burton during his passage of 1860. Drawing on his experience as one of the great travelers of the age—he drew comparisons between buffalo chips and assorted animal dung of Switzerland, Armenia, Tibet, and India—Burton wrote like a precocious and erudite child. He was driven to look at, tell about, and if possible pick up and sniff each piece of this new world—the clotted clay soil, asters and wild parsnips, fossils, beetles, and native artifacts. He described the northern lights and how cooking with sagebrush flavored meat like camphor and turpentine. Occasionally he caught as well the area's more general qualities, as in this view of a sunset opening up the spaciousness of the plains:

> Strata upon strata of cloud-banks [to the west] . . . lay
> piled half way from the horizon to the zenith. . . . Overhead
> floated . . . heavy purple nimbi, apparently turned upside
> down,—the convex bulges below, and their horizontal lines
> high in the air,—whilst, in the East, black and blue were so
> curiously blended, that the eye could not distinguish whether
> it rested upon darkening air or upon a lowering
> thundercloud.[17]

Burton could see the uniqueness of the plains so clearly because his sense of the normal had been shaped elsewhere. By the same token he, and all outlanders, could not help bringing with them other expectations—not topographical, in this case, but cultural and social. Through those expectations they projected deeper meanings onto the physical West they described so vividly. To them, the new country was never just an interesting place to be portrayed in its own right. Differences of terrain were never *only* differences. They were messages and, almost always, imperatives.

Emigrants looked at the West's profound dissimilarity and saw in it two broad and opposing sets of possibilities. In the first, the country's difference invited new arrivals to change it, to transform the West so that it would become like the places they had left in body but which continued to be the measure of what was normal and proper. Because the West was "there," in other words, they felt compelled to change it into "here." In the second case, the West had promise only if it remained different and fundamentally apart. It was "there," and it ought to keep on being "there."

The first response was the most common and the one with the most widespread, visible consequences. The West called out to be changed. It was seen as a series of developments about to occur. The Great Plains grasslands were pastures waiting for cattle; they were corn and wheat fields that needed only to be laid out, plowed, planted, cultivated, weeded, and cropped. The physical expanse was unshaped social potential waiting to be molded according to the familial ideals of communities that newcomers had left in body but not in spirit. The West was an economic and social order asking to happen.

A good bit of what appeared in the first three essays were cases of people acting out that compulsion. In 1853 the Indian agent Thomas Fitzpatrick called the upper Arkansas valley "a disconnecting wilderness"—a land, that is, important insofar as it separated an older civilized order to the east from one just emerging to the west. Its significance was that it had to be passed through and endured; but that would change quickly. By 1855 boosters were predicting that along the river churches and courthouses soon would send their spires toward heaven. In fact, towns were soon laid out and shops were built, false-fronted to look like others in Ohio and lined along the usual eastern grid of streets. On surrounding lands were much larger right-angle patterns of fields that were plowed and planted in ways deemed appropriate and proper in Indiana and Missouri.[18] Within that visible, physical order another was projected, this one summed up best in the familial ideals of America to the east. The family marched westward and made over the country, not just as demographic breadmold and as a chewer of the land, but also as a pattern of behavior and a social arrangement—one that white newcomers tried also to impose on natives whom they looked upon, like the land, as generic western stuff waiting to be transformed.

The second impulse, although not as immediately noticeable, also had a surprisingly powerful hold on the emigrants. In this case the West's difference was exactly what the newcomers liked. They praised the new land for its lack of what they had left behind them. The country's potential, they thought, would be realized if it remained alien.

Specifically, many were smitten by what they perceived as "wild" country and what they believed was its uplifting influence. On the plains, this wildness took form, first of all, in two attributes of the country—its size and emptiness. Climbing a bluff above the Platte, William Lockwood looked west and saw land "as level as a frozen lake." The vista was "right welcome [but] strange," not beautiful, exactly, but stunning in "its vast extent, its solitide and its wilderness." Essential to such feelings was the perception that this land was largely empty of human presence. For Julia Holmes, on her way to Colorado in 1858, the "grandeur" of the "silent, uninhabited plains . . . made my heart leap with joy." Some slipped into unintentional irony. "O solitude solitude, how I love it," a young woman wrote: "If [only] I had about dozen of my acquaintances to enjoy it with me." The obvious exceptions to this human absence—Indians—were considered more like relatively rare fauna, moving here and there with the whims of all predators, an unchanging part of the landscape and no more participants in history than antelopes and gophers.[19]

Many outlanders, but especially men, found that the vastness and the seeming emptiness encouraged the feeling that one was no longer in a world where living was a matter of dealing with other people, coping with rules and institutions, and moving within a web of human actions, past and present. Here, on the plains, a man could believe he had put society and history behind him. Now he stood in confrontation with elemental forces, nose-to-nose with nature—and nobody else. This heady illusion that life had been reduced to its basics had a curious double implication: you were solely responsible for your own fate, but on the other hand nothing you did had any consequences beyond you, beyond the immediate "now." The sense that life was suddenly confined to the present tense could be intoxicating. On a hunting trip in the Smoky Hill valley in 1866, the Prussian diplomat Friedrich von Holstein, later a prominent figure in German diplomacy, wrote to his family that coming onto the plains, being ever watchful for both dangers and prey, had a powerful effect on his self-perception: "One stands there with the Wallenstein-like feeling that 'here a man is still worth something.'" It was exhilarating but sobering: "In the wilderness [is] a deep seriousness from which no one escapes."[20]

All these impressions added up to perhaps the most seductive allure of the plains and the West generally—its offer of simplicity. William Jackson Palmer, railroad executive and Colorado booster, wrote his wife from western Kansas:

Now I seem to vibrate between a life of savagery and civilization. . . . It brings one back . . . to nature in its purest simplicity, before man has even made a foothold. . . . [O]n the Great Plains life seems stripped of its complexity; wood, grass and water, a few wild animals to outwit and shoot, a certain distance to march and then go into camp; a little round of daily duties, a limited number of relations with a very few people . . . does it not all go to make up a more healthful life? . . . Life has never seemed *straighter* to me than when . . . I have been thrown on to the Plains. . . . Is not this perhaps the real source of the fascination which lays hold of everyone who has spent any time on the Plains?[21]

Those who celebrated simplicity, however, had no interest in anything close to full immersion in alien country. Sportsmen like Holstein were well provisioned and never far from settlements. Palmer wrote the letter quoted above not from a lonely bivouac but while riding toward Colorado in a plush railcar of the Kansas Pacific. They and virtually everyone drawn to "wild" landscape wanted to live in reasonable safety but with easy access to a world they could imagine as savage and free of complicating attachments. They wanted, in other words, to live out both of those narratives—the one about people coming into that emptiness and changing it into the place they had left, and the other about escaping into the same country, enjoying its sights, being somehow strengthened and cleansed and liberated from both past and future. What seems especially striking, looking back, is the ability of so many newcomers to keep those two narratives going in their heads, apparently without noticing any contradictions.

Such mental juggling was more understandable among those who had the wherewithal to act out different stories simultaneously. Palmer was a good example. When he wrote admiringly of the plains, where "man has [not] even made a foothold," he was speeding toward the Rockies to create the town of Colorado Springs. His idea for that enterprise is a classic instance of double-vision. The town was to be a resort for well-to-do easterners who wanted to take the western air and to avoid the seedy new immigrants starting to fill the cities of the Atlantic coast. Colorado Springs was designed with broad tree-lined boulevards, fountains, churches, business blocks, and hotels, like the Antlers, a magnificent Queen Anne style resort of shingles and stone that might have been airlifted from Europe, or at least from Connecticut. As Palmer saw it, visitors would also be able to venture onto the neighboring plains, into an extensive "deer park" where wild animals would still graze and a remnant of native peoples would continue to live in primitive simplicity. Two worlds, a transplanted East and pristine West, would exist side by side, seemingly without difficulty.[22]

It is much more surprising to find similar impulses among ordinary settlers caught up in the common tasks of pioneering. In 1877, a few years after Palmer set his fantasy in motion, the newlyweds Gus and Mary Magdalene Brulport started a farm in Rush County, Kansas. Soon afterward they set off for a delayed honeymoon on a rail excursion to the Front Range. In her diary, Mary told of bathing with her husband in hot springs, admiring the primal beauty of the Garden of Gods, and watching the sunrise from Pikes Peak before heading home for more sodbusting. Along the way, at Dodge City, a town that at that moment was generating its own mythic tradition, the Brulports paused to watch a procession of Cheyennes, "like a moving Panarama." That evening they had a greater thrill: "The Indians came over into the town and Danced one of their War dances this PM." Just before that spectacle they had enjoyed the opera, and next morning they attended church, followed by a public lecture on "Morality."[23] In the West, the move between the settled and the savage has always been an easy shuttle, and the twin narratives of civilizer and seeker of the wild are readily at hand.

Those two basic impulses, so different in so many ways, did have certain points in common. In both, as already noted, the West was seen as fundamentally apart in its geography; but the two narratives shared something else. Both defined the West negatively in its record of human experience. The West was the West, that is, because of what had *not* happened, because of the absence of human events, accomplishments and disasters. It was the Land of Isn't, the Empire of Gonna Be. Physical geography became the pure stuff of imagined possibilities, not a reminder of who had been there and what they had done, how they had succeeded and failed.

This point is worth emphasizing in light of the large body of recent work from humanistic geographers—among others, Denis

Cosgrove, Donald W. Meinig, Edward Relph, Douglas Pocock, Fred Lukermann, and, most visibly of late, Yi-Fu Tuan.[24] Of particular interest are their attempts to define what turns out to be one of the most slippery words in the English language: "place." What is "place," and how is it different from mere space, or land? For all their various opinions, most of these writers would agree that a place must have three elements. First, there is its physical setting, its topology and soil and climate that together make it a unique part of the world. Second, a place is its history, all the things that humans have done there, and have had done to them, and the marks and artifacts that its history has left behind. Finally, essential to a place is what that setting and that history have meant to their people. A place is partly its collective human memory, its people's awareness that much has happened there. It is the accumulation over generations of people's responses to the land and its events. We might think of this as emotional strata laid down over time, all the while being bent, fractured, partly eroded, and uplifted like ancient rock to give each place its peculiar mental, mythic shape.

By those terms, what attracted pioneers was the West's placelessness. As they saw it, the West was no past and all possibilities. Those potentials varied; they might want to give the "new land" a shape like the place they had known, or they might want to keep it "new," always available so they might play the primitive; but in all cases they would be working with country that had no past when they came to it.

Maybe this was the larger, truly compelling meaning of the famous phrase that Frederick Jackson Turner used to define the frontier: "free land." In an economic sense, the way it is usually taken, the term implied that no one was inhabiting and using the country the pioneers were taking—notwithstanding the tens of thousands of Indians who were being dispossessed. Similarly, in the context of "place," the words "free land" denied the human experience that lay centuries-deep on the plains. This West was free of memories and lessons, free to be made into places people had left or to be kept simple and free of complications: land free of ghosts. The West was waiting to have history brought to it or to remain without a past. In either case, as the white invaders saw it, the West had no stories of its own, nothing to listen to and learn from, no emotional layering. Pioneers were, in this sense, going No Place, which was exactly where they wanted to be.

This way of thinking about the pioneering impulse has obvious limitations. We should not ride this horse too hard. Nonetheless, we can learn a lot from it. What is especially striking is the remarkable staying power of these traditions. Their persistence, in fact, is arguably one of the West's most distinctive characteristics—and an enduring connection between the frontier experience and the present day. Those lived-out narratives have continued through political upheavals, the Dust Bowl and the drought of the fifties, vast shufflings of population, half a dozen boom-and-bust cycles, revolutions in technology and transportation, and five generations of social change.

The literary tradition of the spellbound outsider is especially vigorous. Several recent books about the plains are by travelers or sojourners. These are often reviewed as original and innovative, but they are really revivals of travel accounts like those of Richard Burton. Their style is updated and streamlined, to be sure, and some of these writers have not just passed through but have stayed and worked awhile, but their outlanders' point of view, wide-eyed tone, and ability to see the plains freshly and perceptively rank them with the best professional travelers of the last century. Probably the best known of these recent rediscoverers is Ian Frazier, staffer for the *New Yorker* whose *Great Plains* has received a wide readership and well deserved awards, but there are others, among them Gretel Ehrlich, Merrill Gilfillan, Dayton Duncan, Pete Davies, and Kathleen Norris. Nobody, not even Burton, has captured better the unsettling, exhilarating impact of the openness of the plains than a friend of Frazier at the end of her first day driving around the Montana flatlands. "It's amazing here!" she telephoned home: "The sky is like a person yawned and never stopped!"[25]

Much more influential has been the persistence of those two stories that oncoming whites have projected onto the West. Among the most enduring forces shaping the visible West has been the passion to remold it by the patterns of other places, not only to pursue economic goals but also to make it look like the world outside. Wherever pioneers and their descendants have lived in any numbers, we can see the cultural deposition from decades of this effort. The pattern is epecially clear in towns, which typically were structured by an imported geometry and garnished with public and private architectural forms meant to replicate the town-builders' origins.[26]

The reiterative wave rolled across the central plains and washed against the base of the Rockies, with consequences still very much with us. Part of this essay was written at the University of Colorado in Boulder. Photos from the 1870s show a campus with one building, a midwestern-style Old Main, set on a shortgrass plain. A ribbon of cottonwoods followed Boulder Creek. That pasture of duns and greys has long since given way to green commons. Students attend lectures, including ones about a distinctive local and regional history, delivered in buildings of Tuscan architecture. Between classes they sunbathe on imported grasses and lounge in the shade of hickories, elms, maples, and oaks kept alive by great disgorgings of water from fat canvas umbilicals. Neighborhoods near campus are lined with more hardwoods and with gabled houses behind lush, well-sprinkled lawns. Southeast of Boulder is Denver. The "Queen City of the Plains" has generous parks with more imported trees, lovely Victorian neighborhoods, and the original business district kept in an "old West" condition through a faithful restoration of architecture that was at the time self-consciously eastern. Baseball fans flock to a stadium nearby to watch the Colorado Rockies. As thousands cheer this, the first major league team of the interior western heartland, vendors work the crowd, selling cappucino.

Just as tenacious has been the tradition of the West as the simple land, a refuge for those looking for the elemental life amidst untouched natural beauty. The search for Eden, Malcolm Clark writes, has been "the major apparition of the American Dream." That ghost still haunts the land, but as the first narrative has increasingly reshaped and built upon the landscape, the fear has grown that paradise, the land before time, has slipped beyond our reach.

This aching concern has inspired one of our most familiar literary genres. We might call it "Old Geezer" fiction: stories that play with that exquisite tension between the two impulses. The Geezers in these stories are men who were there at that moment when people came from the east to reproduce their own world in the innocent, unstoried western paradise—men who then lived long enough to be able to look back and tell us how heavenly it was in that lovely day before history arrived and spoiled everything. Larry McMurtry's novels are a veritable gallery of Geezers: Sam the Lion in *The Last Picture Show*, Wild Horse Homer Bannon in *Horseman, Pass By*, Gus McCrae and Captain Call in *Lonesome Dove*, and Calamity Jane, a kind of Gezerette, in *Buffalo Girls*. The ultimate Geezer, of course, is from the central plains: Jack Crabb in Thomas Berger's *Little Big Man*, the 111-year-old resident of a nursing home who spins a tale of coming west as boy, being captured and adopted by Cheyennes, then meeting and witnessing most of the mythic characters and events of the plains frontier. With this device, Berger portrays the West as two utterly distinct worlds—the static and timeless one of the Cheyennes and the expanding, dynamic, transforming, irresistible one of whites.[27] As we follow Crabb commuting between the two, we watch the second one triumph and the first disappear.

These twin impulses inevitably bring with them their own frustration. The reason is obvious. Stories that presume to be *about* the country they inhabit necessarily must grow out of that country. If they are simply brought into it, after being grown elsewhere, they can certainly have enormous effects, and they will leave their marks; but by definition they cannot be reconciled with the land and people they say they describe. More specifically, Kansas and Utah cannot be made to look like the Ohio valley and upstate New York, no matter how much anybody tries. "There" can never become "here." And neither can anyone ever find in the West that land free of history, that changeless Eden, because it never existed, or at least it has not for at least ten thousand years or so. Consequently, these imported narratives can only keep on striving toward what they can never attain, or look back wistfully at lost opportunities that were never there.

Perhaps this is the burden of western history: not so much shame over mistreatment of others but rather a mix of frustrations: an unappeasable inferiority complex that has left east-to-westerners forever playing cultural catch-up, and a melancholy longing over botched innocence.

On the other hand, some say that timeless, unlayered, storyless West, the land of No Place, might still be with us. Those who hope for it are most likely to look, naturally, where there are fewest people, in the highest country and on the deserts and plains. Those areas are largely empty, of course, because conditions have driven almost everybody away, but for a lot of the new travel writers, like new arrivals a century ago, emptiness is equated with potential for just about anything, and solitude is linked to spiritual enrichment through simplication. "Of all landscapes," Merrill Gilfillan writes, "the open

plain is one of Possibility." Kathleen Norris, who subtitled her book
A Spiritual Geography, compares the plains to a monastery and considers its quiet and lack of human presence an opportunity for wisdom impossible in the New York she fled. Gretel Ehrlich offers a
statement about the open country that would have astounded a lot
of busted ranchers and mothers trying to keep their wits while rearing children on the high plains: "Space represents sanity, . . . a life . . .
that might accommodate intelligently any idea or situation." Visiting her from New York, her dying lover felt something similar: "All
this space reminds me of possibility."[28]

Behind all this is the notion that the dedicated searcher can discover parts of the West where the chains of events that define civi-
lizations have not yet been set in motion. Find them, and you can
pass over into the timeless. "The frontier is a burning edge, a frazzle . . .
between two utterly different worlds," as Gary Snyder put it in his
recent essays, *The Practice of the Wild*. It is a boundary he believes
still can be found in a few parts of the West: "There is an almost
visible line that a person of the invading culture [can] walk across,
out of history and into the perpetual present. . . ."[29]

Snyder, of course, is writing about wilderness, and it is in the
fascination with the wild country that this second impulse survives
most heartily. We are used to thinking of the frontier as destroying
wilderness. Certainly the invaders disrupted existing habitats, killed
off indigenous animals, and triggered all sorts of ecological changes.
Without a doubt the Euro-Americans introduced technologies with
a capacity to alter the non-human world far more quickly and thoroughly than anything Indian peoples had ever known, and whites,
furthermore, showed a far greater enthusiasm to carry out such al-
terations. Certainly there have been—and are now—plenty of good
reasons to try to isolate and protect areas least affected by the changes
that have rolled over the West during the past three centuries; but if
"wilderness" is taken to mean country beyond the reach of change,
that is a dream, and always has been.

In a sense the frontier did not *destroy* wilderness at all; it *created* it.
It did so in two ways. First, whites brought contact diseases that
swept away millions of native residents of the western hemisphere,
making it possible for later invaders to imagine the country as never
touched by human presence. Second, those invaders then projected
into that newly emptied space their need to find Edenic, unstoried

territory, "the perpetual present" as Snyder calls it. That infatuation
might be best defined by Maurice Sendak's classic children's book,
Where the Wild Things Are: a dreamworld we can reach only by crawling out of civilization's window and sailing or walking away from
parents, biological and cultural, into country without rules or lessons rooted in collective experience.[30]

In practice, modern searchers have rarely sought a true break
with their past and its protections, any more than sportsmen and
homesteader-tourists did a century and a half ago. Policies of national parks and monuments, for instance, have always been in tension between the ideal of preserving a pristine wilderness and the
need to assure a visitor access, safety, and a modicum of comfort.
Consequently, parks are best understood as partially constructed
landscapes. Stephen Mather, director of national parks from 1916
to 1929, promoted idyllic, game-filled scenes conforming to romantic preconceptions of untouched beauty. Efforts to snuff out fires
and control insect infestation have been similar, if less obvious,
manipulations.[31] The ironic task has been subtly to create and compose settings that seem to be in contrast to the surrounding "developed" country. The overall effect perpetuates that old illusion of a
dichotomized West, a land divided between the built and the wild,
history and Eden. When tourist-consumers enter a park, a historian
recently wrote, they participate in a time-polished westering ritual,
crossing a "perceptual threshold" and "imaginative border" based
on their "faith in radical difference, a perception that the 'undeveloped' spaces on the far side of the frontier [the park boundary] con-
stitute an exotic other" in stark contrast to the developed East and
the West that has mimicked it.[32]

Sometimes those responsible for these constructed wildlands had
to get rid of what did not fit the imagined country, including people.
It is important to remember that there has been a double Indian
removal policy in the far West, compelled by those twin narrative
impulses. Native Americans were not only taken off land meant to
be made over into fields, towns and cattle pastures. As historian
Mark David Spence notes, Indians were also forced out of some of
white America's sacred wild spaces, such as Yellowstone, Yosemite,
Glacier, and the Black Hills, then penned up in areas less fitted for
the wilderness dream. This was sometimes done with the support of
well-known sympathizers and reformers like George Bird Grinnell

and Helen Hunt Jackson. On a visit to Yosemite, Jackson complained of "filthy" and "uncouth" Indians marring the valley's pristine, primordial beauty.[33]

Obviously there are distinctions among those who have shaped the West out of a search for wilderness. National Parks are not theme parks. Custodians of the Yellowstone backcountry are not like William Jackson Palmer, trying merely to keep a few deer and Indians close at hand to amuse the hotel loungers. Nonetheless, the bedrock assumptions have not been so different. The pervasive belief has been the "faith in radical difference" by which much of the public lands are perceived as separated cleanly from "developed" space by an "imaginary frontier." Beyond that line, "Euro-American fantasies of an unoccupied continent" can still be played out.[34]

That dichotomy and those fantasies continue to play an enormous role in western life. In fact, with the sagging of other aspects of the economy their relative contribution has grown considerably. "It's a product that you don't have to get funding for," observed one authority, Joe Bowlin, owner of Bowlin's Big Red Indian store near Fort Sumner, New Mexico.[35] The particular brand of the product he sells is the myth of Billy the Kid, the wild child on the wide open frontier, but Bowlin's comments apply far more broadly. The myth business has definite advantages. Other resources—oil and cattle, wheat and timber—are subject to erratic swings in outside demand. They are also indigenous goods that are mined and harvested, then taken elsewhere and sold. By contrast, the myth's basic resource— the desire to find and touch a wilder, freer, simpler world—has a demand that is remarkably stable and apparently bottomless. Even better, this resource is the happy opposite of the others: it originates elsewhere, but it can only be truly converted to income in the West. Dude ranching, including the recent "City Slicker" phenomenon of white-collar outlanders paying large sums to act out western fantasies, is a recognition of this economic edge. Ranchers have retooled. As much as they might want to concentrate on raising cattle, many understand that if they sell the myth instead, the money will come to them.[36]

No wonder that tourism and the search for wilderness have proved so vigorous. The numbers alone suggest how much. The annual count of visitations to the four most popular national parks in the West (Grand Canyon, Yellowstone, Yosemite, and Olympia) is greater than the population of New England. Death Valley, the western wild space with the most daunting and inhospitable reputation, last year drew more than four hundred thousand people. It was as if all of Baltimore came out to take a look. In 1955, the last year before restrictions were imposed on rafting through the Grand Canyon, 16,428 people braved the rapids, more than the entire overland migration to Oregon and California before 1849.[37]

The dream of acting out that narrative, of crossing the line and touching wild places forever in the present, partly explains the annual flocking of the RVs. It supports a huge supply industry for the hard core, that army of techno-primitivists who press toward the heart of the dreamspace—and who pay plenty for the chance. Dozens of catalogues offer everything from inflatable sinks and a stove that "cleans itself as you hike" to a variety of "technical socks" (including trekking and "moraine" socks). When the time comes to take a load off in God's cathedral, there is the thirty-four-ounce "Power Lounger."[38] Even without such devices, a modest backpacking outfit can easily surpass the annual per capita gross domestic product of Bolivia ($630 in 1992). The impulse has inspired whole libraries of books. Besides collections of glossy photographs of pristine, isolated beauty, there are dozens of novels and essays that play on the fantasy of outrunning history, most notably those of Edward Abbey, the modern master of the adolescent male escape fantasy. Those who want to act out the story first-hand can browse through shelves of instruction manuals. One really gets down to basics: *How To Shit in the Woods*.[39]

Those two stories—one about replicating other places and the other about finding simpler lives in land free of the past—have been among the unavoidable facts of recent western life. Imported and acted out, they have had a profound and continuing influence. They have proved resilient, powerful, endlessly seductive.

And they are lies. The West has been a place, or rather places, in the fullest human sense of the term for quite a while. It has had its own stories to tell since at least five thousand years before the earliest cities of Mesopotamia. It holds the nation's oldest continuously inhabited sites. The central plains, although not the most ancient West in human terms, have been inhabited for thousands of years; the invasions of the last century and a half have been only the most recent of many human waves that have washed over that country, all with their own stories, each of which has been worn over time to reveal its own particularity.

Among other narratives, the most obvious are those of Indian peoples of the plains and West.[40] These stories are accessible in different forms, including Native American oral tradition and transcriptions and descriptions by non-native observers, some taken recently and others from previous generations. All have their limitations, among them the inability to describe with certainty stories of earlier times. How, for instance, did the Kiowas or Cheyennes consider the plains when they first encountered them? Did they, like later white pioneers, look into them as an empty space to fill with their dreams? Nobody can say. Something else, however, is starkly clear: Native American stories, as told now and recorded along the way, are fundamentally different from pioneer narratives in their stance, messages, and the meanings they take from the country.

Plains Indians, like whites, have surviving traditions of coming into the country. Kiowas recall moving from the snowy mountains around the headwaters of the Yellowstone River to the central and south plains. It was "the great adventure . . . [of] going forth into the heart of the continent," N. Scott Momaday writes.[41] Cheyennes tell of moving from the Great Lakes region to the Missouri valley and then gradually onto the plains, first to the Black Hills before fanning out southward. The stories are of people reaching for better lives and for realization.[42]

In other ways, however, native peoples remember themselves, long ago, as set in the world around them now. Creation accounts, albeit, are usually abstract and unfold in generic landscapes. Both Cheyennes and Kiowas tell of emerging from the dark underground into the light. For the Cheyennes, the creator made a woman and a man and sent one north and the other south to live with Winter Man and Thunder, basic forces who push against one another during every year. Apart from these abstracted stories, which might have unfolded anywhere, native traditions also explain particular landmarks, familiar parts of today's landscape. Those explanations are bound together with actions of ancestors. For the Kiowas, the stars of the Pleiades (or the Big Dipper) are kinsmen, a girl and her brothers (or seven sisters) pursued by a bear (in one variant a woman transformed by her love for a he-bear). To save themselves they scrambled into the heavens up a great rock (or tree stump), which the bear clawed in frustration and rage. The scarred rock-stump remains as Devil's Tower in present-day Wyoming. The immediate setting, furthermore, is continuous with a larger unseen universe. In the deep earth below the Cheyenne's feet are caverns where animal spirits gather and may be withheld or released in physical form into the middle zone, the surface world of plains and rivers and grass. The near sky space holds air, breath, clouds, rain, and thunder. Above it is *otatavoom*, the blue sky space, from mountain peaks to the stars, associated with the All-Father Creator, Maheo. Upon a person's death, his or her immortal spiritual form is freed, perhaps to roam the near and blue sky spaces, or perhaps to be reincarnated with the gift of breath or to remain close, a spirit in physical form, as a helper and guide.

Stories of spiritual ancestry and collective identity are grounded in immediate surroundings, often particular places near at hand. As the Cheyennes came onto the plains and approached the Black Hills, they approached a mountain resembling a slumbering bear. This was the Sacred Mountain, *Noaha-vose*, called Bear Butte by whites. The Cheyenne prophet, Sweet Root Standing (or Sweet Medicine), entered *Noaha-vose* through an opened door. He remained four years with Maheo, the All-Father Creator, as well as the Sacred Powers and the four Sacred Persons. He returned to his people with a divine code of law and the four Sacred Arrows through which the creator continually sent his own sustaining spirit and with which he provided power over other tribes and the herds of bison. Sweet Root Standing also brought word of how his people were to order their society and establish five warrior societies. The Cheyennes became *Votostataneo*, the "singled-out people."

It is important to recognize what these stories are not. Westward-moving whites perceived plains natives as living timeless, change-less lives; but there is nothing static about these stories. To the contrary, Indian narratives are full of dynamic changes—rivalries and collective squabbles, alliances, victories and calamitous losses, adaptations and shifting relations among spirits and men. The Kiowas tell of leaving the Yellowstone valley over a fight with another tribal faction over some antelope udders. There followed friendly relations with the Crows, bitter conflict with the Sioux, and a mixed history with the Comanches before a long-term alliance around 1790. The Cheyennes' story of themselves, as noted several times in these essays, is one of movement, political fission, and intratribal tensions.

There are struggles and an armistice with the Comanches and Kiowas and continuing warfare with the Pawnees, and territorial pulling and shoving. Traditions recognize the adjustment and give-and-take that came with the move onto the plains. One story tells of the Cheyennes' first encounter with horses while still living in lodges along eastern rivers. For four days their holy men prayed to Maheo, who answered at last:

> You may have horses. . . . You may even go with the Comanches to take them. But remember this: If you have horses everything will be changed for you forever.
>
> You will have to move around a lot to find pasture for your horses. You will have to give up gardening and live by hunting and gathering, like the Comanches. And you will have to come out of your earth houses and live in tents. I will tell your women how to make them, and how to decorate them.
>
> And there will be other changes. You will have to have fights with other tribes, who will want your pasture land or the places where you hunt. You will have to have real soldiers, who can protect the people. Think, before you decide.

The choice, of course, is for horses; but in return Maheo demands the Cheyennes never forget who they are and where they have come from, and he gives them the Sun Dance as a guide and a sacred remembrance.[43]

Nothing in these stories, furthermore, suggests that the people who tell them necessarily will live in peace and in balance with their country. There is plenty of room for foul-ups. Relationships among humans, animals, and spirits need close attention precisely because they can so easily go awry. Tomorrow's conditions depend upon today's decisions—actions that can be wise and proper or dead wrong. People's relations with their surroundings, in fact, are in many ways quite dynamic. Things happen. Consequences are felt.

Place, as a result, is inseparable from discrete developments that have occurred there. Events—individual achievements, encounters with spirits, miscalculations and terrible violations of proper order, magnificent victories and tragic disasters, heinous crimes, withdrawal and return of divine favors—are essential elements of a homeland's definition. A place is what it is, partly, because of the deep strata of stories that are still being laid down, and will continue to be, presumably forever.

There is, however, an unchanging aspect of place in these stories. The world immediately around the Cheyennes is the only possibility they have for a sustaining force in their lives. From it must come, not only the means of day-to-day survival, but more fundamentally the spiritual power that created them as a people, that has set the basic terms of their existence, and that continues to provide the basis of their sense of themselves. The Cheyenne story recognizes an earlier life elsewhere, but its central moment—Sweet Root Standing's time with Maheo inside the Sacred Mountain—tells of finding an identity that emanates, quite literally, from the plains to which the Cheyennes have come. Their idea of who they are, their means of self-conception, cannot be told apart from this country and what has happened there.

This unbreakable relation, so basic that it is easy to pass over it, is ubiquitous in Amerindian narratives on the plains and elsewhere. Keith Basso has noted that the oral narratives of Western Apaches are grouped in four categories: myths, historical tales, sagas, and gossip, each distinguished by its placement in time and its purpose. Narratives of the second group, historical tales, are brief stories set "long ago," when Apaches were establishing their culture and lifeways, and they are intended to define and criticize social misconduct. These tales always start and end with a statement establishing the precise location where the story occurred. One begins: "It happened at 'coarse-textured rocks lie above in a compact cluster,'" and another: "It happened at 'big cottonwood trees stand spreading here and there.'" Both the lesson and its placement are essential elements in establishing proper Apache behavior. Morality, identity, history, and place are of a piece.[44] As with the Cheyennes, who is bound up inextricably with where.

That perspective is behind one of the most persistent patterns in contemporary Native American fiction. In many such stories, the protagonists have left the place of their origins, frequently to chase success or to meet some duty prescribed by white American mores. They become soldiers and lawyers, or they just take off to look for a job or something different. Most stories open with them sick, physically or spiritually—usually both—but they are drawn back irresistably to their beginnings; the "tribal past," as William Bevis puts it, is "a gravity field stronger than individual will."[45] The plot centers on the rebirth of an understanding that the character's identity—in a basic sense, his meaning—can exist only in the nexus of a particular place and in relation to people bound to him in common laws and history.

Several of the most celebrated Native American novels are variations of this pattern: N. Scott Momaday's *House Made of Dawn*, Leslie Silko's *Ceremony*, and James Welch's *Winter in the Blood*, among others. An example from the central plains is Linda Hogan's *Mean Spirit*, set in Oklahoma during the oil boom of the 1920s. Stace Red Hawk, a Lakota Sioux working for the Bureau of Investigation, is sent from Washington to look into the deaths of Indians resisting the surrender of oil leases. What he finds (besides the murderers) are webs of Osage Indian families, flesh-and-blood ghosts, spirit villages, and caves of old bones and bat kinsmen—and, with all that, the knowledge that severing himself from his own people and place has hollowed him out. At the end, Red Hawk leaves with an Osage family, the Grayclouds. We are not sure where he is heading, but it is not back to Washington.[46]

This pattern is exactly opposite from that in white narratives. White protagonists are forever leaving home to seek fortune and adventure and to "find themselves," which means going west to escape family, society, and history. Unlike the Indian characters, leaving home does not make them a spiritual mess. Lighting out for the wilderness is what they are supposed to do. Their beginnings are the last things they want to discover; their hope for satisfaction is through eluding the past. Whites run away to the West to pursue what might be done in country stripped free of limits and entanglements. Indians return to the West to reintegrate their individuality into an old, complex world.

Indian and white stories, then, might be pictured through a series of paired meanings. For native peoples, the West is a place of origins; for whites, it is where one breaks generational and social bonds. For Indians, it offers the opportunity of enmeshing within intricate connections of land, kinship, history, ritual, rules of behavior, and enduring spiritual forces; for whites, it is the chance to shuck off complicating relationships and find pure possibility, the raw makings of what has not yet happened. For Native Americans, fulfill-ment there is achieved by learning—by getting exactly right—the old story that has come out of the place and continues to grow from it; for whites, full satisfaction will come either by playing out a story carried in from elsewhere, or by finding that unhistoried West where narratives never take hold, in land where ghosts can never be.

These distinctions can help explain what might otherwise seem baf-fling aspects of contemporary native and white fiction. Why, for in-stance, do white storytellers, whose forebearers, after all, *won* the struggle for control of the West, so seldom write about the presumably triumphant results? Why do they most often look back longingly to-ward the early days of their arrival, or write so depressingly of those pioneers, the Geezers, whose cruel fate has been to survive frontier victories? Why, conversely, do Native American novelists so seldom spin tales from the glory days before their Sand Creeks and Washitas and write instead about the recent West of reservations and poverty?

Part of the answer, as already suggested, lies in the logic of pio-neer narratives. The freer one is to pursue the implications of those stories, the clearer and more unavoidable the contradictions be-come. Just as important, the people who tell those narratives today will find nothing to root themselves into the past of where they are. No present-day consequence of acting out those stories can possibly fit into a pattern of meaning that explains the uniqueness of the place where the storyteller is living out his days.

On the other hand, that organic connection among the narrator, the distinctive setting of the telling and the details of present and past, is the most fundamental feature of Native American stories. Current circumstances might be grim and disturbing, but they rep-resent one more successive layering of the story, which has grown up out of the place and will continue to do so. As such, conditions just are. Telling them—setting them in place—is as natural as keeping your name and parentage in your head.

Precisely because the landscape is integral to the stories, its de-tails never seem as remarkable as they often do in traditional white narratives. Writers in the pioneer tradition, whether Richard Burton or modern sojourners or novelists of the mountain man and cowboy genres, seem always to be pointing at the land, observing and com-menting. Addressing the country that way, they tell us that they see themselves apart from it. To Indian narrators, however, the particulars are simply there, part of the neighborhood. A good example is the opening paragraph of James Welch's *Winter in the Blood*. In six sentences Welch mentions several familiar elements of the pioneer's mythic West—a horse and colt, a log cabin, wind-blown tumbleweed, and barbed wire—but the scene that Welch makes of those details does not feel in the slightest like a "western." It is just the Earthboy place, a particular spot in Montana's Milk River valley where the story starts for the unnamed narrator.[47]

Native American narratives, however, are no longer the only alternatives. There is now, and has been for decades, a flourishing of stories from the descendants of nineteenth-century white newcomers. These are part of the West's continuing, sequential aging. Like all migrants, the sodturners, herders, town-makers, and their children and grandchildren came to their own terms with the country. Over time the new land has become the home place.

With that, the narrative perspective has shifted around. In the stories told from these generations, the West is not a destination, an undeveloped realm where one can seek out whatever is needed. Now it is the initial vantage point. In Eric Dardel's term, the West is the "*here* from which the world discloses itself." On the plains and in the West at large, this perspective has gradually found its voice.

We can listen for it in many places, starting with the archives of historical societies and universities throughout the West. In their vaults are hundreds of reminiscences and oral histories, from a page or so of dim pencil scrawlings to book-length manuscripts, all of them largely passed over by scholars in favor of more traditional sources. With titles like "Father Came West" and "Prairie Children," they often provide materials and points of view not found in accounts from the generation immediately preceding—vivid and detailed environmental descriptions of particular places, a sense of discovery relatively free of preconceptions, and ambivalent loyalties toward native country and the forces transforming it.[48]

Some such sources, slightly more polished, are more readily available. Virtually every western state has its small private presses that over the past fifty years have published dozens of memoirs. The titles are often overly cute, the style folksy, and the contents sugared with sentiment, but these books are nonetheless a reservoir of

material on the experiences and perceptions of those who have lived
across those years that connect the frontier—the invaded West—
with the place we know today. A small portion with higher literary
quality have been picked up by university and commercial presses
with larger audiences. A superb example is *An Owl on Every Post*,
Sanora Babb's account from her homesteading girlhood in the Arkansas River valley just prior to World War I. Other examples from
the plains include two by prominent historians: Edward Everett Dale's
The Cross Timbers and Marquis James's *The Cherokee Strip*.[49]

I mention these collections and books to make a point. During
the past few years critics and literary historians have hailed a flowering of new western writing—fiction, essays, and, perhaps most common, memoirs—by authors whose popularity is at least one welcome
aspect of the present fascination with the West. They come from
various parts of the region: Mary Clearman Blew, Ivan Doig, Teresa
Jordan, and Cyra McFadden from the northern plains and Rockies;
William Kittredge and Sallie Tisdale from the great northwest; and Terry
Tempest Williams from the Great Basin.[50] Their works are praised,
quite properly, for their eloquence, insights, and powerful evoca-
tions of life in the twentieth-century West. Occasionally these memoirists are also described, quite improperly, as if they have come out of
nowhere. In fact, these new stars are best understood as just a few voices
among hundreds, all of them native children, who have been trying to
get our attention for at least a few decades. Most of these voices are still
entirely unheard when the air is filled with complaints about the lack of
work on the post-frontier West and about how little we know about the
experiences of commonfolk during the past few generations.

These are the testimonies of the daughters and sons and grandchildren of the Geezer generation. The stories they tell are not of
paradise lost but of places known from the ground up. Reading
through them, some in best sellers and some in Big Chief tablets, a
few themes appear over and over, ones reflecting not fantasies of the
West but what it has meant to live there. In some ways they could
not be more different from the usual frontier narratives.

They are, first of all, almost always about families and the insepa-
rability of family from people's workaday lives and their reckoning
of who they are and where they fit in this world. The subtitle of
Mary Blew's reminiscence is *A Memoir of Five Generations in the Life
of a Montana Family*; Teresa Jordan's is *A Western Family Album*; for

Terry Tempest Williams, it is *An Unnatural History of Family and Place*. If the frontier myth has involved running away from family and community, these stories tell us that life outside family is a contradiction in terms.

A second point is bound up with the first: these narratives express the authors' intimate, sensual connections with particular places. In the older tradition, western settings were largely generic. They found their meaning either as spaces to be made over or as uncorrupted landscapes. Because they were important for what they were *not*, the specifics of these places were relatively unimportant. The West was the West was the West. The new narratives, by contrast, are nearly always grounded in settings that are utterly particular. Each story could have happened only where it did; each place is defined through its unique details that in turn are bound up with its characters' memories. James Galvin's *The Meadow* is the story of one piece of land in northern Colorado and one family's attempt to make a go of it for nearly a hundred years. In *Going Over East*, Linda Hasselstrom walks us across her ranch, gate by gate, stopping each time to tell about pastures, family, neighbors, critters, cattle, grass, water, bones, and what they have all meant to her.[51]

Despite their rooting in diverse, unique places, these stories come up with similar lessons never found in traditional east-to-west narratives. The reader will not find any expansive imaginings, no hopes of ultimate wisdom and boundless possibilities. Feelings toward the West are at once more hardened and forgiving. The prime values are endurance and accommodation. The people in these stories all live by an iron, hard-earned lesson: if you want to survive over the long haul, you must pay both dues and attention. The context is an instinctive sense of boundaries and a wary affection for beautiful places that sometimes will turn around and slap you silly.

Interestingly, these writers often say their piece in two or more genres. Besides his memoir, Kittredge has given us short stories and essays, Doig several novels and *Winter Brothers*, a rumination and a dialogue with a Bostonian confronting the northwest coast in the 1850s. Jordan's first book was *Cowgirls*, sketches of ranch women, most of whom grew up on the northern plains. Blew published two collections of short stories before *All But the Waltz*.[52] Eight years before her memoir, Terry Tempest Williams wrote *Pieces of White Shell*. Drawing on her time as a schoolteacher on the Navajo reservation, it mixes reminiscent reflection with Navajo mythology and natural history. Williams is quick to point out, however, that the Navajos' stories are not hers, or ours. "Their stories hold meaning for us only as examples," she writes. Stories "grow from the inside out," and we are responsible for finding our own, "embedded in the landscapes," so "we will better know how to live our lives in the midst of change."[53] The result of her own search was *Refuge*.

It is as if Williams and the others are using various modes of telling and multiple angles of vision to tease out what is "embedded in the landscapes." The result is to see particular places in intrinsically different ways. In what is often called "nature writing," for instance, the western country usually has been seen as a dwindling reserve of "nature," which is defined in an introduction to a highly regarded collection of writing as "everything that exists on this planet (or elsewhere) that was not made by man" and all things in which humans have had no part. That leaves a few islands beyond human touch: "Only a wilderness area is not at least partly a collaboration [between people and the natural world]."[54] That's real escape country. *Desert Solitaire*, a sacred text among contemporary preservationists, is Edward Abbey's account of flight to the Utah outback to evade "the clamor and filth and confusion of the cultural apparatus" while confronting "the bare bones of existence, the elemental and fundamental." His goal was to go where he could look at a piece of quartz, a spider, or a vulture "devoid of all humanly described qualities."[55] Abbey usually is portrayed as an outrageous iconoclast, but his refrain would ring familiar and true to thousands before him, those seekers of the wild like Friedrich von Holstein, who have pictured themselves as standing alone in the West's big spaces, drunk with "the Wallenstein-like feeling that 'here a man is still worth something.'" Nothing could be more traditional—more hidebound—than Abbey's old, longing dream.

Nothing could be more wrenchingly different than some recent writing on the physical world of the West. A fine example is that of Gary Paul Nabhan. Nabhan's desert is the last place one would go to escape society. It has plenty of people, present and past, and plenty of what they have done. Distinctions between "nature" and "cultural apparatus" make no sense. Far from trying to look at juniper and snakes as "devoid of all humanly described qualities," Nabhan sees the desert as woven tight with exchanges among plants, spirits, rituals, stones, seeds, stories, experience, and sensations. He writes of Papago Indians who classify saguaro cactus as part of humankind, who harvest its fruit to ferment into sweet wine, which they drink from Hormel frankfurter cans then vomit back to cleanse themselves and to bring forth renewing, cooling rains. Nabhan's desert is crowded with memory and noisy with conversations among its parts, people included. It is an ancient, continuing collaboration.[56]

Nabhan's essays, seemingly gentle explorations of melon seeds and native traditions, are in fact profoundly radical, in an etymologically truer sense than Abbey and other angry nature-seekers can ever be. Like others of this bent (Williams's *Pieces of White Shell* is close kin), they force the reader into a fundamentally different stance, one that looks from the West outward instead of gazing into it as a playground for needs cultivated elsewhere. They are explicitly radical—as in the word's Latin origin, *radix*, or "root"—because they reach deep into the place that they describe and from which they grow. Reading them, it is easy to regret and resist many of the changes afoot. This West needs defending from blind greed and bungling and dangerous illusions. However, it would never dawn on Nabhan's readers, and certainly not on the native people he writes about, to see his books as an elegy to a doomed land and a vanishing life or to consider them what Abbey called *Desert Solitaire*: "a tombstone . . . a bloody rock" to throw at the modern world.[57] What we see in these essays has come out of what used to be, and it will be part of something else yet to come. It's an old place. Things persist.

That perspective of rooted continuity distinguishes the alternate western narrative and unites its various genres. In "Chant the Creation," Gary Holthaus sees mountains and plains, past and present blend together:

The basement gneiss and granite
Of the Beartooths, seventy million years old,
Their topmost sedimentary layers now
Washed away to Laurel, holding up
The Owl Cafe, Open All Night. . . .[58]

Ron Hansen, having written an excellent Geezer novel on the Dalton brothers, *Desperadoes*, went on to a collection of stories, *Nebraska*, that ends with an impressionistic word portrait of a plains town. The passing outsider "is only aware of what isn't . . . no

bookshop, no picture show . . . motels, hotels . . . theories about
Being and the soul." What are there, however, are people in place:
"Everyone is famous in this town. And everyone is necessary." They
go to the grocery store for news and "for history class" to the Home
Restaurant, where in the evening the owner, Mrs. Antoinette Heft

> plac[es] frozen meat patties on waxed paper, pausing at times
> to clamp her fingers under her arms and press the sting from
> them. She stops when the Union Pacific passes, then picks a
> cigarette out of a pack of Kools and smokes it on the back
> porch, smelling air as crisp as Oxydol, looking up at stars the
> Pawnee Indians looked at, hearing the low harmonica of big
> rigs on the highway, in the town she knows like the palm of
> her hand, in the country she knows by heart.[59]

The stories of Hansen, Holthaus, and Blew, of Nabhan, Kittredge,
Williams, and the authors of dozens of archive reminiscences are
centered in the West. They sit firmly, like a tub on its own bottom.
In these narratives the frontier invasion from the east becomes
one other episode, albeit an enormously influential one, rather
than the defining perspective itself. Boundaries between the pioneer experience and the contemporary West blur over or disappear
entirely. There is a lot of room for anger, but none for the psychological dislocation that comes from imported dreams that can only
be frustrated.

The sense of identity among these white post-frontier storytellers
is closely akin to the westerners regarded by pioneers as the ultimate
"others"—the Indians. Look, for instance, at the relationship white
writers discover among themselves, their home places, and the world
outside. There is a striking parallel with the theme of "homing in"
found in so much recent Native American fiction.[60] Characters in
novels by Welch and Silko tell of Indians leaving home in search of
accomplishment or some vague something, only to find understanding when they return home and fit their own stories into older ones
of their birth country. So it is with the white memoirists. Doig went
to Northwestern University, Kittredge to Iowa, Jordan to Yale.

These writers follow the example of the man who in many ways
broke the path for new writing and thinking about the West. Wallace
Stegner, who examined western land and life through fiction, essays,
biography, and history, grew up in Montana, Saskatchewan, and Utah.

As a young man he felt confined and cornered by what he saw as his homeland's cultural sterility: "I wanted to hunt up and rejoin the civilization I had been deprived of;" so he went, first to Iowa and then to Illinois, Wisconsin and Massachusetts. At Harvard he finally recognized that he belonged where he had come from. Stegner moved to California and proceeded to write some of the most revealing and perceptive views of the West we will ever have, mixes of fictional vision, familial remembrance, personal examination, environmental analysis, and literary criticism. He considered this remarkable body of work, however, simply the epilogue to his life's most significant insight. "[This] is essentially the whole story," he wrote in 1989. "I grew up western, and the very first time I moved out of the West I realized what it meant to me. The rest is documentation, detail."[61]

The pattern in the lives and writing of Stegner, Doig, Kittredge and others is obvious. Turnabouts all, they came back to reintegrate into the place they had left. As they do that, all tell their individual stories and those of their families, but in the process, because who they are is inseparable from where they are, they also describe the country of their origins in ways that establish its particular identity. The usual frontier east-to-west presumptions are treated as simply another force, often an alienating and destructive one, that has worked on the land and its people. Like Native American stories, in other words, these post-pioneer memoirs can tell about individuals only by simultaneously naming the place, recognizing a kinship to it, and granting to it its own narrative integrity.

This sort of joint declaration of personal and local identity is present, too, among the "new" western historians. Patricia Nelson Limerick frequently mixes the testimonial and historical. After "homing in" from an ivy league sojourn, she draws on experiences growing up in Banning, California, to cast a quadruple whammy on the traditional frontier narrative: it has done a lot of damage, it leaves out too many important actors, it needlessly isolates the present West from its past, and it cannot possibly tell westerners today who they are. The native westerner Donald Worster, who recalls his parents being driven by drought from western Kansas to California, rejects the Turnerian view for a regionally based history of "a distinct place inhabited by distinct people," a West of discrete environments with inherent limitations. He draws this understanding from his own experience and that of his family: "I know in my bones, if not always through my education" that this approach cuts closer to the truth.[62]

Worster's remark was specifically in praise of Walter Prescott Webb, whose career from the early 1930s until his death in 1963 in many ways helped bring this new western narrative into focus.[63] Webb was one of the first to write West-centered history. He was among the earliest to insist that any part of the region has to be understood on its own terms, including the limits imposed by its environment. That understanding, he said, should involve looking at successive strata of geology, climate, various flora and fauna, and whatever human groups have been there, their physical impact and their cultural institutions. Webb came to these views from a conversion that was as much personal as scholarly. His "homing in" would become a minor academic legend. Webb left his native Texas for the University of Chicago to earn a doctorate—the key, he was told, to his professional respectability. There he flunked his qualifying examinations. Webb walked away from the university, vowing henceforth to think and write on his own terms about what he knew best (and, it was implied, what his Chicago professors misunderstood completely).

What, specifically, would he have to say? The answer, Webb's intellectual epiphany, came one rainy evening while he was reading in a back room of his Austin home. The book in his hands was Emerson Hough's *The Way to the West*, a stirring but standard frontier narrative set in trans-Appalachia. Webb considered what Hough's book could, and more often could not, explain about Webb's own West—the plains—and it came to him: the plains story would be more truly told by someone with his feet planted there and looking out, accounting for the place's enduring singular features and its unique pattern of experience. Webb set out to tell that story that way.

The result, *The Great Plains*, was a marriage of history and lived insight; Webb was fond of saying he began researching it at the age of five when his family moved from east Texas to the edge of the high plains.[64] The same could be said of most of Webb's writing. He seemed always to try simultaneously to figure out where he and his part of the West had come from; the two stories were inextricably tangled. It was no coincidence that of all presidential addresses of the American Historical Association over the past fifty years, his was the most avowedly autobiographical.[65] It summed up Webb's message to the academic establishment: everything genuinely important he had to say had come, not from received scholarly truth, but from looking inside his own experience as a westerner.

The essential point was not simply that he drew on what had happened to him. Rather, the merging of the story of person and place established a narrative in fundamental opposition to another, imposed from elsewhere, that had dominated the West and the way its history had been told for a century and a half. Webb was well known for his blunt and angry denunciations of outsiders' economic control of his beloved home country, most notably in *Divided We Stand*. *The Great Plains* should be read as something similar, but in this case the issues were not economic but narrative. It was a declaration of storytelling independence, a passionate rejection of imagining the West from the outside in. For all its many flaws and shortcomings, *The Great Plains* ought to be recognized as a landmark in the way westerners have regarded themselves. It encouraged a narrative that stands within the West and draws deeply on its roots. It urges us to know the place and its story by telling its many parts and how they fit together.

Here, perhaps, is part of the modern West's distinctiveness. Besides all the other tusslings—economic, ethnic, subregional, and the rest—there is this conflict between sources of narrative power. Westerners today live with the region's opposed ways of thinking about itself: the West as place, old and tangled in lessons, and the West as space, empty room to escape old limits, to do anything, to lose the past, to dance with wolves.

This is no abstract distinction. It is entwined with much of the region's public policy. Take, for instance, national parks, those portions of the West intricately bound up with both its economy and its perceived meaning. Looking back after a hundred years on the story of Yosemite National Park, an environmental historian recently pointed to its greatest lesson: "what was saved were the natural objects of that park, *saved to be themselves* [emphasis in original]." That, he added, has been the grand principle of the modern preservation movement.[66] However, that familiar idea raises thorny questions. Most obviously, when we draw a clear distinction between humans and nature, how are those "natural objects . . . *saved to be themselves*" when millions of people crowd into a park every year and when development is proceeding full tilt just outside the gates? More fundamentally, what exactly is nature "being itself?" If nothing else, this implies a world utterly apart from human influence; but such a world has not existed, in Yosemite or anywhere else in the West, for thousands of years.

National parks, like every acre of the region, are thick with human experience. Native peoples, after all, had to be booted out of Yosemite (something unmentioned in the essay just cited) before it could be reimagined as nature "being itself." Park environments have always been interactions among thousands of species. For scores of generations people have been prominent players in those exchanges, and their influence, for good or ill, has increased vastly during the past century. Managing parks as if they were wilderness, letting them "be themselves," can turn them into elk-ravaged, desiccated disaster zones.[67] Administrators are facing up to other contradictions. If Canyonlands National Park or the Gila wilderness is a pristine and preservable non-human setting, then where did all those ruins come from? And what are the obligations to living westerners who trace their own stories to that undeniable ancient human presence? The National Park Service now has Native American officials working to balance the demands of tourism with Indian interests and prerogatives, including the right to inform visitors that they are camping not in the virgin wilds but on some of North America's oldest inhabited ground.[68]

Other difficulties, ones not so easily compromised, are likely to crop up. Once native rights are recognized—once, that is, we begin to acknowledge the narrative of a West deep in history—what will be done with places that are not merely old habitations but sacred, inviolate sites? How do we answer people who look at a scene of happy vacationers as we would a Ford Bronco inside the cathedral at Chartres? What about hunting rights? How might campers react when they look out of their nylon dome tent to see local Native Americans (presumably not wearing breach clouts and hunting with atlatls) taking down an elk?

Variations of these conflicts show up throughout the region. On the plains, a complicated example is the controversial proposal for a "buffalo commons." From one angle, the plan, the brainchild of Rutgers professors Frank and Deborah Popper, is a hardheaded recognition that the pioneers' heady dreams have proved disastrous.[69] The previous community of plains life has been largely displaced by one that cannot sustain itself. Most counties have lost population as thousands of farms have gone belly-up. Fresh generations look for their future elsewhere. Central Kansas, where an army of optimistic young families settled in the last century, is today the oldest part of America, demographically speaking, with a higher percentage of persons over eighty-five than anywhere else, including the snowbird country of Arizona and Florida.[70] The Poppers are saying, in other words, that one of the two old western narratives, working to turn pure possibility into a vision of another place, has failed calamitously. Their option is to vacate roughly 140,000 square miles of ten states, an area larger than New York, Pennsylvania and Virginia combined. This territory, roughly a fourth of the plains, would revert to an earlier condition, a vast domain of indigenous life. It would be the world's largest natural preserve.

But this answer itself appeals in part through the western's other fantasy—of a flight into a mythic land free from history. The Poppers take a hardboiled look at the present, then suggest a future vision of visiting a West in perfect stasis and somehow free of human touch. They look into the country with the old outlanders' optimism. The West is interesting because "change still feels possible there, unlike the bleak and difficult East." At its most unrecognizable, in the Texas panhandle, it stuns them as it did the first white settlers: "This is terrible country! . . . There is *nothing here*. This is un-country."[71] This West, in short, is No Place.

The problem is, there are families living there. Some are into their fourth generation of hanging on. Their local history, that is, runs deeper than that of the Cheyennes when they were ordered onto reservations. These people justify staying with a mix of stubbornness, faith in ingenuity, and, perhaps most of all, an emotional rootedness. "That's my mama's country there, Ellis County!" a Kansan called out during one of the Poppers' lectures, not as an observation but an explanation of why leaving was unthinkable. Another summed up a widespread response: "Maybe a hundred years ago this would make sense, now, no."[72] Bound to the place by experience, memory, and familial identity, their response is a lot like that of plains Indians of the 1860s when they were told that their outmoded, unproductive lifeways had to give way to something more sensible. There may be better lives, they say, but this one is ours, and we want to keep it.

From this angle, the "buffalo commons" looks like a reprise of events a century and a half ago. Once again the western stomps out of the east and onto the plains, this time wearing not its make-the-land-over but its back-to-nature hat. Once again hard-pressed natives are told that they will simply have to go. The story demands it.

If we hope to know the West, we at least need to recognize the forces at work there. Among them are the human use of the land, the climate, and the behavior of plants and animals, including the perverse interactions that brought disaster to Cheyenne pastoralists, the plains bison, and then to white farmers and ranchers. Social forms like the family and the values embedded in them also play their parts. Just as important are stories. They both express and inspire the ways that people act on their immediate world.

Until recently the most noticeable story has been the western. It is best understood as a national phenomenon, and an astonishingly resilient one. It is the closest thing we have to a national myth. In folklore, poetry, novels, fashions, plays, political bunkum, arena performances, movies, songs, and advertisements many Americans have used it to explain themselves to themselves and to others. Westerns are the nation's Greek chorus, and they won't shut up.

What about the western's relationship to the West? There is no *necessary* connection at all. So entrenched is the western in the popular mind that it is entirely independent of the country it is supposedly about. If our region were suddenly sealed off and all its gateways boarded and padlocked, with no one allowed to enter or leave or even peek in, the western would keep sailing along, sustained by a certain level of loyalty, its popularity dipping and rising with puffs of fashion. Millions would hum its tunes, wear its duds and ape its postures. Truck drivers, hairdressers, accountants and presidents would still devour gargantuan numbers of pulp paperbacks about steely-eyed strangers under skies of brass.

That said, however, it is equally clear that westerns and the West *are* connected; but westerns have not come out of that land across the wide Missouri. The movement has been largely the other way. The far West, that is, has not been the subject of the western. It has been its object.

The two basic narratives that compose the western—that of imposing an outside order and that of escape into prehistory—have been carried into the country and acted out upon it. The result has been a kind of narrative colonialism, but in this case outlanders have not extracted valuable resources. Instead they have exploited the West by using it as a blank screen where they can project and pursue their fantasies. (As always, colonials have figured out how to manipulate the colonizers and squeeze out some profits for themselves.) The consequences have been incalculable. Pioneer narratives have molded the land, shaped social relations, and fed dream-based economies that continue to thrive. In those ways the western has been one of America's pre-eminent examples of stories as power.

However, in other ways the western is impotent. It has not the slightest power to convey identity by explaining how western places and people have come to be. Because its guiding principles come from the outside in, not the inside out, it cannot help people in Satanta, Kansas, or Arabia, Nebraska figure out, literally, who in the world they are. It is a narrative import with no inherent kinship with the western country. It just lies there, like syrup on a rump roast.

Thus, while we can let the western entertain us, we also ought to recognize its profound limitations and potential dangers. "The imposed view, however innocent, always obscures," Barry Lopez reminds us. If we hope to imagine truly any place, he adds, we have to work hard "to understand why a region is different, to show an initial deference toward its mysteries. . . ."[73] Until westerners find their own stories, they will have no power to name themselves. People and places will never be, in the biblical sense, justified.

Luckily, such stories are around. Native American narratives old and new, white post-frontier reminiscences and memoirs, some of the recent historical and naturalist writing—these suggest another vision of the West and of how to live with its changes. They offer a sense of limits as well as possibilities. The liberties they allow come from recognizing that any place has to be understood as a meshing of family, society, history, and natural setting in which everyone, like it or not, is implicated. They give us the power to know where we stand.

"Life has never seemed *straighter* to me . . . [It] seems stripped of its complexity," William Jackson Palmer wrote of coming onto the plains. In that simple life, he thought, one needed only "wood, grass and water, a few wild animals to outwit and shoot." Today's western enthusiasts, to quote that consumer survey, are after "less stress, . . . escape—ways to simplify their lives." Palmer's way to the West is a powerful, enduring dream, but those who have tried to live it out, those actors in real-life frontier narratives, have found that this is the last place to look for simplicity, and if Palmer had stopped his train, gotten off in western Kansas, and asked the Cheyennes, they could have explained that merely getting the basics of life ("wood, grass . . .") is a complicated, chancy business; and Lord knows, they could have told today's computer programmers, homemakers, and CEOs a thing or two about stress.

Life is not "straighter" here. The way to understanding the West is never by clean lines but by indirection and by webs of changing connections among people, plants, institutions, animals, politics, soil, weather, ambitions, and perceptions. That way is rarely traced by clear distinctions but by ambiguities and by blurred, evolving identities. Its stories—not those brought in but the ones built from the roots up—will never offer the pleasures of simple lessons and inspirations; but it is through those stories, the weathered surface of a very old layering, that westerners can tell where and who they are. If we are to find our way to the West, they are the ones we have to listen to.

NOTES

Notes to Introduction

1. Merrill J. Mattes, ed., "Capt. L. C. Easton's Report: Fort Laramie to Fort Leavenworth Via Republican River in 1849," *Kansas Historical Quarterly*, 20, no. 6 (May 1953): 404.
2. For a small sampling of the literature on the natural history of the plains, see J. E. Weaver and F. W. Albertson, *Grasslands of the Great Plains* (Lincoln: Johnsen Publishing Co., 1956) and J. E. Weaver, *North American Prairie* (Lincoln: Johnsen Publishing Co., 1954); J. Richard Carpenter, "The Grassland Biome," *Ecological Monographs* 10 (1940): 617–84; D. I. Axelrod, "Rise of the Grassland Biome, Central North America," *Botanical Review* 51 (1985): 163–202; O. E. Sala, et al., "Primary Production of the Central Grassland Region of the United States," *Ecology* 69 (1988): 40–45; James C. Malin, *History and Ecology: Studies of the Grassland*, ed. Robert P. Swierenga (Lincoln: University of Nebraska Press, 1984); F. E. Clements and R. W. Chayney, *Environment and Life in the Great Plains* (Washington, D.C.: Carnegie Institution, 1936); Scott L. Collins and Linda L. Wallace, eds., *Fire in the North American Tallgrass Prairies* (Norman: University of Oklahoma Press, 1990); Carl O. Sauer, "Grassland Climax, Fire and Man," *Journal of Range Management* 3 (1950): 16–21; Robert T. Coupland, "The Effects of Fluctuations in Weather Upon the Grasslands, of the Great Plains," *Botanical Review* 24, no. 5 (May 1958): 273–317.
3. In its investigations the Indian Claims Commission estimated that of the portion of the plains given to the Cheyennes and Arapahoes in 1865, grasslands constituted about 38.3 million acres and river bottoms about 3 million acres. See LeRoy R. Hafen and Zachary Gussow, *Arapaho-Cheyenne Indians* [reports and findings of United States Indian Claims Commission] (New York: Garland Publishing Inc., 1974), 244.
4. Roger Thomas Trindell, "Sequent Occupance of Pueblo, Colorado," M.A. thesis, University of Colorado, 1960, 18.
5. Anyone interested in the history of the central plains before European contact should begin with several works by Waldo R. Wedel: *Prehistoric Man on the Great Plains* (Norman: University of Oklahoma Press, 1961); *Central Plains Prehistory:*

Holocene Environments and Culture Change in the Republican River Basin (Lincoln: University of Nebraska Press, 1986); "Some Problems and Prospects in Kansas Prehistory," *Kansas Historical Quarterly* 7 (May 1938): 115–32; "Toward a History of Plains Archeology," *Great Plains Quarterly* 1 (Winter 1981): 16–38. See also George E. Hyde, *Indians of the High Plains: From the Prehistoric Period to the Coming of Europeans* (Norman: University of Oklahoma Press, 1959); E. B. Renaud, *Archaeological Survey of Eastern Colorado*, Reports 1–3 (Denver: University of Denver, 1931–33) and Etienne B. Renaud, "Archaeology of the High Western Plains: Seventeen Years of Archaeological Research," publication of the Department of Anthroplogy, University of Denver, 1947; Roger Douglas Grosser, "Late Archaic Subsistence Patterns from the Central Great Plains," Ph.D. dissertation, University of Kansas, 1977; Patricia J. O'Brien, *Archaeology in Kansas* (Lawrence: University of Kansas Museum of Natural History, 1984).

6. Waldo R. Wedel, *Central Plains Prehistory: Holocene Environments and Culture Change in the Republican River Basin* (Lincoln: University of Nebraska Press, 1986), 72.

7. Waldo R. Wedel, *Environment and Native Subsistence Economies in the Central Great Plains*, Smithsonian Miscellaneous Collections 101, no. 3 (Washington: Smithsonian Institution, 1941), 16.

8. Waldo R. Wedel, "The High Plains and their Utilization by the Indian," *American Antiquity* 29, no. 1 (July 1963): 1–16.

9. Timothy G. Baugh, "Ecology and Exchange: The Dynamics of Plains-Pueblo Interaction" and Katherine B. Spielmann, "Coercion or Cooperation? Plains-Pueblo Interaction in the Protohistoric Period," both in *Farmers, Hunters, and Colonists: Interaction Between the Southwest and the Southern Plains*, Ed. Katherine B. Spielmann (Tucson: University of Arizona Press, 1991); Darrell Creel, "Bison Hides in Late Prehistoric Exchange in the Southern Plains," *American Antiquity* 56, no. 1 (1991): 40–49; Susan C. Vehik, "Late Prehistoric Plains Trade and Economic Specialization," *Plains Anthropologist* 35:128 (May 1990): 125–45; Wedel, *Central Plains Prehistory* 89, 91, 111; Frank F. Schambach, "Some New Interpretations of Spiroan Culture History," in *Archaeology of Eastern North America: Papers in Honor of Stephen Williams*, ed. James B. Stoltman, Archaeological Report No. 25 (Jackson: Miss.: Mississippi Department of Archives and History, 1993), 187–230.

10. "Letter of Thomas S. Twiss, Indian Agent at Deer Creek, U.S. Indian Agency on the Upper Platte," *Annals of Wyoming* 17, no. 2 (July 1945): 149–50.

11. The classic account is Joseph Jablow, *The Cheyenne in Plains Indian Trade Relations, 1795–1840*, Monographs of the American Ethnological Society, XIX (New York: J. J. Augustin, 1951).

12. For a discussion of this and other dilemmas in the writing of environmental history, see William Cronon, "A Place for Stories: Nature, History, and Narrative," *Journal of American History* 78 (March 1992): 1347–76.

Notes to Chapter 1

1. Lewis Thomas, *Lives of a Cell: Notes of a Biology Watcher* (New York: Viking Press, 1974), 145.

2. For various accounts of the peace of 1840, see George Bird Grinnell, *The Fighting Cheyennes* (Norman: University of Oklahoma Press, 1985), 63–69; Donald Berthrong, *The Southern Cheyennes* (Norman: University of Oklahoma Press, 1963), 82–84; Joseph Jablow, *The Cheyenne in Plains Indian Trade Relations, 1795–1840* (New York: J. J. Augustin, 1951), 72–77; James Mooney, *Calendar History of the Kiowa Indians*, (Washington, D. C.: Smithsonian Institution Press, 1979; originally published 1898), 275–76; Father John Peter Powell, *People of the Sacred Mountain: A History of the Northern Cheyenne Chiefs and Warrior Societies*, Vol. 1 (San Francisco: Harper and Row, 1981); George Bent to George Hyde, 23 January, 1905, George Bent Papers, Denver Public Library.

3. Joseph Jablow, *The Cheyenne in Plains Indian Trade Relations, 1795-1840*, Monographs of the American Ethnological Society, XIX (New York: J. J. Augustin, 1951), 58-60; Donald J. Berthrong, *The Southern Cheyennes* (Norman: University of Oklahoma Press, 1963), 17–22; Jacob Fowler, *The Journal of Jacob Fowler*, ed. Elliott Coues (Lincoln: University of Nebraska Press, 1970), 65.

4. For an analysis of the distribution of horses and the horse culture stressing the climatic congeniality of the more southern portions of the plains, see Alan J. Osborn, "Ecological Aspects of Equestrian Adaptations in Aboriginal North America," *American Anthropologist* 85, no. 3 (September 1983): 563–91.

5. Estimating the population of semi-nomadic peoples living where head-counters observed them only sporadically is necessarily chancy. No single estimate during these years covered all the central plains. On the upper Arkansas in 1821, early in the Cheyenne's migration into this area, Jacob Fowler found a great gathering of Comanches, Kiowas, Cheyennes and Arapahoes that included from seven hundred to nine hundred lodges that would have held between 4,900 and 5,600 persons if figured at the usual ratio of eight persons per lodge. It is impossible to say what portion of the region's population was included here. Estimates from a quarter-century later suggest more than five thousand Cheyennes and Arapahoes on the high plains, with twenty thousand to twenty-five thousand Sioux to the north, some bands of which ranged down into this area. Ten years later, after the Cheyennes and Arapahoes had divided into northern and southern branches, one agent estimated seventy-five hundred to nine thousand Cheyennes, Arapahoes, and Sioux along the South and North Plattes and another agent estimated nearly 11,500 Cheyennes, Arapahoes, Comanches, Kiowas, and Plains Apaches on the upper Arkansas. By then, as will be noted later in this essay, pressure from the south meant that more Comanches and Kiowas were spending more time in the Arkansas valley. In 1859, William Bent reported twenty-five hundred warriors of these groups at Walnut Creek; the full population, of course, would have been several times that number. Given these estimates, a guess of twenty thousand native peoples using the central plains by the mid-1850s does not seem unreasonable.

   On various estimates and comments on population, see Fowler, *Journal*, 65; *Report of the Commissioner of Indian Affairs, 1845*; Thomas Fitzpatrick to Thomas H. Harvey, 18 September, 1847, in *Report of Commissioner of Indian Affairs, 1847*, 243–49; Thomas S. Twiss to Col. Cumming, 14 November, 1855, Office of Indian Affairs, Letters Received, Upper Platte Agency, 1855; J. W. Whitfield to

Superintendent of Indian Affairs, 5 January, 1856, Office of Indian Affairs, Letters Received, Upper Arkansas Agency, 1856; Thomas S. Twiss to Secretary of Interior, *Report of Commissioner of Indian Affairs, 1856*, 96–98; William Bent Annual Report in *Report of Commissioner of Indian Affairs, 1859*, 137–39.

6. J. Evarts Greene, *The Santa Fe Trade: Its Route and Character* (Worcester, Mass: Charles Hamilton, 1893); Thomas D. Hall, *Social Change in the Southwest, 1350–1880* (Lawrence: University Press of Kansas, 1989), 150–54; Walker Wyman, "Freighting: A Big Business on the Santa Fe Trail," *Kansas Historical Quarterly* 1, no. 1 (November 1931): 17–27.

7. William Thompson, *Reminiscences of a Pioneer* (San Francisco: [s.n.], 1912), 5.

8. For estimates of overland migration, see John D. Unruh, Jr., *The Plains Across: The Overland Emigrants and the Trans-Mississippi West, 1840–60* (Urbana: University of Illinois Press, 1982), 84–85; Merrill J. Mattes, *Platte River Road Narratives: A Descriptive Bibliography of Travel Over the Great Central Overland Route to Oregon, California, Utah, Colorado, Montana, and Other Western States and Territories, 1812–1866* (Urbana: University of Illinois Press, 1988), 2–5.

9. The most explicit discussion of this theme is in John H. Moore, "Cheyenne Political History, 1820–1894," *Ethnohistory* 21, no. 4 (Fall 1974): 329–59. Every history of the Cheyennes on the plains, however, touches on this problem to some degree.

10. For examples of the literature on pastoralism in other settings, see Louis E. Sweets, "Camel Pastoralism in North Arabia and the Minimal Camping Unit," in *Man, Culture, and Animals: The Role of Animals in Human Ecological Adjustments*, eds. Anthony Leeds and Andrew P. Vayda (Washington D.C.: American Association for the Advancement of Science, 1965), 129–52; Andrew B. Smith, *Pastoralism in Africa: Origins and Development Ecology* (London and Athens: Hurst & Co. and Ohio University Press, 1992); John G. Galaty, *The World of Pastoralism: Herding Systems in Comparative Perspective* (Belhaven Press, 1991); Tim Ingold, *Hunters, Pastoralists, and Ranchers: Reindeer Economics and their Transformations* (Cambridge: Cambridge University Press, 1980); Lawrence A. Kuznar, "Transhumant Goat Pastoralism in the High Sierra of the South Central Andes: Human Responses to Environmental and Social Uncertainty," *Nomadic Peoples* 28 (1991): 93–104; Steven Webster, "Native Pastoralism in the South Andes," *Ethnology* 12 (April 1973): 115–33; Robert Brainerd Ekvall, *Fields on the Hoof: Nexus of Tibetan Nomadic Pastoralism* (New York: Holt, Rinehart and Winston, 1968); David Western, "The Environment and Ecology of Pastoralists in Arid Savannas," *Development and Change* 13, no. 2 (1982): 159–82; Katherine Homewood and W. A. Rodgers, "Pastoralism and Conservation," *Human Ecology* 12, no. 4 (1984): 431–41; Robert Netting, *Balancing on an Alp: Ecological Change and Continuity in a Swiss Mountain Community* (Cambridge: Cambridge University Press, 1981). For an interesting recent discussion of the economy that replaced the plains Indians–cattle ranching–within the context of other pastoral peoples, see Donald Worster, "Cowboy Ecology," in *Under Western Skies: Nature and History in the American West* (New York: Oxford University Press, 1992), 34–63.

11. For estimates of horses per person based on numerous observations of Cheyennes, see Jurgen Doring, *Kulturwandel bei den Nordamerikanischen Plainsindianern: Zur*

Rolle des Pferdes bei den Comanchen und den Cheyenne (Berlin: Dietrick Reimer, 1984). For discussions of the needs of the horse culture as a key to understanding plains Indian adaptation and patterns of life, see H. Clyde Wilson, "An Inquiry into the Nature of Plains Indian Cultural Development," *American Anthropologist* 65, no. 2 (April 1963): 355–69; James F. Downs, "Comments on Plains Indian Cultural Development," *American Anthropologist* 66, no. 2 (April 1964): 421–22; Alan J. Osborn, "Ecological Aspects of Equestrian Adaptations in Aboriginal North America," *American Anthropologist* 85, no. 3 (September 1983): 563–91; R. Brooke Jacobsen and Jeffrey L. Eighmy, "A Mathematical Theory of Horse Adoption on the North American Plains," *Plains Anthropologist* 25, no. 90 (November 1980): 333–41.

12. Downs, "Comments," 421.

13. James Sherow has taken an interesting and provocative look at some of the implications and difficulties of this transition to pastoralism. He is currently at work on a broader examination of this topic. I have benefitted greatly from his analysis and advice. See James Sherow, "Workings of the Geodialectic: High Plains Indians and their Horses in the Region of the Arkansas River Valley, 1800–1870," *Environment History Review* Summer 1992.

14. Percival G. Lowe, "P. G. Lowe's Journal of the Sumner Wagon Train," in *Relations with the Indians of the Plains, 1857-1861*, eds. LeRoy R. Hafen and Ann W. Hafen (Glendale: Arthur H. Clark Company, 1959), 61, reprinted from Percival G. Lowe, *Five Years a Dragoon ('49 to '54) and Other Adventures on the Great Plains* (Kansas City, Mo.: Franklin Hudson Publishing Co., 1906).

15. "Journal of Two Expeditions From Boone's Lick to Santa Fe, By Capt. Thomas Becknell," in *Southwest on the Turquoise Trail: The First Diaries on the Road to Santa Fe*, ed. Archer Butler Hulbert (Colorado Springs: The Stewart Commission of Colorado College and Denver Public Library, 1933), 61.

16. Later settlers would learn of the continuing dangers of sudden storms. In late March of 1931, twenty-two schoolchildren and their bus driver were stranded when their bus stalled in a snowdrift during a ferocious blizzard. The children improvised a stove from a milk can and burned all their books, tablets, parts of the seats, even their pencils. Nonetheless, by the time a rancher found the bus thirty-three hours after it stalled, five children and the driver, who had set out for help, had frozen to death. *Denver Post*, 28 March, 1931, Denver *Rocky Mountain News*, 30 March, 1931.

17. The quotation is from Louise Barry, *The Beginning of the West: Annals of the Kansas Gateway to the American West* (Topeka: Kansas State Historical Society, 1972), 663. On burned wagons, see H. M. T. Powell, *The Santa Fe Trail to California, 1849–1852. The Journal and Drawings of H. M. T. Powell*, ed. Douglas S. Watson (San Francisco: The Book Club of California, 1931), 41; William W. Hunter, *Missouri '49er: The Journal of William W. Hunter on the Southern Gold Trail* (Albuquerque: University of New Mexico Press, 1992). Richens "Uncle Dick" Wootton once drove his cattle to shelter during a storm, then returned to find stage passengers had corralled their team and were warming themselves on a fire made from his ox yokes. Another traveler watched a freighter gradually dismantle his prairie schooner and burn it to stay alive during a blizzard. Howard

Louis Conard, *Uncle Dick Wootton: The Pioneer Frontiersman of the Rocky Mountain Region*, ed. Milo Milton Quaife (Chicago: Lakeside Press; R. R. Donnelley and Sons Company, 1957), 339; Daniel Kellogg, "Across the Plains in 1858," *The Trail* 5, no. 7 (December 1912): 11.

18. G. S. McCain, "A Trip from Atchison, Kansas, to Laurette, Colorado: Diary of G. S. McCain," *Colorado Magazine* 27, no.2 (April 1950): 99–100.

19. "Report on Winter Travel, 1852," in *On the Santa Fe Trail*, ed. Marc Simmons (Lawrence: University Press of Kansas, 1986), 11–17.

20. *New York Weekly Tribune*, 26 February, 1848. South of this spot, along the Cimarron River, a large contingent of troops was caught in a storm in 1865–66 and lost about six hundred horses to starvation and freezing. Richard Irving Dodge, *The Hunting Grounds of the Great West. A Description of the Plains, Game, and Indians of the Great North American Desert* (London: Chatto and Windus, 1877), 39.

21. From the *Manhattan Standard* of Manhattan, Kansas, of 2 January, 1869, excerpted in Jimmy Breslin, *Damon Runyon* (New York: Tichnor & Fields, 1991), 32. Damon Runyon's father, who spelled his last name with an "a," was a printer and sometime journalist in several towns and cities of the central plains. So it happened, by wonderful coincidence, that Runyon, who would make his name and fortune writing romanticized stories of gangsters on the streets of Manhattan, New York, was born and spent his early years in Manhattan, Kansas.

22. Richard Irving Dodge, *Our Wild Indians: Thirty-Three Years' Personal Experience among the Red Men of the Great West* (Hartford: A. D. Worthington and Co., 1883), 501.

23. Zebulon Pike was well east of the present Kansas-Colorado line when he reported groves of young cottonwoods in 1806. After only another day's travel, he found both banks entirely covered with thick woodlands. When Jacob Fowler reached this same area in 1821 he also saw copses of trees, brush, and tangles of wild grapes, although he noted more growth on islands than on the shore. Donald Jackson, ed., *Journals of Zebulon Montgomery Pike, with Letters and Related Documents*, 2 vols. (Norman: University of Oklahoma Press, 1966), I, 344–45; Jacob Fowler, *The Journal of Jacob Fowler*, ed. Elliott Coues (Lincoln: University of Nebraska Press, 1970), 41–44.

24. Philip V. Wells, "Scarp Woodlands, Transported Grassland Soils, and Concept of Grassland Climate in the Great Plains Region," *Science* 148 (1965): 246–49.

25. Fowler, *Journal*, 41–43; Donald Jackson, ed., *The Journals of Zebulon Montgomery Pike with Letters and Related Documents*, Vol. 1 (Norman: University of Oklahoma Press, 1966), appendix, map 4. On this map Pike marks many "Spanish camps," although they likely were mostly those of Indians. Colonel Thomas Mather, "Diary of Colonel Thomas Mather, Santa Fe Road Commissioner," September 3–10, typescript, Newberry Library, and "Field Notes by Joseph C. Brown, United States Surveying Expedition, 1825–1827," *Eighteenth Biennial Report of the Board of Directors of the Kansas State Historical Society* (Topeka: State Printing Office, 1913), 120. Brown recommended travelers stock up on wood along the shore at Choteau's Island, "where fuel is plenty." Ibid., 121.

26. From Pike's Peak, Edwin James saw that "the Arkansa [sic], with several of its tributaries, and some of the branches of the Platte, could be distinctly traced as

on a map, by the line of timber along their courses." Shortly afterward he descended to the Arkansas and along the stream above the junction of the Purgatory found "trees of considerable size" covering islands and at many points on the bank. Edwin James, *Account of an Expedition From Pittsburgh to the Rocky Mountains, Performed in the Years 1819, 1820* (Cleveland: Arthur H. Clark Company, 1905), in *Early Western Travels*, Vol. xvi, Thwaites, 20, 31, 63. See also Dodge, *Journal of the March of a Detachment of Dragoons*, 28. Even in 1845 a government party found the river seventy miles above Bent's Fort "well timbered." See "Abstract of Journals kept by Lt. Turner, adjutant 1st dragoons, and Lt. Franklin, Top. Eng., during an expedition performed in the summer of 1845, by five companies of the 1st dragoons under the command of Colonel S. W. Kearny." U. S. Congress, 29th Cong., 1st sess., H. E. Doc. 2, 216.

27. Thomas J. Farnham, *Travels in the Great Western Prairies, The Anahuac and Rocky Mountains, and in the Oregon Territory* (London: Richard Bentley, 1843), I, 54, 91.

28. George Bent, probably the best single source for the location of features and events of the 1850s and 1860s along the Arkansas, placed the lower end of the Big Timbers here. See his map and his comments to George Hyde in folders 14, 20, and 22, Bent-Hyde Papers, Western History Collection, University of Colorado Library. Sources suggest a successive shrinkage of the grove. As late as 1839, a diarist wrote of first encountering the Timbers sixty miles below Bent's Fort, which would have had the grove extending downstream from the mouth of Sand Creek but still well above where they had been described twenty years earlier; given that the diarist passed Bent's Fort two days later, the distance was likely closer to fifty miles. See J. Nielson Barry, "An Excerpt From the Journal of E. Willard Smith, 1839–1840," *Annals of Wyoming*, 15, no. 3 (July 1943): 288. Seven years later, A. J. Johnston, who recorded precisely the length of each march and the location of notable sites, placed the lower end of the Big Timbers at a point five miles upstream from the mouth of Sand Creek and its upper limit thirty-seven miles downstream from Bent's Fort—exactly where George Bent indicated for the 1850s. See A. R. Johnston journal, July 27–28, 1846, in *Marching*, 90, as well as George Rutledge Gibson, *Journal of a Soldier Under Kearny and Doniphan, 1846–47*, ed. Ralph P. Bieder (Glendale: Arthur H. Clark, 1935), 163. As for the stretch below the Timbers, Josiah Bell in 1841 wrote that "No trees are to be seen"; Lieutenant Turner in 1845 reported "little timber"; Marcellus Edwards in 1846 found "a few scattering groves of cottonwoods" mostly on the southern bank; H. M. T. Powell and William Hunter in 1849 complained of "scarcely any timber" and "scarcely a stick of timber" along the river. Josias Bell, "Sketches of a Journey From Smithsboro, Pa., to California and Return," entry for 1 September, 1841, manuscript journal, Newberry Library; "Abstract of Journals kept by Lt. Turner, adjutant 1st dragoons, and Lt. Franklin, Top. Eng., during an expedition performed in the summer of 1845, by five companies of the 1st dragoons under the command of Colonel S. W. Kearny," U. S. Congress, 29th Cong., 1st Sess., H. E. Doc. 2, 216–17; Marcellus Ball Edwards Journal, in *Marching With the Army of the West, 1846–1848*, ed. Ralph P. Bieber (Glendale: Arthur H. Clark Company, 1936), 138; H. M. T. Powell, *The Santa Fe Trail to California, 1849–1852. The Journal and Drawings of H. M. T. Powell*, ed.

Douglas S. Watson (San Francisco: The Book Club of California, 1931), 45; William W. Hunter, *Missouri '49er: The Journal of William W. Hunter on the Southern Gold Trail*, ed. David P. Robrock (Albuquerque: University of New Mexico Press, 1992), 23.

29. David Lindsey, ed., "The Journal of an 1859 Pike's Peak Gold Seeker," *Kansas Historical Quarterly* 22, no. 4 (Winter 1956): 331; Charles Post diary, June 12, 1859, in *Overland Routes to the Gold Fields, 1859, From Contemporary Diaries* ed. LeRoy R. Hafen (Glendale: Arthur H. Clark Company, 1942), 44–45.

30. Susan Shelby Magoffin, *Down the Santa Fe Trail and Into Mexico. The Diary of Susan Shelby Magoffin, 1846–1847* (New Haven: Yale University Press, 1926), 57–58; Lt. E.G.Beckwith, *Report of Exploration for a Route for the Pacific Railroad, by Capt. J. W. Bunison, Topographical Engineers, near the 38th and 39th Parallels of North Latitude, from the Mouth of the Kansas River, MO, to the Sevier Lake, in the Great Basin*, U. S. Congress, 33rd Cong., 2nd sess., 1855, H. Doc. 91, 27–28; Charles Post Diary, 44-45. George Willing in 1859 found the lower end of the Big Timbers "mostly dead." Ralph P. Bieber, ed., "Diary of a Journey to the Pike's Peak Gold Mines in 1859," *Mississippi Valley Historical Review* 14, no. 3 (December 1927): 365.

31. Edwin James, *Account of an Expedition from Pittsburgh to the Rocky Mountains. . . .* , (Philadelphia: H. C. Carey and I. Lea, 1823), Vol. I, 454, Vol. II, 353–54.

32. Colonel Henry Dodge. *Report of the Secretary of War . . . Journal of the March of a Detachment of Dragoons, Under the Command of Colonel Dodge, During the summer of 1835*. U. S. Congress, 24th Cong., 1st sess., H. E. Doc. 181, 13–14.

33. Osborne Cross Diary, 8 June, 1849, in *The March of the Mounted Riflemen: First United States Military Expedition to Travel the Full Length of the Oregon Trail . . .* , ed. Raymond W. Settle (Glendale: Arthur H. Clark Company, 1940), 71; Leo M. Kaiser and Priscilla Knuth, eds., "From Ithaca to Clatsop Plains: Miss Ketcham's Journal of Travel," *Oregon Historical Quarterly* 62, no. 3 (September 1961): 273; Lydia Milner Waters, "Account of a Trip Across the Plains in 1855," *Quarterly of the Society of California Pioneers* 6, no. 2 (June 1929): 64; "Diary of E. H. N. Patterson," in *Overland Routes to the Gold Fields, 1859, From Contemporary Diaries*, ed. LeRoy R. Hafen (Glendale: Arthur H. Clark Company, 1942), 130; George Soule, "Pike's Peak, Valley of the Platte," in *Western Reserve Chronicle* [Warren Ohio], 21 September, 1859, copy in Beinecke Library, Yale University.

34. Donald Jackson and Mary Lee Spence, *The Expeditions of John Charles Fremont . . . Travels from 1838 to 1844*, Vol. I (Urbana: University of Illinois Press, 1970), 194.

35. Sir Richard Burton, *The Look of the West, 1860: Across the Plains to California* (Lincoln: University of Nebraska Press, n. d.), 66.

36. William K. Sloan referred to the "Lone Tree Crossing" of the South Platte in his "Autobiography of William K. Sloan," *Annals of Wyoming* 4 (1926): 253–61. The well-known lone tree's demise was noted by William Richard Brown in *An Authentic Wagon Trail Journal of 1853* (Mokelumne Hill, California, 1985).

37. Calvin Clark, for instance, wrote that he "waded the a.k. [Arkansas] river to get a peace [sic] of wood to cook supper, for we are mighty hungry." Calvin Clark Diary, 29 May, 1859, Western History Collections, Denver Public Library. See also

Ralph P. Bieber, "Diary of a Journey to the Pike's Peak Gold Mines in 1859," *Mississippi Valley Historical Review* 14, no.3 (December 1927): 363, entry for 27 May, 1859.

38. Gibson, *Soldier*, 144, 147, 164–65. The journal of A. R. Johnston, another officer with the Army of the West, shows the same patchy pattern: "good bottom for grass, although it was reported that there was none for many miles above the crossing," then "grass is plenty," then "the grass is not very good." Abraham Robinson Johnston Journal, in *Marching with the Army of the West, 1846–1848*, ed. Ralph P. Bieber (Glendale: Arthur H. Clark Company, 1936), 87–90.

39. George Willing Diary, June 1–2, 1859, in "Diary of a Journey to the Pike's Peak Gold Mines," ed. Bieber, 368–69; "Diary of Mrs. A. C. Hunt, 1859," *Colorado Magazine* 21, no. 5 (September 1944): 161–70.

40. Thomas J. Farnham, *Travels in the Great Western Prairies, The Anahuac and Rocky Mountains, and in the Orego Country*, 2 vols. (London: Richard Bentley, 1843), 109.

41. Osborne Cross Diary, 6 June and 8 June, 1849, and George Gibbs diary, 28 May and 7 June, 1849, in *March of the Mounted Riflemen*, ed. Settle, 68, 71, 298, 308.

42. J. Robert Brown, "Journal of a Trip Across the Plains of the U.S. from Mo. to Cal.," entry for 1 June, 1856, copy of manuscript journal, Newberry Library; Kaiser and Knuth, eds., "Miss Ketcham's Journal of Travel," 279.

43. The photograph is reproduced in several sources, including William E. Brown, *The Santa Fe Trail* (St. Louis: The Patrice Press, 1988), 106.

44. Gibbs Diary, 28 May, 1849, 298; Rebecca Ketcham Journal, 14 June, 1853, 278; Lydia Milner Waters, "Account of a Trip Across the Plains in 1855," *Quarterly of the Society of California Pioneers* 6, no. 2 (June 1929): 64.

45. H. L. Shantz, "Plant Succession on Abandoned Roads in Eastern Colorado," *Journal of Ecology* 5, no. 1 (March 1917):19–42.

46. Louise Barry, *Beginning of the West*, 1158; James Ure Journal, 1856, Historical Department, Church of Jesus Christ of Latter-Day Saints, Salt Lake City; Arthur M. Menefee, "Arthur M. Menefee's Travels Across the Plains, 1857," *Nevada Historical Society Quarterly* 9. no. 1 (Spring 1966): 11. The ratio for 1851 was about two animals per person, that of 1852 was roughly four-to-one. See Barry, *Beginning of the West*, 1008, 1081–84.

47. William Hawking Hedges, *Pike's Peak . . . or Busted! Frontier Reminiscences of William Hawkins Hedges*, ed. Herbert O. Brayer (Evanston, Illinois: Branding Iron Press, 1954), 13–14.

48. Freighting train manifest, folder 50, Moses U. Payne Papers, Missouri Historical Society; George Stephens to William Stephens, 4 March, 1860, George Stephens file, Nebraska State Historical Society; D. P. Rolfe, "Overland Freighting From Nebraska City," *Proceedings and Collections of the Nebraska State Historical Society*, Series II, Vol. V (1902): 282; Alexander Majors, *Seventy Years on the Frontier, Memoirs of a Lifetime on the Border* (Minneapolis: Ross & Haines, Inc., 1965), 102, 105.

49. Fowler, *Journal*, 65; Hyde, *Life of George Bent*, 37; James Bordeaux to Superintendent of Indian Affairs, *Report of the Commissioner of Indian Affairs*, 1854.

50. J. W. Abert, *Journal of Lieutenant J. W. Abert from Bent's Fort to St. Louis, in 1845*, U.S. Senate, 29th Cong., 1st sess., S. Doc. 438, 9. The next year Abert noted

that "This morning I got two species of willow and some of the cottonwood tree, here called sweet cottonwood, as it forms a very palatable food for animals. . . . The Indians frequently winter animals on the sweet cottonwood." John Galvin, ed., *Western America in 1846–1847: The Original Travel Diary of Lieutenant J. W. Abert, Who Mapped New Mexico for the United States Army* (San Francisco: John Howell, 1966), 25.

51. LeRoy R. Hafen and Ann W. Hafen, eds., *Rufus B. Sage, His Letters and Papers, 1836–1847*. . . . (Glendale: Arthur H. Clark Company, 1956), 194. For other comments on the use of cottonwood for feeding horses, see Fowler, *Journal* 60–61; W. H. Emory, *Lieutenant Emory Reports: A Reprint of Lieutenant W. H. Emory's Notes of a Military Reconnoissance* [sic] (Albuquerque: University of New Mexico Press, 1951), 30. George Custer also saw Indian camps littered with trunks and branches stripped of their bark, and Richard Dodge told of "acres and acres" of cottonwoods cut down as feed for Indian horses. George A. Custer, *My Life on the Plains* (Norman: University of Oklahoma Press, 1962), 7; Richard Irving Dodge, *Our Wild Indians*, 588.

52. Barry, *Beginning of the West*, 781, 787; Thomas J. Fitzpatrick to Thomas H. Harvey [?], 24 June, 1848, Bureau of Indian Affairs, Letters Received, Upper Platte Agency, 1848.

53. For one bibliography on the scientific literature on grasslands, far from complete but including nearly seven thousand entries, see Mohan K. Wali, ed., *Native Grassland Ecosystems East of the Rocky Mountains in North America: A Preliminary Bibliography. A Supplement to Prairie: A Multiple View* (Grand Forks: University of North Dakota Press, 1975). See also K. Blanchet, et al., comps., *An Abstract Bibliography on Shortgrass and Mixed-grass Prairie Ecosystems*, U.S. IBP Grassland Biome Tech. Rep. 236 (Fort Collins: Colorado State University, 1973), and J. S. Singh, *U.S. IBP Grassland Biome Tech. Rep. No. 155* (Fort Collins: Colorado State University, 1972).

54. Among the many studies of the effects of overgrazing on grasses and grass systems, here are some that I found especially useful: F. W. Alberston, Andrew Riegel, and John L. Launchbauch, Jr., "Effects of Different Intensities of Clipping on Short Grasses in West-Central Kansas," *Ecology* 34, no. 1 (January 1953): 1–20; Harold H. Biswell and J. E. Weaver, "Effect of Frequent Clipping on the Development of the Roots and Tops of Grasses in Prairie Sod," *Ecology* 14, no. 4 (October 1933): 368–90; F. S. Bukey and J. E. Weaver, "Effects of Frequent Clipping on the Underground Food Reserves of Certain Prairie Grasses," *Ecology* 20, no. 2 (April 1939): 246–52; Farrell Branson and J. E. Weaver, "Quantitative Study of Degeneration of Mixed Prairie," *Botanical Gazette* 114, no. 4 (June 1953): 397–416; J. D. Beebe and G. R. Hoffman, "Effects of Grazing on Vegetation and Soils in Southeastern South Dakota," *American Midland Naturalist* 80, no. 1 (July 1968): 96–110; W. B. Gernert, "Native Grass Behavior as Affected by Periodic Clipping," *Journal of the American Society of Agonomy* 28, no. 6 (June 1936): 447–56; J. E. Weaver "Summary and Interpretation of Underground Development in Natural Grassland Communities," *Ecological Monographs* 28, no. 1 (January 1958): 55–78; J. E. Weaver, "Underground Plant Development in its Relation

to Grazing." *Ecology* 11, no. 3 (July 1930): 543–57; J. E. Weaver, "Replacement of True Prairie by Mixed Prairie in Eastern Nebraska and Kansas," *Ecology* 24, no. 4 (October 1943): 421–34.

55. A. O. Weese, "The Effect of Overgrazing on Insect Population," Oklahoma Academy of Science *Proceedings* 19 (1939): 95–99.

56. On Cooke's march, see Hamilton Gardner, ed., "March of the 2nd Dragoons: Report of Lieutenant Colonel Philip St. George Cooke on the March of the 2nd Dragoons from Fort Leavenworth to Fort Bridger in 1857," *Annals of Wyoming* 27, no. 1 (April 1955): 43–60.

57. Thomas J. Fitzpatrick to D. D. Mitchell, 29 May, 1849, Bureau of Indian Affairs, Letters Received, Upper Platte Agency, 1849; William Bent annual report in *Report of the Commissioner of Indian Affairs, 1859*, 137–39. In 1848 Fitzpatrick wrote that the Kiowas had already taken up residence among the Cheyennes and Arapahoes. See Thomas Fitzpatrick to Thomas H. Harvey, in *Report of Commissioner of Indian Affairs, 1848*.

58. Merlin Paul Lawson, *The Climate of the Great American Desert: Reconstruction of the Climate of Western Interior United States, 1800–1850* (Lincoln: University of Nebraska Press, 1974). A more localized tree ring study was conducted around North Platte, Nebraska, near the forks of the Platte, an area traversed by the Pacific trails and especially popular as a hunting and camping area for the newly arrived native groups. This study showed an eighteen-year stretch free from drought after the opening of the nineteenth century (1804–21), followed by eleven dry years (1822–32), and then, coinciding with the great overland migration and movement of larger numbers of Indians into the area, a quarter-century without drought (1833–57). After that, at the time of the Colorado gold rush and Indian wars, there was another very dry period, this time nine years (1858–66). See Harry Weakly, "A Tree Ring Record of Precipitation in Western Nebraska," *Journal of Forestry* 41 (1943): 816–19. Yet another investigation, correlating sunspot occurrence with drought cycles, as indicated through tree ring analysis, finds conclusive evidence of severe drought from 1859 to 1861 and suggestions of a major dry spell from 1846 to 1851: Frederick E. Clements, "Drought Periods and Climatic Cycles," *Ecology* 2, no. 3 (July 1921): 181–88. See also Edmund Schulman, *Dendroclimatic Changes in Semiarid America* (Tucson: University of Arizona Press, 1956), especially 85–89.

59. On the effects of drought on the high central plains, see, F. W. Albertson and J. E. Weaver, "History of the Native Vegetation of Western Kansas During Seven Years of Continuous Drought," *Ecological Monographs* 12, no. 1 (January 1942): 23–53; J. E. Weaver and F. W. Albertson, "Nature and Degree of Recovery of Grassland from the Great Drought of 1933 to 1940." *Ecological Monographs* 14, no. 4 (October 1944): 393–479; Robert T. Coupland, "The Effects of Fluctuations in Weather Upon the Grasslands of the Great Plains," *Botanical Review* 24, no. 5 (May 1958): 273–317.

60. James Mooney, *Calendar History of the Kiowa Indians* (Washington, D. C.: Smithsonian Institution Press, 1979), 300; "J. E. B. Stuart's Official Journal," in *Relations With the Plains Indians*, Hafen and Hafen, entries for 5 August and 10 August 1860, 242–43. "In wet weather there are holes along to-day's march,"

Stuart also wrote, "*No* doubt abundantly supplied with water," entry for 9
August, 1860, 243.

61. H. T. Clarke, "Freighting—Denver and Black Hills," *Proceedings and Collections
    of the Nebraska State Historical Society*, Series II, vol. V (1902): 301–02.

62. During his tour of the Platte in 1842, John Charles Fremont wrote that an
    intense dry spell had left little grass for his horses. In a recently vacated Indian
    camp he made a useful discovery: "Boughs of the cottonwood yet green covered
    the ground, which the Indians had cut down to feed their horses upon. It is only
    in the winter that recourse is had to this means of sustaining them; and their
    resort to it at this time was a striking evidence of the state of the country. We
    followed their example and turned our horses into a grove of young poplars."
    Donald Jackson and Mary Lee Spence, *The Expeditions of John Charles Fremont,
    Volume 1, Travels from 1838 to 1844* (Urbana: University of Illinois Press, 1970),
    entry for 23 July, 1842, 235–36.

63. Wyman Walker, "Freighting: A Big Business on the Santa Fe Trail," *Kansas
    Historical Quarterly* 1, no. 1 (November 1931): 19; J. W. Whitfield to Superin-
    tendent of Indian Affairs, 15 August, 1855, Bureau of Indian Affairs, Letters
    Received, Upper Arkansas Agency, 1855; Thomas Fitzpatrick to D. D. Mitchell,
    24 September, 1850, *Report of Commissioner of Indian Affairs, 1850*, 50–51.

64. Dodge, *Journal of Dragoons*, 16–17.

65. J. W. Abert, *Journal of Lieutenant J. W. Abert from Bent's Fort to St. Louis, in 1845*,
    U. S. Senate, 29th Cong., 1st sess., S. Doc. 438.

66. D. D. Mitchell to Orlando Brown, in *Annual Report of Commissioner of Indian
    Affairs, 1849—50*, 132. Mitchell may well have relied on the opinions of his
    agent on the upper Arkansas, Thomas Fitzpatrick, who made the same point in
    the same year. The Indians' "complaints are increasing yearly and the grievances
    of which they complain becoming more sensibly felt. . . . [I]t must be acknowl-
    edged that they have full grounds for their complaints, which are as follows. The
    disturbance and dispersion of game. The cutting down and destroying [of] wood."
    Thomas J. Fitzpatrick to D. D. Mitchell, 29 May, 1849, Bureau of Indian Affairs,
    Letters Received, Upper Platte Agency, 1849. On other occasions Fitzpatrick
    warned that construction of military posts in the region would heighten ill
    feeling, since the Indians knew full well that such installations would consume
    great numbers of trees and much game. Thomas Fitzpatrick to D. D. Mitchell,
    24 September, 1850, in *Report of Commissioner of Indian Affairs, 1850*, 55, and
    Thomas Fitzpatrick to A. Cumming, 19 November, 1853, in *Report of Commis-
    sioner of Indian Affairs, 1853*, 362.

67. J. C. Baird, "First Gold Find in the Mountains," *The Trail* 14, no. 9 (February
    1922): 4–5; William K. Sloan, "Autobiography of William K. Sloan, Western
    Pioneer," *Annals of Wyoming* 4, no. 1 (July 1926): 243–44.

68. Thomas Fitzpatrick to A. Cumming, 19 November, 1853, *Report of Commissioner
    of Indian Affairs, 1853*, 363.

69. Abert, *Journal of Lieutenant J. W. Abert*, 438.

70. Robert C. Miller to A. M. Robinson, Superintendent of Indian Affairs, 21 July,
    1858, Office of Indian Affairs, Letters Received, Upper Arkansas Agency, 1858.
    To arrive at these averages, I have used the population figures from an agent's

report in 1855: J. W. Whitfield to Superintendent of Indian Affairs, 5 January, 1856, Office of Indian Affairs, Letters Received, Upper Arkansas Agency, 1856.

71. D. P. Rolfe, "Overland Freighting from Nebraska City," *Proceedings and Collections of the Nebraska State Historical Society*, Series II, vol. V (1902): 287–88.

72. S. A. Bemis to Jenny, 12 June, 1860, Bemis Family Papers, Missouri Historical Society.

73. William K. Sloan, "Autobiography of William K. Sloan, Western Pioneer," *Annals of Wyoming* 4, no. 1 (July 1926): 243–44; W. B. Napton, *Over the Santa Fe Trail, 1857* (Kansas City: Franklin Hudson, 1905), 28–32. The Pawnees, ravaged by disease, denied access to bison by the Lakota, and suffering heavy losses in warfare, were most notorious for pressing emigrants for food and supplies. Fitzpatrick wrote in 1848 that travelers had lost more in the last year than in any other at the hands of the Pawnees, who, he was told by military officials, were "starving and destitute." Sarcastically noting this "philanthropic view" of the Pawnees' plight, he called for more protection from overlanders as they proceeded on "one of the most arduous land journeys ever undertaken by man . . ." Thomas Fitzpatrick to Thomas H. Harvey, 6 October, 1848, in *Report of Commissioner of Indian Affairs, 1848*, 471.

74. Wyman Walker, "Freighting: A Big Business on the Santa Fe Trail," *Kansas Historical Quarterly* 1, no. 1 (November 1931): 22.

75. J. W. Whitfield to Superintendent of Indian Affairs, 15 August, 1855, Office of Indian Affairs, Letters Received, Upper Arkansas Agency; Thomas S. Twiss to Secretary of Interior, 10 October, 1855, *Report of Commissioner of Indian Affairs, 1855*, 82–84.

76. Wyman Walker, "Freighting: A Big Business on the Santa Fe Trail," *Kansas Historical Quarterly*, 1:1 (November 1931): 19; Thomas Fitzpatrick to D. D. Mitchell, in *Report of Commissioner of Indian Affairs, 1850*, 50–51.

77. Thomas J. Fitzpatrick to D. D. Mitchell, 29 May, 1849, Bureau of Indian Affairs, Letters Received, Upper Arkansas Agency, 1849.

78. Robert Miller to Superintendent of Indian Affairs, 20 July, 1857, Office of Indian Affairs, Letters Received, Upper Arkansas Agency, 1857; Robert Miller to Superintendent of Indian Affairs, 29 August, 1856, Office of Indian Affairs, Letters Received, Upper Arkansas Agency, 1856. See also Claim of P. Chouteau Jr. and Co., 20 December, 1854, received 26 March, 1854, Office of Indian Affairs, Letters Received, Upper Arkansas Agency, 1854.

79. Dr. Augustus M. Heslep quoted in Barry, *Beginning of the West*, 867.

80. William Bent to Robinson, 17 December, 1858, Office of Indian Affairs, Letters Received, Upper Arkansas Agency, 1858.

81. Henry Pickering Walker, *The Wagonmasters: High Plains Freighting from the Earliest Days of the Santa Fe Trail to 1880* (Norman: University of Oklahoma Press, 1966), 194–95.

82. Wyman, "Freighting," 25.

83. For business records revealing the extent and variety of this trade, see ledger and account books in John Bratt Papers, Nebraska State Historical Society; Barnard Silvaeir Blondeau account books, 1858–1867, Nebraska State Historical Society; Penniston and Miller General Store Day Books, 1867–71, Nebraska State

Historical Society; Charles McDonald Ledger and Cash Book, Charles McDonald Papers, Nebraska State Historical Society.

84. George A. Root and Russell K. Hickman, "Pike's Peak Express Companies: Part I—Soloman and Republican Route," *Kansas Historical Quarterly* 13 (August 1944): 163–95.

85. Mooney, *Kiowa Calendar*, 306.

86. Thomas Fitzpatrick to D. D. Mitchell, 24 September, 1850, in *Report of Commissioner of Indian Affairs, 1850*, 55, and Thomas Fitzpatrick to A. Cumming, 19 November, 1853, in *Report of Commissioner of Indian Affairs, 1853*, 362.

87. In his memoir the trapper turned merchant Richens "Uncle Dick" Wootton recalled that one of the principal complaints of the Arapahoes was the cutting of the Smoky Hill's timbers, which they used both for wintering and for burials: "The contractors who built Fort Wallace, cut down the fine old trees and entirely destroyed the grove. . . . Then the Indians . . . declared that for every tree the white men had cut down they would kill a white man, and I reckon they did it before they were finally subdued and forced to quit the country." Howard Louis Conard, *Uncle Dick Wootton: The Pioneer Frontiersman of the Rocky Mountain Region*, ed. Milo Milton Quaife (Chicago: Lakeside Press; R. R. Donnelley and Sons Company, 1957), 387–88. Among those killed was a French emigrant, Joseph Faivre, who had contracted to supply wood for Fort Wallace. He was killed in 1867. Cragin Notebooks, Vol. 18, 2, Western History Collections, Denver Public Library.

88. John Bratt, *Trails of Yesterday* (Lincoln: The University Publishing Company, 1921), 146.

89. Field notes of surveys of what had been the Big Timbers of the Arkansas in General Land Office Records, Bureau of Land Management Office, Denver, Colorado. See especially records for three townships—T23S R50W in Vol. R7, 201—03; T23S R51W and T23S R52W in Vol. RA10, 118–19, 125–26, 132–33, 146–48. For the former timbers of the Smoky Hill, field notes and surveys are in General Land Office Records, Bureau of Land Management Office, Santa Fe, New Mexico. See especially township T13S R39W, Vol. 59.

90. Daniel Kellogg, "Across the Plains in 1858," *The Trail* 5, no. 7 (December 1912): 10–11.

91. Justus von Liebig, *Die Organische Chemie in Ihrer Anwendung auf Agricultur und Physiologie* (Braunsweig: F. Viewig und Sohn, 1840). The first edition in English was *Organic Chemistry and its Applications to Agriculture and Physiology* (London: Taylor and Walton, 1840).

Notes to Chapter 2

1. The most extensive bibliography, although far from complete, contains more than twenty-five hundred entries. George W. Arthur, *A Buffalo Round-up: A Selected Bibliography* (Regina: Canadian Plains Research Center and University of Regina, 1985). For a shorter bibliography of technical literature, see Glenn E. Plumb, Jerrold L. Dodd, and J. Brad Stelfox, "A Bibliography on Bison (*Bison bison*)," University of Wyoming Experiment Station Publication, MP-71, June 1992.

2. For a discussion of the pitfalls and difficlties of modern estimations, see Lee R. Dice, "Methods for Estimating Populations of Mammals," *Journal of Wildlife Management* 5, no. 4 (October 1941): 398–407.

3. Tom McHugh, *The Time of the Buffalo* (New York: Alfred A. Knopf, 1972), 16–17; Dan Flores, "Bison Ecology and Bison Diplomacy: The Southern Plains from 1800 to 1850," *Journal of American History* 78, no. 2 (September 1991): 470–71. Calculations are more complicated than I have presented in the text. After considering the various grazing capacities of the tallgrass, mixed, and shortgrass regions, McHugh writes that on the average the plains could support about twenty-six buffalo per square mile. Flores relies on county reports from the 1910 agricultural census for the area that is the focus of his study, the bison range south of the Arkansas. From that he compiles the number of "cattle-equivalent" grazers, then increases that total (roughly 7 million) by eighteen percent to account for the wild bison's greater efficiency at using native grasses. The resulting total for the south plains is 8.2 million. Based on that, he projects a general speculation for the entire plains of 24 million to 26 million.

4. John Charles Fremont, *Narrative of the Exploring Expedition to the Rocky Mountains in the Year 1842.* . . . (London, 1846), 142; John Bidwell, *A Journey to California, 1841: The First Emigrant Party to California by Wagon Train* (Berkeley: Friends of the Bancroft Library, 1964), 13–14, entry for 8 June, 1841

5. Raymond W. Settle, ed., *The March of the Mounted Riflemen: First United States Military Expedition to Travel the Full Length of the Oregon Trail* . . . (Glendale, Calif.: Arthur H. Clark Company, 1940), 72–73, entry for 9 June, 1849; Howard Stansbury, *An Expedition to the Valley of the Great Salt Lake of Utah.* . . . (Philadelphia: Lippincott, Grambo and Co., 1855), 29, entry for 29 June, 1849.

6. Thomas S. Twiss to Secretary of Interior, *Report of Commissioner of Indian Affairs*, 1855, 82–84; Thomas Fitzpatrick to Colonel A. Cumming, *Report of Commissioner of Indian Affairs*, 1853, 368; James Mooney, *Calendar History of the Kiowa Indians* (Washington, D. C.: Smithsonian Institution Press, 1979), 287–90. See also Thomas Fitzpatrick to Thomas H. Harvey, 18 September, 1847, in *Report of Commissioner of Indian Affairs*, 342; D. D. Mitchell to Orlando Brown in *Annual Report of Commissioner of Indian Affairs, 1849–50*, 133; Jonathan W. Whitfield to Colonel A. Cumming, Superintendent of Indian Affairs, *Annual Report, Commissioner of Indian Affairs*, 1854, 94–95; J. W. Whitfield to Superintendent of Indian Affairs, August 15, 1855, Office of Indian Affairs, Letters Received, Upper Arkansas Agency; Thomas Twiss to Secretary of Interior, *Report of Commissioner of Indian Affairs*, 1856, 96–98; Report of William Bent in *Report of Commissioner of Indian Affairs*, 1859, 137–39.

7. Thomas S. Twiss, "Proceedings of a Treaty Council," 18 September, 1859, Office of Indian Affairs, Letters Received, Upper Platte Agency. In correspondence the previous month, Twiss wrote that some Sioux believed that the mere smell of a white person would keep bison away from a place forever. "Letter of Thomas S. Twiss, Indian Agent at Deer Creek, U.S. Indian Agency on the Upper Platte." *Annals of Wyoming* 17, no. 2 (July 1945): 148.

8. George Bird Grinnell, *The Fighting Cheyennes* (Norman: University of Oklahoma Press, 1985), 99.

9. Howard Stansbury, *An Expedition to the Valley of the Great Salt Lake of Utah.* . . . (Philadelphia: Lippincott, Grambo and Co., 1855), 29. Osborne Cross

also thought that the "immense emigration" of 1849 had forced buffaloes "far beyond the bluffs." Cross, *Mounted Riflemen*, 72–73.

10. Thomas J. Fitzpatrick to D. D. Mitchell, 29 May, 1849, Bureau of Indian Affairs, Letters Received, Upper Platte Agency, 1849; Thomas Fitzpatrick to A. Cumming, 19 November, 1853, *Report of Commissioner of Indian Affairs*, 1853, 368.

11. Robert Thoroughman Reminiscence, Montana State University Library, Bozeman, Montana. The brutal wear on horses, valuable assets of the overlanders, was a major deterrent against hunting along the trails. When Lieutenant W. H. Emory's command first met buffaloes near the Pawnee Fork of the Arkansas, his men killed two, "at the expense of a couple of fine horses, which never recovered from the chase." Grass-fed horses, he concluded, should never be subjected to such "quick work," a tough lesson that had brought "trouble without end on many inexperienced travellers." W. H. Emory, *Lieutenant Emory Reports: A Reprint of Lieutenant W. H. Emory's Notes of a Military Reconnoissance* [sic] (Albuquerque: University of New Mexico Press, 1951), 29.

12. A mature bison can run about thirty to thirty-five miles per hour, only slightly slower than a racehorse in its prime. Even more impressive is its ability to keep up such a speed over distances far greater than the best horse can manage, all the while avoiding the holes and low spots that often trip its pursuers. If shot in the head or face, a buffalo would only shake its head, "as if dislodging a fly," and run faster as the bullet glanced harmlessly off the dense bone and thick matting of hair. Elizabeth B. Custer, *Following the Guidon* (Norman: University of Oklahoma Press, 1966), 206–07; Edwin Bryant, *What I Saw in California: Being the Journal of a Tour . . . in the Years 1846, 1847* (London: Richard Bentley, 1849), 77, and for modern confirmation, Tom McHugh, *The Time of the Buffalo* (Lincoln: University of Nebraska Press, 1979), 170–71, 266.

13. Incidents in which even a modest number were slain were typically cases of strange happenstance. Marcellus Ball Edwards, for instance, wrote of twenty-five bison killed when a herd, pursued by hired hunters, ran directly into a column of soldiers, who broke rank and fired bullets, "thick as hail," into the stampeding beasts. Apart from such assaults at close quarters, buffalo were far more often shot at than shot. See Ralph P. Bieber, ed., *Marching With the Army of the West, 1846–1848* (Glendale, Calif.: Arthur H. Clark Company, 1936), 129–30.

14. Sir Richard Burton, *The Look of the West, 1860: Across the Plains to California* (Lincoln: University of Nebraska Press, n. d.), 60.

15. In 1846, fourteen years before Burton, at a time when scarcely eight thousand pioneers had gone up the Platte road, Edwin Bryant found buffalo skeletons every few yards, "ghastly witnesses . . . of a retreating and fast perishing race." Military officers traveling the Arkansas in the same year described a similar sight. A young officer's comment of bison remains "in every state of decay" suggests at least some fresh kills. However, his belief that everything was attributable to wanton destruction by soldiers ahead of him does not hold up. Among the many comments of soldiers breaking ranks to chase and fire at animals, there are precious few accounts of any successes, certainly far too few to account for the "slaughter yard" of skeletons. In fact, a close reading of the documents fails to show when the bones were *not* along the Santa Fe and Platte roads. A diarist

among the first party making the trip to California, in 1841, was shocked by "the immense quantity of buffalo bones, which are everywhere strewed with great profusion. . . . The valley . . . is nothing but one complete slaughter yard." He was one of the first seventy emigrants to use the overland trail. Edwin Bryant, *What I Saw in California: Being the Journal of a Tour . . . in the Years 1846, 1847* (London: Richard Bentley, 1849), 63, 65; George Rutledge Gibson, *Journal of a Soldier Under Kearny and Doniphan, 1846–47*, ed. Ralph P. Bieber (Glendale, Calif.: Arthur H. Clark Company, 1935), 153; John Bidwell, *A Journey to California, 1841: The First Emigrant Party to California by Wagon Train* (Berkeley: Friends of the Bancroft Library, 1964), 13.

16. I am using here an estimate of 3 million buffaloes for the central plains—a figure well below even cautious guesses and one roughly equal to those reported killed in the great hunt of the early 1870s. The heaviest traffic before 1859 came in 1850, when about fifty thousand persons made the crossing. Thus, to harvest five percent of the herd, or 150,000 animals, each person would have to kill three.

17. Between twenty-seven hundred and twenty-eight hundred persons crossed the plains in each of those years. The distance from Fort Kearny to Independence Rock was roughly five hundred miles. To account for 150,000 dead bison, then, every emigrant would have had to kill more more than fifty animals, or about one per ten miles.

18. Frank Gilbert Roe, *The North American Buffalo: A Critical Study of the Species in its Wild State* (Toronto: University of Toronto Press, 1970), 188.

19. Entry for 12 July, 1820, in Edwin James, *Account of an Expedition From Pittsburgh to the Rocky Mountains, Performed in the Years 1819, 1820* (Cleveland: Arthur H. Clark Company, 1905), in Thwaites, Early Western Travels, Vol. XV, 255–56; Colonel Henry Dodge, *Report of the Secretary of War . . . Journal of the March of a Detachment of Dragoons, Under the Command of Colonel Dodge, During the Summer of 1835*, U. S. Congress, 24th Cong., 1st sess., H. E. Doc. 181, 139.

20. F. A. Wislizenus, *A Journey to the Rocky Mountains in the Year 1839* (St. Louis: Missouri Historical Society, 1912), 136; LeRoy R. Hafen and Ann W. Hafen, eds. *Rufus B. Sage, His Letters and Papers, 1836–1847 . . .* (Glendale, Calif.: Arthur H. Clark Company, 1956), 191, 194; Donald Jackson and Mary Lee Spence, *The Expeditions of John Charles Fremont. Volume 1, Travels from 1838 to 1844* (Urbana: University of Illinois Press, 1970), 435–37; Joseph Williams, *Narrative of a Tour from the State of Indiana to the Oregon Territory in the Years 1841–2* (Cincinnati: J. B. Wilson, 1843), 41–43.

21. A chronicler of S. W. Kearny's 1845 march down the Front Range through the area visited a few years earlier by Fremont, Sage, and others mentioned no bison until the party had traveled down the Arkansas below Bent's Fort. See "Abstract of Journals kept by Lt. Turner, adjutant 1st dragoons, and Lt. Franklin, Top. Eng. . . . ," U.S. Congress, 29th Cong., 1st sess., H. E. Doc. 2, 216–17.

22. *The Huntsman's Echo*, quoted in E. Douglas Branch, *The Hunting of the Buffalo* (New York: D. Appleton and Company, 1929), 123–24.

23. Two military expeditions are especially helpful here. In August of 1849, Captain L. C. Easton traveled south from Fort Laramie to the South Platte, then eastward across the highlands to the Republican and down it to the Smoky Hill.

Except for a small herd on the South Platte, he reported the buffalo range began where the Arikara Fork entered the Republican, just west of the 101st meridian. Lieutenant Francis Bryan, covering almost exactly the same ground in 1856, first found bison a bit farther east and wrote that the greatest concentration was well downstream. Merrill J. Mattes, ed., "Capt. L. C. Easton's Report: Fort Laramie to Fort Leavenworth Via Republican River in 1849," *Kansas Historical Quarterly* 20, no. 6 (May 1853): 404; Report of Lt. Francis T. Bryan, *Report of the Secretary of War*, 1857, U. S. Congress, 35th Cong., 1st sess., H. E. Doc. 473–76. These reports were confirmed by Colonel E. V. Sumner's troops in their 1857 campaign against the Cheyenne and Sioux. On their way west along the Platte they saw no buffaloes beyond Fremont's Springs, just past the forks, and as they looped to the south and then moved eastward by Bryan's route they saw no signs of bison until they approached the Republican River. William Y. Chalfant, *Cheyennes and Horse Soldiers: The 1857 Expedition and the Battle of Soloman's Fork* (Norman: University of Oklahoma Press, 1989), 143. Members of two surveying parties working farther east in the Republican valley in 1858 and 1859 both told of huge numbers of the animals along the river and on the surrounding prairie. Augustus Ford Harvey Journal, 23 September, 3 October, 1858, copy of transcript, Kansas State Historical Society; Justus L. Cozad Reminiscence, Nebraska State Historical Society.

24. James B. Hamm, "Plains Indian Plant Usage," and Kelly Kindscher, "The Ethnobotanical Use of Native Prairie Plants," in *The Prairie: Roots of Our Culture; Foundation of Our Economy*, Proceedings of the Tenth North American Prairie Conference (Dallas: Native Prairies Association of Texas, 1988), papers 02.03 and 02.04; George Bird Grinnell, *The Cheyenne Indians: Their History and Ways of Life*, Vol. 2 (Lincoln: University of Nebraska Press, 1972), 166–91.

25. Elbridge Gerry Account Books, Colorado State Historical Society.

26. Honora DeBusk Smith, "Early Life in Trinidad and the Purgatory Valley," M.A. thesis, University of Colorado, 1930, 43–44; Janet Lecompte, *Pueblo, Hardscrabble, Greenhorn: Society on the High Plains, 1832–1856* (Norman: University of Oklahoma Press, 1978), 74–85. Within these trading networks Indians also operated modestly as middlemen. On his trading expeditions from Santa Fe in the 1850s, for instance, Rafael Chacon found that the Cheyennes, Arapahoes, and Comanches typically had a surplus of coffee, which they exchanged, measure for measure, for New Mexican cornmeal. Smith, "Early Life in Trinidad," 44.

27. Hafen, *Fremont's Fourth Expedition* (Glendale, Calif.: Arthur H. Clark Company, 1960).

28. The largest loads came from around Fort Laramie, which drew from both north and south of the Platte. On 6 July, 1846, for instance, the St. Louis *Missouri Republican* reported that eleven hundred packs of robes, presumably one of several shipments, had just arrived from Fort John (the earlier name for Fort Laramie). Amounts moving down the Arkansas to Westport and St. Louis were somewhat smaller, but the trade in that area might well have been as great, since robes and meat were also being traded in the other direction, to New Mexico. LeRoy R. Hafen and Francis Marion Young, *Fort Laramie and the Pageant of the West, 1834–1890* (Glendale, Calif.: Arthur H. Clark Company, 1938),

115–16,121–22; Louise Barry, *The Beginning of the West: Annals of the Kansas Gateway to the American West, 1540–1854* (Topeka: Kansas State Historical Society, 1972), 431, 449, 522, 548.

29. Edwin Bryant, *What I Saw in California: Being the Journal of a Tour . . . in the Years 1846, 1847* (London: Richard Bentley, 1849), 64–66; H. M. T. Powell, *The Santa Fe Trail to California, 1849–1852*, ed. Douglas S. Watson (San Francisco: The Book Club of California, 1931), 41; William W. Hunter, *Missouri '49er: The Journal of William W. Hunter on the Southern Gold Trail*, ed. David P. Robrock (Albuquerque: University of New Mexico Press, 1992), 29; David Brainard Journal, June 12, 1849, State Historical Society of Wisconsin.

30. Lewis H. Morgan, *Ancient Society, or Researches in the Lines of Human Progress from Savagery, through Barbarism to Civilization* (New York: Henry Holt and Company, 1877), 112.

31. See Harold Hickerson, "The Virginia Deer and Intertribal Buffer Zones in the Upper Mississippi Valley," in *Man, Culture, and Animals: The Role of Animals in Human Ecological Adjustments*, eds. Anthony Leeds and Andrew P. Vayda (Washington, D.C.: American Association for the Advancement of Science, Publication No. 78, 1965), 43–66, and Charles Watrall, "Virginia Deer and the Buffer Zone in the Late Prehistoric-Early Protohistoric Periods in Minnesota," *Plains Anthropologist* 13 (1968): 81–86.

32. Dodge, *Journal of Dragoons*, 6 July, 1835, 18–19.

33. Flores, "Bison Ecology," 483.

34. Donald Jackson and Mary Lee Spence, eds., *The Expeditions of John Charles Fremont. Volume 1, Travels from 1838 to 1844* (Urbana: University of Illinois Press, 1970), 437.

35. Byers's statement is in a letter to J. A. Allen found in Allen's *The American Bisons, Living and Extinct*, Memoirs of the Museum of Comparative Zoology, at Harvard College. Vol. 4, no. 10 (Cambridge: University Press, 1876), 150–51.

36. J. W. Whitfield to Superintendant of Indian Affairs, 5 Janaury, 1856, Office of Indian Affairs, Letters Received, Upper Arkansas Agency.

37. William R. Brown, Jr., "*Comancheria* Demography, 1805–1830," *Panhandle-Plains Historical Review* 59 (1986): 1–17.

38. J. W. Whitfield to Superintendant of Indian Affairs, 5 January, 1856, Office of Indian Affairs, Letters Received, Upper Arkansas Agency.

39. Thomas S. Twiss to Secretary of Interior, 10 October, 1855 in *Annual Report of the Commissioner of Indians Affairs . . . 1855*, Report to Secretary of the Interior (Washington, 1856), 83.

40. Richard Irving Dodge, *The Hunting Grounds of the Great West. A Description of the Plains, Game, and Indians of the Great North American Desert* (London: Chatto and Windus, 1877), 321; Colonel Henry Dodge, *Report of the Secretary of War . . . Journal of the March of a Detachment of Dragoons, Under the Command of Colonel Dodge. . . .* U. S. Congress, 24th Cong., 1st sess., H. E. Doc. 181, 24; Donald Jackson and Mary Lee Spence, *The Expeditions of John Charles Fremont. Volume 1, Travels from 1838 to 1844* (Urbana: University of Illinois Press, 1970), 219.

41. Thomas J. Fitzpatrick to Thomas H. Harvey, 24 June, 1848, Letters Received, Upper Arkansas Agency, Bureau of Indian Affairs, 1848. After this exchange in a

village along the South Platte, Fitzpatrick proceeded downriver, where he met a trader heading for the Indian camp with two kegs of raw alcohol, which Fitzpatrick dumped.

42. Father Peter John Powell, *People of the Sacred Mountain: A History of the Northern Cheyenne Chiefs and Warrior Societies*, Vol. 1 (San Francisco: Harper and Row, 1981), 175.

43. Ibid., 177.

44. Thomas Fitzpatarick to D. D. Mitchell, 24 September, 1850, *Report of Commissioner of Indian Affairs . . . 1850*, 50–51.

45. Robert C. Miller to A. M. Robinson, 21 July, 1858, Office of Indian Affairs, Letters Received, Upper Arkansas Agency; James H. Pierce, "With the Green Russell Party," *The Trail* 13, no. 12 (May 1921): 6. Other accounts from that period make the same point. Julia Holmes last reported Indians a week's travel downstream from Bent's Fort. Although she had been mightily impressed with the herds of bison, and so probably would have noted them when she saw them, she reported none past her last sight of the Indians. Julia Archibald Holmes, *A Bloomer Girl on Pike's Peak 1858*, ed. Agnes Wright Spring (Denver: Denver Public Library, 1949), 24. Based on the tribal calendar and informants, James Mooney also wrote that for several years before 1861 the Kiowas had been drifting eastward down the Arkansas. James Mooney, *Calendar History of the Kiowa Indians* (Washington, D. C.: Smithsonian Institution Press, 1979; originally published 1898), 310–11.

46. Father Peter John Powell, *People of the Sacred Mountain: A History of the Northern Cheyenne Chiefs and Warrior Societies*, Vol. 1 (San Francisco: Harper and Row, 1981), 111–12.

47. Cheyenne accounts of these years are in Father John Peter Powell, *People of the Sacred Mountain: A History of the Northern Cheyenne Chiefs and Warrior Societies* (San Francisco: Harper and Row, 1981).

48. Ibid., 115–16, 162–63.

49. James Bordeaux to A. Cumming, *Annual Report of Commissioner of Indians Affairs . . . 1854*. See also George Bent to George Hyde, 7 January, 1905, George Bent Letters, Denver Public Library, and Powell, *People of the Sacred Mountain*, Vol. 1, 173–74.

50. J. W. Whitfield to Superintendent of Indian Affairs, 15 August, 1855, Office of Indian Affairs, Letters Received, Upper Arkansas Agency.

51. J. W. Whitfield to Superintendent of Indian Affairs, 5 January, 1856, Office of Indian Affairs, Letters Received, Upper Arkansas Agency.

52. Flores, "Bison Ecology," 476–78.

53. Flores, "Bison Ecology," 481; Joseph Chapman and George Feldhamer, eds., *Wild Mammals of North America: Biology, Management, and Economics* (Baltimore: Johns Hopkins University Press, 1982), 991–94; Major L. Boddicker and Ernest J. Hugghins, "Helminths of Big Game Mammals in South Dakota," *Journal of Parasitology* 55, no. 5 (October 1969): 1067–74; Stacy V. Tessaro, "Review of the Diseases, Parasites and Miscellaneous Pathological Conditions of North American Bison," *Canadian Veterinarian Journal* 30, no. 5 (May 1989): 416–22; Seymour Hadwen, "Tuberculosis in the Buffalo," *Journal of the American Veterinary Medical Association* 100, no. 778 (January 1942): 19–22.

54. Kirsten Krueger, "Feeding Relationships Among Bison, Pronghorn, and Prairie Dogs: An Experimental Analysis," *Ecology* 67, no. 3 (June 1986): 760–70; D. V. Ravendal, "Interspecific Nutritional Facilitation: Do Bison Benefit From Feeding on Prairie Dog Towns?" Unpublished M. A. thesis, Colorado State University, 1985; T. A. and J. K. Detling, "Grassland Patch Dynamics and Herbivore Grazing Preference Following Urine Deposition," *Ecology* 71, no. 1 (February 1991): 180–88; J. K. Detling, et al., "Examination of North American Bison Saliva for Potential Plant Growth Regulators," *Journal of Chemical Ecology* 7, no. 2 (March 1981): 239–46.

55. F. G. Roe, *The North American Buffalo*, 84. Roe's remark was specifically directed at the conclusion of Ernest Thompson Seton in his *Life-Histories of Northern Animals*, 2 vols. (New York, 1910). When observers insisted that migrations occurred, even when face to face with evidence to the contrary, the results could be bizarre. A leading buffalo hunter of the south plains concluded the plains bison were divided into three great herds. One in Canada came south to the Platte in summer and returned north in fall; another in west central Texas went north to the Platte in summer and returned in fall; the third, on the staked plains, moved north, south, east or west, depending on which way the wind blew. John R. Cook, *The Border and the Buffalo, An Untold Story of the Southwest Plains* (Topeka: Crane and Company, 1907), 152.

56. The quoted phrases are from McHugh, *Time of the Buffalo*, 173, Roe, *North American Buffalo*, 552.

57. Jeffrey R. Hanson, "Bison Ecology in the Northern Plains and a Reconstruction of Bison Patterns for the North Dakota Region," *Plains Anthropologist* 29 (May 1984): 111.

58. All modern accounts of bison describe this annual cycle of movement. McHugh, *Time of the Buffalo*, provides a brief and highly readable account, while that in Roe, *North American Buffalo*, is much more detailed. Some of the closest studies and observations have come from the Canadian plains, and although the specifics differ from those of the central plains, those studies are still extremely helpful in understanding the generic pattern of bison behavior. See especially J. Dewey Soper, "History, Range, and Home Life of the Northern Bison," *Ecological Monographs* 11, no. 4 (October 1941): 348–412, and R. Grace Morgan, "Bison Movement Patterns on the Canadian Plains: An Ecological Analysis, " *Plains Anthropologist* 25, no. 88, Part 1 (May 1980): 143–60.

59. The role of protein is crucial to understanding the annual grazing cycle, as well as the limits of the bison's overall range. A bison requires one part protein for every six parts fuel nutrients in its diet. Without protein, those nutrients, usually in the form of carbohydrates, cannot be digested and are therefore useless. In general, furthermore, the taller a grass grows the greater its carbohydrate content in relation to protein. Thus, in early spring when the forage along the rivers had just begun to grow, the infant tallgrasses had a double appeal: besides being about the best meal in town, they also offered an excellent protein-carbohydrate balance. Once those grasses rose above a certain height, however, a buffalo could only partially digest each bellyful of forage. Grazing entirely on the seemingly lush tallgrasses thus became inefficient and potentially dangerous; theoretically, in fact,

a bison could fill its stomach with fuel nutrients, crowd out new protein, and starve to death by overeating. Shortgrasses, on the other hand, reach an almost perfect one-to-six ratio of protein-to-carbohydrates at maturity, and, again unlike the taller species, they retain a high protein content throughout the winter. For these reasons the bison began looking fondly toward the uplands by early June. See Charles W. Johnson, "Protein as a Factor in the Distribution of American Bison," *Geographical Review* 41, no. 2 (April 1951): 330–31.

60. Glenn E. Plumb and Jerrold L. Dodd, "Foraging Ecology of Bison and Cattle on a Northern Mixed Prairie: Implications for Natural Area Management," paper in possession of the author, in press for the journal *Ecological Applications*.

61. James Clyman Memorandum Book and Diary, 1840, Graff Collection, Newberry Library.

62. LeRoy and Ann W. Hafen, eds., *Rufus B. Sage, His Letters and Papers, 1836–1847* . . . (Glendale, Calif.: Arthur H. Clark Company, 1956), Vol. 2, 191; Reuben Gold Thwaites, *Early Western Travels*, 23, 245.

63. Alexander Toponce, *Reminiscences of Alexander Toponce, Pioneer* (Salt Lake City: Century Printing Company, 1923), 122.

64. For an excellent description and discussion of these points, see R. Grace Morgan, "Bison Movement Patterns on the Canadian Plains: An Ecological Analysis," *Plains Anthropologist* 25, no. 88, Part 1 (May 1980): 143–60. See also Charles C. Schwartz and James E. Ellis, "Feeding Ecology and Niche Separation in Some Native and Domestic Ungulates on the Shortgrass Prairie," *Journal of Applied Ecology* 18, no. 2 (August 1981): 343–53, D. G. Peden et al., "The Trophic Ecology of *Bison Bison* L. on Shortgrass Plains," *Journal of Applied Ecology* 11, no. 2 (August 1974): 489–97, and S. E. Clark, et al., "The Effects of Climate and Grazing Practices on Short-Grass Prairie Vegetation," Canadian Department of Agriculture Technical Bulletin 46, Ottawa, Canada, 1943.

65. Joel Palmer, *Journal of Travels Over the Rocky Mountains, to the Mouth of the Columbia River, Made During the Years 1845 and 1846* . . . Cincinnati: J. A. and U. P. James, 1847), 48.

66. On relative selectivity of cattle and bison, see D. G. Peden et al., "The Trophic Ecology of *Bison Bison* L. on Shortgrass Plains," *Journal of Applied Ecology* 11, no. 2 (August 1974): 489–97, and Glenn E. Plumb and Jerrold L. Dodd, "Foraging Ecology of Bison and Cattle on a Northern Mixed Prairie: Implications for Natural Area Management," paper in possession of the author, in press for the journal *Ecological Adaptations*.

67. W. H. Emory, *Lieutenant Emory Reports: A Reprint of Lieutenant W. H. Emory's Notes of a Military Reconnoissance* [sic] (Albuquerque: University of New Mexico Press, 1951), 30.

68. Travelers in 1859, for instance, rarely reported bison in the immediate area of Fort Kearny, yet J. L. Cozad, surveying the country immediately to the south, found massive herds between the Platte and Republican. When he turned north and drew close to the Platte road, the bison suddenly vanished. As early as 1846 a traveler thought that buffaloes had been "driven . . . into the hills" by parties like his. Daniel Kellogg, moving down the Platte in the spring of 1859, similarly found a buffalo to kill only when he rode just above the bluffs, and although

Richard Burton saw virtually no bison the next year, he wrote that "buffalo herds were behind the hills, but we were too full of sleep to follow them." Edwin Bryant, *What I Saw in California: Being the Journal of a Tour . . . in the Years 1846, 1847* (London: Richard Bentley, 1849), 68; J. L. Cozad Reminiscence, Nebraska State Historical Society; Daniel Kellogg, "Across the Plains in 1858," *The Trail* 5, no. 7 (December 1912): 11; Burton, *Look of the West* 60.

69. As usual, this kind of generalization hides something more complicated. Because shortgrasses on the western plains are better adapted to drought than the taller grasses from the east, tallgrasses and midgrasses died off even more rapidly. Shortgrasses, therefore, expanded their domain during prolonged dry spells, becoming the most common plant in areas where a mixture of types flourished in wetter times. Thus, the acreage dominated by shortgrasses, the bison's favored food, actually increased during droughts. Unfortunately for the bison, however, the percentage of ground cover on any given acre was shrinking at a rate much greater than that by which the range of shortgrasses was expanding, and to make matters worse the nutritional value of shortgrasses' upper storey was dropping as well. The bottom line was simple: buffaloes had a lot less to eat. See J. E. Weaver, "Replacement of True Prairie by Mixed Prairie in Eastern Nebraska and Kansas," *Ecology* 24, no. 4 (October 1943): 421–34.

70. There is considerable debate around the apparently simple statements in this paragraph. See Tom D. Dillehay, "Late Quaternary Bison Population Changes on the Southern Plains," *Plains Anthropologist* 19, no. 65 (August 1974): 180–96; Darrell Creel, Robert F. Soctt IV, and Michael B. Collins. "A Faunal Record from West Central Texas and Its Bearing on Late Holocene Bison Population Changes in the Southern Plains," *Plains Anthropologist* 35, no. 127 (February 1990): 55–69; Susan S. Hughes, "Bison Diminution on the Great Plains," in *Wyoming Contributions to Anthropology*, eds. F. E. Smiley and Jack L. Hofman, 42, no. 1 (Spring 1978): 38–47; Stephen A. Hall, "Environment and Archaeology of the Central Osage Plains," *Plains Anthropologist* 33: 203–18; Douglas B. Bamforth, "An Empirical Perspective on Little Ice Age Climatic Change on the Great Plains," *Plains Anthropologist* 35, no. 132 (November 1990): 359–66.

71. Robert MacArthur, "Species Packing and Competitive Equilibrium for Many Species," *Theoretical Population Biology* 1, no. 1 (May 1970): 1–11. See also the chapter on "Niche Overlap" in *Stability and Complexity in Model Ecosystems*, Robert M. May (Princeton: Princeton University Press, 1973).

72. Lewis H. Garrard, *Wah-To-Yah and the Taos Trail*, ed. Ralph P. Bieber, Vol. 6 of Southwest Historical Series (Glendale, Calif.: Arthur H. Clark Company, 1938), 83.

Notes to Chapter 3

1. For a partial bibliography suggesting the range of literature on the history of the family, see Gerald L. Soliday, ed., with Tamara K. Hareven, Richard T. Vann, and Robert Wheaton, *History of the Family and Kinship: A Select International Bibliography* (Millwood, New York: Kraus-International Publications, 1980).

2. For recent surveys of the considerable literature on Native American demography, see John W. Verano and Douglas H. Ubelaker, eds., *Disease and Demography in the*

Americas (Washington, D.C.: Smithsonian Institution Press, 1992), and Russell Thornton, *American Indian Holocaust and Survival: A Population History Since 1492* (Norman: University of Oklahoma Press, 1987). As its title suggests, the latter tends to accept the larger estimates of losses from disease. For an analysis and critique of methods used in calculating Indian population at the time of Columbian contact, see John D. Daniels, "The Indian Population of North America in 1492," *William and Mary Quarterly*, 3rd series, 49, no. 2 (April 1992): 298–320.

3. Garrick Mallery, *Picture-Writing of the American Indians* in *Tenth Annual Report of the Bureau of Ethnology to the Secretary of the Smithsonian Institution, 1889–1889* (Washington, D.C., 1898), 308, 317, 323, 325; Alexis Praus, *The Sioux, 1798–1922: A Dakota Winter Count* (Bloomfield Hills: Cranbrook Institute of Science, 1962), 10.

4. James Mooney, *Calendar History of the Kiowa Indians* (Washington, D.C.: Smithsonian Institution Press, 1979; originally published 1898), 168; E. Wagner Stearn and Allen E. Stearn, *The Effect of Smallpox on the Destiny of the Amerindian* (Boston: Bruce Humphries, Inc., 1945), 76; Alice C. Fletcher and Francis La Flesche, *The Omaha Tribe* (Lincoln: University of Nebraska Press, 1972), Vol. I, 86-87.

5. Jedediah Morse, *A Report to the Secretary of War of the United States on Indian Affairs* (New Haven, 1822), 259; Mooney, *Calendar History of Kiowas*, 168.

6. Praus, *Sioux Winter Count*, 16; Margot Liberty, "Population Trends Among Present-Day Omaha Indians," *Plains Anthropologist* 20, no. 69 (August 1969): 225–30; John C. Ewers, "The Influence of Epidemics on the Indian Populations and Cultures of Texas," *Plains Anthropologist* 18, no. 60 (May 1973): 104-15.

7. Fletcher and La Flesche, *The Omaha Tribe*, Vol. II, 620.

8. Louise Amelia Knapp Clappe, *The Shirley Letters from California Mines in 1851–52* (San Francisco: T. C. Russell, 1922), 322.

9. Mooney, *Kiowa Calendar*, 289–90; Father John Peter Powell, *People of the Sacred Mountain: A History of the Northern Cheyenne Chiefs and Warrior Societies*, Vol. 1 (San Francisco: Harper and Row, 1981), 93–99; George Bent to George Hyde, 23 January, 1905, George Bent Letters, Western History Collection, Denver Public Library.

10. Howard Stansbury, *An Expedition to the Valley of the Great Salt Lake of Utah. . . .* (Philadelphia: Lippincott, Grambo and Co., 1855), 43–44; Lee Whipple-Haslam, *Early Days in California: Scenes and Events of the '50s As I Remember Them* (Jamestown, California: [s.n.], 1925), 20; Adrietta Applegate Hixon, *On to Oregon! A True Story of a Young Girl's Journey Into the West*, ed. Waldo Taylor (Weiser, Idaho: Signal-American Printers, 1947), 37.

11. A. Cumming to Comissioner of Indian Affairs, *Report of Commissioner of Indian Affairs, 1856*. The previous year Thomas Twiss of the Upper Platte Agency reported that the Arapahoes had told him that "smallpox was raging in their lodges," preventing them even from hunting buffalo. Thomas S. Twiss to Secretary of Interior, *Report of Commissioner of Indian Affairs, 1855*, 82.

12. Mooney, *Calendar History of Kiowas*, 311.

13. Alfred Barnitz to wife, 13 August, 1867, 3 September, 1867, Alfred Barnitz Papers, Beinecke Library, Yale University. Barnitz's troops were skirmishing with the Cheyennes along the Smoky Hill River. Warfare may actually have offered

Indians a measure of protection by minimizing their contact with whites. The effects of the epidemics of 1866 and 1867 on Indians not at war are better documented. Skeleton Creek in southern Kansas got its name after a party of Wichitas, under military escort to the Washita River, lost so many persons so quickly that the corpses were left untended. Arrival of survivors at the Washita triggered a new round of the disease there. Ramon Powers and Gene Younger, "Cholera On the Plains: The Epidemic of 1867 in Kansas," *Kansas Historical Quarterly* 37, no. 4 (Winter 1971): 377–78.

14. Dr. H. T. Ketchum to William P. Dole, 30 September, 1863, Bureau of Indian Affairs, Letters Received, Colorado Agency, 1863.

15. George E. Hyde, *The Pawnee Indians* (Norman: University of Oklahoma Press, 1951), 181, 197–98.

16. Fletcher and La Flesche, *The Omaha Tribe*, 86–87.

17. Census of Cheyennes and Arapahoes of upper Arkansas in A. G. Boone to Commissioner of Indian Afffairs, 16 November, 1861, Office of Indian Affairs, Letters Received, Upper Arkansas Agency, 1861. A census of the Pawnees in 1859 shows an even more troubling erosion. Their population of 3,111 was almost precisely half that reported in 1840. Of these, there were nearly twice as many women as men (1,505 to 820). Children numbered only 786, or barely a fourth of the whole. William W. Dennison to Commissioner of Indian Affairs, 16 July, 1859, Bureau of Indian Affairs, Letters Received, Otoe Agency, 1859. A missionary census of 1840 reported 6,244 Pawnees. That figure, in turn, was barely half of the government population estimate of several years earlier (twelve thousand). The 1840 census also showed a substantial female majority (2,185 to 1,449), suggesting the Pawnees already had paid a considerable price in men in their struggles with the Sioux. See Hyde, *Pawnee Indians*, 364.

18. A. Cumming to Commissioner of Indian Affairs in *Report of Commissioner of Indian Affairs, 1856*.

19. Richard A. Easterlin has estimated that in newly settled portions of Kansas in 1860, there were between 2.2 and 2.4 children nine years and younger for every woman between the ages of twenty and forty-nine. According to the United Nations *Demographic Yearbook* for 1992, the corresponding numbers for Ethiopia, Columbia, and the United States were 2.21, 1.11, and 0.64. See Richard A. Easterlin, "Factors in the Decline of Farm Family Fertility in the United States: Some Preliminary Research Results," *Journal of American History* 63, no. 3 (December 1976): 600–14; *Demographic Yearbook/Annuaire demographique* (New York: United Nations/Nations Unies, 1992).

20. Because laryngeal diphtheria, the hungriest killer of white children in the West, was common in eastern cities, families there were often relatively immune, yet they still could carry the disease with them when they moved elsewhere. Those urban centers became deep disease pools from which city emigrants dipped and distributed infections among new neighbors in the West who were unexposed and vulnerable. A diphtheria epidemic in 1880 devastated families in parts of western Kansas, accounting for more than half of all deaths in some counties. This process, of contagion imported into virgin soil, was a grim mimicry of the Indian experience. Kansas manuscript mortality schedules, 1870, National

Archives; John W. Florin, *Death in New England: Regional Variations in Mortality* (Chapel Hill: University of North Carolina Press, 1971).

21. Quoted in Deborah Fink, *Agrarian Women: Wives and Mothers in Rural Nebraska, 1880–1940* (Chapel Hill: University of North Carolina Press, 1992), 137.

22. One document in particular offers a fascinating glimpse into the complex and interwoven tasks of a farmstead. A scrapbook of the A. B. Duncan family, who settled on the south plains of Texas, consists of a listing and description of various types of farm work, comments on seasonal cycles, hints and lore of planting, harvesting, animal care, household work, and other aspects of farm life. It contains a catalogue of labor and examples of information passed from one generation to the next. The scrapbook is found in the A. B. Duncan Collection, Southwest Collection, Texas Tech University.

23. Venola Lewis Bivens, ed., "The Diary of Luna E. Warner, a Kansas Teenager of the Early 1870s," *Kansas Historical Quarterly* 35, no. 4 (Winter 1969): 420.

24. Christopher James Huggard, "The Role of the Family in Settling the Cherokee Outlet," M.A. thesis, University of Arkansas, 1987.

25. Bivens, ed., *Diary of Luna Warner*, 276–77.

26. On 4 May, 1871, Luna wrote: "Alpheus plowed about an acre for us. The men worked on the timber. Papa got us some good butter." On Howard's bout with the bottle, see entries for 4–11 November, 1871, all in Bivens, ed., *Diary of Luna Warner*, 283, 295–96.

27. Uriah Oblinger to family, 28 October, 1872 [1874?], Uriah W. Oblinger Papers, Nebraska State Historical Society.

28. For an example of a family that relied during the first period of settlement on cooperation with relatives and financial support sent by relatives, see Glenda Riley, ed., "The Morse Family Letters: A New Home in Iowa," *Annals of Iowa* 45 (Winter 1980): 551–67.

29. S. W. James, "Soil Nitrogen, Phosphorus and Organic Matter Processing by Earthworms in Tallgrass Prairie," *Ecology* 72 (1991): 2101–10.

30. See, for instance, series of maps, each entitled *Map Showing the Progress of the Public Surveys in Kansas and Nebraska, to Accompany the Annual Report of the Surveyor General . . . ,*" numbered sequentially, illustrating the survey of the central and western portions of those states in the 1860s, in Kansas Collection of University of Kansas Library.

31. U.S. Census Office, *Statistics of the Population of the United States at the Tenth Census,* 1 June, 1880 (Washington: Government Printing Office, 1883), 60–61; U.S. Census Office, *Report on the Productions of Agriculture as Returned at the Tenth Census,* 1 June, 1880 (Washington: Government Printing Office, 1883), 115–16, 153–54. For statistics on the same period in southern Nebraska, see *Biennial Report of the Secretary of State of the State of Nebraska . . .* (Omaha: Omaha Republic Company, 1887). For a more detailed look at the makeup of new emigrants, see manuscripts of County Organizational Censuses, 1867–1887, Kansas State Historical Society.

32. Soloman Gorgas Diary, 30 June, 1850, Henry E. Huntington Library.

33. David DeWolf to Matilda, 17 June, 1849, David DeWolf Letters, Henry E. Huntington Library. Husbands and fathers who homesteaded alone had the same

response. For a poignant series of letters from an early Kansas settler to his wife and children, see Charles Athearn Letters, Beinecke Library, Yale University.

34. Entry for 13 June, 1849, in Helen S. Giffen, ed., *The Diaries of Peter Decker* (Georgetown, Calif.: Talisman Press, 1966), 94.

35. On mobility on the central plains, see D. Aidan McQuillan, "The Mobility of Immigrants and Americans: A Comparison of Farmers on the Kansas Frontier," *Agricultural History* 53, no. 3 (July 1979):576–96; James C. Malin, "The Turn-over of Farm Population in Kansas," in *History and Ecology: Studies of the Grassland,* ed. Robert P. Swierenga (Lincoln: University of Nebraska Press, 1984), 269–99.

36. Arensberg is quoted in Faragher's "Americans, Mexicans, Metis: A Community Approach to the Comparative Study of North American Frontiers," in *Under An Open Sky: Rethinking America's Western Past,* eds. William Cronon, George Miles, and Jay Gitlin (New York: Oxford University Press, 1992), 93. See also Faragher's "Open Country Community: Sugar Creek, Illinois, 1820–1850," Steven Hahn and Jonathan Prude, *The Countryside in the Age of Capitalist Transformation: Essays in the Social History of Rural America* (Chapel Hill: University of North Carolina Press, 1985), 233–58. The term "familialism" is from my personal correspondence with Faragher.

37. Harley P. Tripp Reminiscence, Kansas State Historical Society.

38. In 1880 Kansas had twenty schools per one thousand school-age children; Nebraska had twenty-four. The corresponding ratios for Michigan and Massachu-setts were nineteen per thousand and fifteen per thousand. U.S. Tenth Census, 1880, Vol. 1, 646, 916.

39. This is not to say women were entirely excluded from the formal political structure. For a list of women who held county and city offices in early Kansas, see "Women in Office," *Kansas Historical Collections* 12 (1911–1912): 396–401.

40. For an example from the central plains, see June O. Underwood, "Civilizing Kansas: Women's Organizations, 1880–1920," *Kansas History* 7, no. 4 (Winter 1984/85): 291–306.

41. Carol Leonard and Isidor Willimann, "Prostitution and Changing Morality in the Frontier Cattle Towns of Kansas," *Kansas History* 2, no. 1 (Spring 1979): 39.

42. Ibid., ; Robert R. Dykstra, *The Cattle Towns* (New York: Alfred A. Knopf, 1968), 259–62; Theophilus Little, "Early Days of Abilene and Dickenson County," *Pioneer History of Kansas* (Denver: Great Western Publishing Co., 1933), 38. In his memoir of these years, McCoy does not discuss this dispute or the position he took as mayor but notes only that in frontier towns like Abilene the "natural result" of commerce like the cattle trade is the appearance of men "whose heart-strings are but a wisp of base-sounding chords" and women "who have fallen low—alas, how low!" See Joseph G. Mccoy, *Historic Sketches of the Cattle Trade of the West and Southwest,* Vol. VII, Southwest Historical Series, ed. Ralph P. Bieber (Glendale, California: Arthur H. Clark Company, 1940), 205–06.

43. C. Robert Haywood, *Victorian West: Class and Culture in Kansas Cattle Towns* (Lawrence: University Press of Kansas, 1991), 31.

44. Leonard and Wallimann, "Prostitution and Changing Morality," 43.

45. Haywood, *Victorian West,* 162.

46. Ibid, 165–66, 171.
47. E. C. "Teddy Blue" Abbott and Helena Huntington Smith, *We Pointed Them North: Recollections of a Cowpuncher* (Chicago: The Lakeside Press, R. R. Donnelly and Sons, 1991), 171.
48. Anne M. Butler, *Daughters of Joy, Sisters of Misery: Prostitutes in the American West, 1865–90* (Urbana: University of Illinois Press, 1985), 27.
49. Werner J. Einstadter, "Robbery-Outlawry on the U.S. Frontier, 1863–1890," in *Violent Crime: Historical and Contemporary Issues*, eds. James A. Inciardi and Anne E. Pottieger (Beverly Hills: Sage Books, 1978), 21–35.
50. Cited in Fink, *Agrarian Women*, 79.
51. For examples of studies of central plains Indian mythology, see James R.Walker, *Lakota Myth*, ed. Elaine A. Jahner (Lincoln: University of Nebraska Press, 1983); Maurice Boyd, *Kiowa Voices: Ceremonial Dance, Ritual, and Song* (Fort Worth: Texas Christian University Press, 1981) and *Kiowa Voices: Myths, Legends, and Folktales* (Fort Worth: Texas Christian University Press, 1983); John Stands-in-Timber and Margot Liberty, *Cheyenne Memories* (New Haven: Yale University Press 1967); Peter J. Powell, *Sweet Medicine: The Continuing Role of the Sacred Arrows, the Sun Dance, and the Sacred Buffalo Hat in Northern Cheyenne History*, 2 vols. (Norman: University of Oklahoma Press, 1980); George B. Grinnell, *By Cheyenne Campfires* (New Haven: Yale University Press, 1962); Alfred L. Kroeber, "Cheyenne Tales," *Journal of American Folklore* 13 (1900): 161–90; Alice Marriott and Carol K. Rachlin, *Plains Indian Mythology* (New York: Thomas Y. Crowell Company, 1975) and the same authors' *American Indian Mythology* (New York: Thomas Y. Crowell, 1968). The quotation is from Marriott and Rachlin, *Plains Indian Mythology*, 42.
52. Rodolphe C. Petter, *English-Cheyenne Dictionary* . . . (Kettle Falls, Washington: Valdo Petter, 1915), 900; E. Adamson Hoebel, *The Cheyennes: Indians of the Great Plains* (Fort Worth: Harcourt Brace Jovanovich, 1978), 29–31; Fred Eggan, "The Cheyenne and Arapaho Kinship System," in *Social Anthropology of North American Tribes*, ed. Fred Eggan (Chicago: University of Chicago Press, 1955), 33–95.
53. Fred Eggan, "Social Anthroplogy: Methods and Results," in *Social Anthropology of North American Tribes*, ed. Fred Eggan (Chicago: University of Chicago Press, 1955), 519.
54. The same tendency seems to have been found among others who switched from farming to hunting in very different environments, the Montagnais and other Algonkians of eastern Canada. For a taste of the considerable discussion and debate on this question, see Alfred Goldsworthy Bailey, *The Conflict of European and Eastern Algonkian Cultures, 1504–1700: A Study in Canadian Civilization* (Toronto: University of Toronto Press, 1969), 87–88; Eleanor Leacock, "The Montagnais 'Hunting Territory' and the Fur Trade," American Anthropologist Association *Memoir* No. 78 (1954).
55. Oscar Lewis, *The Effects of White Contact Upon Blackfoot Culture, With Special Reference to the Role of the Fur Trade*, Monographs of the American Ethnological Society, VI (New York: J. J. Augustin, 1942), 38–40; Joseph Jablow, *The Cheyenne in Plains Indian Trade Relations, 1795–1840*, Monographs of the American Etnological Society, 19 (New York: J.J. Augustin, 1951), 20-21. John

H. Moore has studied the family structure of Cheyennes during this period and the reservation era and traced the continuing significance of polygyny among prominent families. See John H. Moore and Gregory R. Campbell, "An Ethnohistorical Perspective on Cheyenne Demography," *Journal of Family History* 14, no. 1 (1989): 17–42 and John H. Moore, "The Developmental Cycle of Cheyenne Polygyny," *American Indian Quarterly* 15 (Summer 1991): 311–28.

56. For an admiring listing of goods acquired at the Treaty of Fort Laramie (called by the Cheyennes the Horse Creek Treaty) of 1851, see a rare reminiscence of a native plainswoman: "Iron Teeth, A Cheyenne Old Woman," in Thomas B. Marquis, *The Cheyennes of Wyoming*, ed. Thomas D. Weist (Algonac, Michigan: Reference Publications, 1978), 57, originally published as "Red Ripe's Squaw" in *Century Magazine* June 1929, 201–09.

57. John C. Ewers, "Climate, Acculturation, and Costume: A History of Women's Clothing Among the Indians of the Southern Plains," *Plains Anthropologist* 25, no. 87 (February 1980): 63–82.

58. W. Eugene Hollon and Ruth Lapham Butler, eds., *William Bollaert's Texas* (Norman: University of Oklahoma Press, 1956), 375n.

59. For examples of this subject's considerable literature, which stresses the complex interplay of economic structure and production, cultural variables, and religiousspiritual factors, see Peggy R. Sanday, "Toward a Theory of the Status of Women," *American Anthropologist* 75, no. 5 (October 1973): 1682–700; Carol Devens, "Separate Confrontations: Gender as a Factor in Indian Adaptation to European Colonization in New France," *American Quarterly* 38, no. 3 (1986): 460–80; Eleanor Leacock, "Women's Status in Egalitarian Society: Implications for Social Evolution," *Current Anthropology* 19 (1978): 247–75; Karen Anderson, "Commodity Exchange and Subordination: Montagnais-Naskapi and Huron Women, 1600–1650," *Signs* 11, no. 1 (Autumn 1985): 48-62; Richard J. Perry, "The Fur Trade and the Status of Women in the Western Subarctic," *Ethnohistory* 26 (1979): 363–75; Judith Brown, "Iroquois Women: An Ethnohistorical Note," in *Toward an Anthropology of Women*, ed. Rayna B. Reiter (New York: Monthly Review Press, 1975), 77–109. For an interesting instance in a non-American context, see Mona Etienne, "Women and Men, Cloth and Colonization: The Transformation of Production-Distribution Relations among the Baule (Ivory Coast)," in *Women and Colonization: Anthropological Perspectives*, eds. Mona Etienne and Eleanor Leacock (New York: Praeger, 1980), 214–38.

60. In a cross-cultural survey, Peggy Sanday argues that women in horticultural economies like those along the Missouri contributed more to their people's subsistence than in any other economies she examined—more than nonagricultural peoples on one extreme, of which plains pastoralists would be an example, and intensive and irrigated agriculture on the other. Although she stresses "that female productive activities may be a *necessary* but not a *sufficient* precondition for the development of female power," such a system certainly encouraged a higher status for women. Sanday, "Theory of the Status of Women," 1690–91, 1697.

61. Margot Liberty, "Hell Came With Horses: Plains Indian Women in the Equestrian Era," *Montana, The Magazine of Western History* 32, no. 3 (Summer 1982):

14–15, and Margot Liberty, "Plains Indian Women Through Time: A Preliminary Overview," in *Lifeways of Intermontane and Plains Montana Indians: In Honor of J. Verne Dusenberry*, ed. Leslie B. Davis, Occasional Papers of the Museum of the Rockies No. 1 (Bozeman: Montana State University, 1979), 138–41. Commenting on the Okipa, a central ceremony of the Mandans, E. Adamson Hoebel wrote that "it was driven home to all Mandans that this was indeed a matrilocal, matrilineal, matrifocal, matridominated society." See *Anthropology: The Study of Man*, 4th Ed. (New York: McGraw-Hill Book Company, 1972), 571.

62. Margot Liberty, "Hell Came With Horses: Plains Indian Women in the Equestrian Era," 13.

63. Jurgen Doring, *Kulturwandel bei den Nordamerikanischen Plainsindianern: Zur Rolle des Pferdes bei den Comanchen und den Cheyenne* (Berlin: Dietrick Reimer, 1984), 214–15.

64. Agent J. W. Whitfield estimated the Cheyenne had nine hundred warriors and half again as many women, or about 1,350. Their annual take in buffaloes was set at forty thousand, or roughly twenty-five for each woman. J. W. Whitfield to Supertintendant of Indian Affairs, 5 January, 1856, Office of Indian Affairs, Letters Received, Upper Arkansas Agency, 1856.

65. I have taken this phrase from an excellent discussion of this neglected topic: Patricia K. Townsend and Ann McElroy, "Toward an Ecology of Women's Reproductive Health," *Medical Anthropology* 14, no. 1 (1992): 9–34.

66. Ibid., 21.

67. A. Robert Frischo, A. Robert, Jane E. Klayman, and Jorge Matos, "Symbiotic Relationship Between High Fertility, High Childhood Mortality and Socio-Economic Status in an Urban Peruvian Population," *Human Biology* 48, no. 1 (February 1976): 101–11; K. P. Singh, "Child Mortality, Social Status, and Fertility in India," *Social Biology* 21 (Winter 1974): 385–88.

68. Jonathan W. Whitfield to Colonel A. Cumming, *Annual Report of the Commissioner of Indian Affairs, 1854*.

69. Alice B. Kehoe, "The Function of Ceremonial Sexual Intercourse among the Northern Plains Indians," *Plains Anthropologist* 15, no. 48 (May 1970): 99–103.

70. George A. Dorsey, *The Arapaho Sun Dance: The Ceremony of the Offerings Lodge*, Field Columbian Museum Publication 75, Anthropological Series, Vol. 4 (Chicago: Field Columbian Museum, 1903), 172–77.

71. Kehoe, "Ceremonial Sexual Intercourse," 101.

72. Jean Baptiste Trudeau, for instance, wrote that Mandan girls and married women "seem to be common property. . . . Fathers, brothers and even husbands offer and take the most beautiful daughters, sisters and wives to the White Men for the diversion . . .," and the American Patrick Gass also thought a woman was treated as "an article of traffic, and *indulgences* are sold at a very moderate price." He attributed this situation to the "loathsome effects *of certain French principles*." Mrs. H. T. Beauregard, trans., "Journal of Jean Baptiste Trudeau Among the Arikara Indians in 1795," *Missouri Historical Society Collections* 4 (1912–1923): 30–31; Patrick Gass, *A Journal of the Voyages and Travels of the Corps of Discovery, Under the Command of Capt. Lewis and Capt. Clarke [sic] of the Army of the United States. . . .* (Minneapolis: Ross & Haines, Inc., 1958).

73. Margaret G. Hanna, "Do You Take This Woman? Economics and Marriage in a Late Prehistoric Band." *Plains Anthropologist* 29, no. 104 (May 1984): 115–29. (The quotation is from page 127.) Hanna's approach was ingenious. By categorizing surviving examples of pottery by geochemical analysis and subtleties of style, she distinguished between ceramics distributed by trade and that dispersed by movement of women, presumably through exogamous marriage.

74. Edward M. Bruner, "Mandan," in *Perspectives in American Indian Culture Change*, ed. Edward H. Spicer (Chicago: University of Chicago Press, 1961), 201. Referring to the period after the appearance of European goods but before the extensive direct involvement of white traders on the plains, Bruner writes that such adoption was "the key mechanism of social structure which enable members of warring tribes to trade in peace. . . . Plains Indian trade was accomplished by barter between fictitious relatives. From a larger perspective, a vast network of rital kinship relationships extended throughout the entire Plains."

75. Polly Pope, "Trade in the Plains: Affluence and Its Effects," Kroeber Anthropological Society, Publication No. 34 (Spring 1966): 53–61.

76. John H. Moore, *The Cheyenne Nation: A Social and Demographic History* (Lincoln: University of Nebraska Press, 1987), 262–63.

77. Lewis, *Effects of White Contact*, 38–40.

78. Status usually depended on several factors, including military accomplishments, lineage and connection to respected families, spiritual powers and priestly office, specialized skills, and personal attributes like generosity, wisdom, common sense and good looks. Wealth was another important measure of standing. Accumulation of property, especially horses, brought a rise in status in itself. Goods could also be parlayed into greater prestige, for instance, by increasing the chances of courageous wartime deeds, since one could not fight without horses, and by opening opportunities of marriage into high-ranking families. Wealth could even enhance spiritual standing because medicine bundles, shields with special powers in battle, other ceremonial objects, and even visions could be bought and sold. These possessions then might further increase income, since owners of bundles and other sacred objects were often paid for performing religious services. For a clear and concise discussion of the various makings of status among the Kiowas, see Jane Richardson, *Law and Status Among the Kiowa Indians*, Monographs of the American Ethnological Society, No. 1 (New York: J. J. Augustin Publisher, 1940), 12–16. See also Bernard Mishkin, *Rank and Warfare Among the Plains Indians*, Monographs of the American Ethnological Society, No. 3 (New York: J. J. Augustin Publisher, 1940); Polly Pope, "Trade in the Plains: Affluence and Its Effects," Kroeber Anthropological Society, Publication No. 34 (Spring 1966): 57–58. See also Lewis, *Effects of White Culture*, 44-45.

79. Richardson, *Law and Status Among the Kiowa Indians*, 102.

80. George E. Hyde, *Life of George Bent, Written From His Letters* (Norman: University of Oklahoma Press, 1968), 323–24; Moore, *The Cheyenne Nation* 223–24.

81. The differing marital patterns of the Dog Soldiers and other bands of this period is the subject of a vigorous and fascinating debate barely touched upon here. John Moore has argued that the Dog Soldiers, as part of a fundamental restructuring of

Cheyenne society, were moving toward a patrilineal and patrilocal system reflecting a more male-dominated warrior culture. While praising Moore's emphasis on dynamic historical changes in native political structure, E. Adamson Hoebel replied that Moore oversimplified those changes and misread some of the evidence. For their exchange, see John H. Moore, "Cheyenne Political History, 1820–1894," *Ethnohistory* 21, no. 4 (Fall 1974): 329–59; E. Adamson Hoebel, "On Cheyenne Sociopolitical Organization," *Plains Anthropologist* 25, no. 88, Part 1 (May 1980): 161–69; John H. Moore, "Evolution and Historical Reductionism," *Plains Anthropologist* 26, no. 94, Part 1 (November 1981): 261–69. See also Moore's extended discussion in *The Cheyenne Nation*, especially 197–204, 253–66.

82. Moore's argument is in "Cheyenne Political History," cited in the previous note. It is important to remember that the practice had been used as a punishment for adultery among Indians of the Illinois country for quite a while. See Lawrence A. Conrad, "Comment: An Early Eighteenth Century Reference to 'Putting a woman on the Prairies' Among the Central Algonquians and Its Implications for Moore's Explanation of the Practice Among the Cheyenne," *Plains Anthropologist* 28, no. 100 (May 1983): 141–42. On the custom, see also Karl N. Llewellyn and E. Adamson Hoebel, *The Cheyenne Way: Conflict and Case Law in Primitive Jurisprudence* (Norman: University of Oklahoma Press, 1941), 202–10; Margot Liberty, "Plains Indian Women Through Time: A Preliminary Overview," in *Lifeways of Intermontane and Plains Montana Indians*, ed. Leslie B. Davis, Occasional Papers of the Museum of the Rockies No. 1 (Bozeman: Montana State University, 1971), 142; S. C. Simms, "A Crow Monument to Shame," *American Anthropologist* 5 (1903): 374–75.

83. Donald Jackson and Mary Lee Spence, eds., *The Expeditions of John Charles Fremont, Volume 1, Travels From 1838 to 1844* (Urbana: University of Illinois Press, 1970), 202–03.

84. W. Raymond Wood and Thomas D. Thiessen, eds., *Early Fur Trade on the Northern Plains: Canadian Traders Among the Mandan and Hidatsa Indians, 1738–1818* (Norman: University of Oklahoma Press, 1985), 42–47. George Catlin wrote that on the plains and the upper Missouri "it becomes . . . almost [an] absolute necessity, for the white men who are Traders in these regions to connect themselves . . . to one or more of the most influential families in the tribe, which in a measure indentifies their interest with that of the nation, and enables them, with the influence of their new family connexions [sic], to carry on successfully their business transactions with them." George Catlin, *Letters and Notes on the Manners, Customs, and Condition of the North American Indians*, Vol. I (London: Tosswill and Myers, 1841), 120.

85. Keith Algier, "Robert Meldrum and the Crow Peltry Trade," *Montana, The Magazine of Western History* 36, no. 3 (Summer 1986): 36–47; Lewis H. Morgan, *Systems of Consanguinity and Affinity of the Human Family* (Oosterhout, The Netherlands: Anthropological Publications, 1970), 133, 186.

86. Thomas Fitzpatrick to Thomas H. Harvey in *Report of the Commissioner of Indian Affairs, 1847*. See also Janet Lecompte, *Pueblo, Hardscrabble, Greenhorn: Society on the High Plains, 1832-1856* (Norman: University of Oklahoma Press, 1978), 65–66.

87. LeRoy R. Hafen, "Elbridge Gerry, Colorado Pioneer," *Colorado Magazine* 29, no. 2 (April 1952): 137–49; Merrill J. Mattes, "Seth E. Ward," in *The Mountain Men and the Fur Trade of the Far West*, ed. LeRoy R. Hafen, Vol. 3 (Glendale, California: Arthur H. Clark Co., 1966), 356–84. For a record of Gerry's trading activities, including those with Ward and Guerrier and with John Simpson Smith, see his account books, 1854–60 in Elbridge Gerry Collection, Colorado State Historical Society.

88. Geminian Beauvais File, Nebraska State Historical Society.

89. Sarah Hively Joural, 5 May, 1863, Western History Collections, Denver Public Library.

90. John Mack Faragher, "Americans, Mexicans, Metis: A Community Approach to the Comparative Study of North American Frontiers," in *Under an Open Sky: Rethinking America's Western Past*, eds. William Cronon, George Miles, and Jay Gitlin (New York: W. W. Norton and Co., 1992), 90–109.

91. Merrill J. Mattes, "Seth E. Ward," in *The Mountain Men and the Fur Trade of the Far West*, ed. LeRoy R. Hafen, Vol. 3 (Glendale, California: Arthur H. Clark Co., 1966), 356–84. For one of Ward's enthusiastic endorsements of ranching, see Hiram Latham, *Trans-Missouri Stock Raising. The Pasture Lands of North America: Winter Grazing* (Denver: Fred A. Rosenstock and the Old West Publishing Co., 1962, reprint of 1871 edition), 22–23.

92. Percival G. Lowe, "P. G. Lowe's Journal of the Sumner Wagon Train," in *Relations with the Indians of the Plains, 1857–1861*, eds. LeRoy R. Hafen and Ann W. Hafen (Glendale, California: Arthur H. Clark Company, 1959), 71.

93. David Lavdender, *Bent's Fort* (Garden City, New York: Doubleday and Company, 1954), 174–76, 239, 301–02, 362; Quantrille D. McClung, *Carson-Bent-Boggs Geneaology* (Denver: Denver Public Library, 1962) and supplement, published in 1973.

94. The information in the next two paragraphs was gathered from the following sources: John W. Prowers file, FF 397, and Judge R. M. Moore file, FF 392, Charles W. Hurd Collection, Colorado State Historical Society; Quantrille D. McClung, *Carson-Bent-Boggs Geneaology* (Denver: Denver Public Library, 1962); Fred S. Bande, "Edmund Gasseau Guerrier: French Trader," *Chronicles of Oklahoma* 47, no. 4 (Winter 1969–70): 360–76; Cragin Notebooks, 3: 32, 34; 8: 43–44, 23: 27–28, Western History Collections, Denver Public Library; Mary Prowers Hudnall, "Early History of Bent County," *Colorado Magazine* 22, no. 6 (November 1945): 233–47; H. L. Lubers, "William Bent's Family and the Indians of the Plains," *Colorado Magazine* 13, no. 1 (January 1936): 19–22; Ida Ellen Rath, *The Rath Trail* (Wichita: McCormick-Armstrong, Co., Inc., 1961); Janet Lecompte, "John Poisal," in *The Mountain Men and the Fur Trade of the Far West*, ed. LeRoy R. Hafen, Vol. 6 (Glendale, California: Arthur H. Clark Company, 1968); Stan Hoig, *The Sand Creek Massacre* (Norman: University of Oklahoma Press, 1961); Stan Hoig, *The Western Odyssey of John Simpson Smith, Frontiersman, Trapper, Trader and Interpreter* (Glendale, California: A. H. Clark, 1974).

95. Sopris was interviewed by LeRoy Hafen. A copy of a portion of the interview, conducted on 28 January, 1930, is in Marcellin St. Vrain file, FF 406, Charles W. Hurd Collection, Colorado State Historical Collection. See also W. R. Sopris,

"My Grandmother, Mrs. Marcellin St. Vrain," *Colorado Magazine* 22, no. 1 (March 1945): 63–68; *The Trail* 8, no. 9 (February 1916): 25; William R. Sopris and Elizabeth Sopris File, Biographical Files, Colorado State Historical Society; Paul Augustus St. Vrain, *Genealogy [sic] of the Family of De Lassus and Saint Vrain* (Kirksville, Missouri, [s.n.], 1943).

96. Lucille Lemmon to Carolyn H. Taylor, 1 August, 1954, 4 August, 1954, 11 October, 29 October, 1954, 13 January, 1955, Bent-St. Vrain Papers, Western History Collection, University of Colorado Library.

Notes to Chapter 4

1. *Entertainment Weekly*, 20 August, 1993, 13; "Moviemakers Return to Boots and Saddles," *New York Times*, 3 May, 1993, B-1.

2. *The Wild West* (New York: Time-Life Books, 1993). The *Life* special issue on "The Wild West, Yesterday and Today" was that of 3 April, 1993.

3. "The Wild West!" special issue of *Architectural Digest*, June 1992.

4. "Denim Definition," *New York Times*, 12 January, 1993, B-1. The sociologist quoted is Fred Davis of the University of Southern California.

5. Cormac McCarthy, *All the Pretty Horses* (New York: Alfred Knopf, 1992).

6. Matthew Kreitman, "Free-Range Verse," London *Times Literary Supplement*, 26 February, 1993, 14.

7. Gail Gilchriest, *The Cowgirl Companion: Big Skies, Buckaroos, Honky Tonks, Lonesome Blues, and Other Glories of the True West*, with introduction by Dale Evans (New York: Hyperion Books, 1993); Gladiola Montana, *Never Ask a Man the Size of His Spread: A Cowgirl's Guide to Life* (Salt Lake City: Gibbs-Smith, 1993).

8. "Ninja Turtle Man Has a New Concept He Thinks Will Sell," *Wall Street Journal*, 7 October, 1992, A-1, A-8.

9. Emett C. Murphy, with Michael Snell, *The Genius of Sitting Bull: Thirteen Heroic Strategies for Today's Business Leaders* (Englewood Cliffs: Prentice Hall, 1993).

10. Yves Montand, with Herve Hamon and Patrick Rotman, *You See, I Haven't Forgotten*, trans. Jeremy Leggatt (New York: Knopf, 1992), 53, 55. On European fascination with western themes, see Ray Allen Billington, *Land of Savagery/Land of Promise: The European Image of the American Frontier in the Nineteenth Century* (New York: Norton, 1981), Rob Kroes, ed., *The American West As Seen by Europeans and Americans* (Amsterdam: Free University Press, 1989), Gerald D. Nash, "European Images of America: The West in Historical Perspective," and Julian Crandall Hollick, "The American West in the European Imagination," both in *Montana, The Magazine of Western History* 42, no. 2 (Spring 1992): 2–16, 17–20.

11. Quoted in Clifford P. Westermeier, "Cowboy Sexuality: An Historical No-No?" *Red River Valley Historical Review* 2, no. 1 (Spring 1975): 105.

12. The most ambitious study of the western myth is Richard Slotkin's trilogy: *Regeneration through Violence: The Mythology of the American Frontier, 1600–1860* (Middletown, Connecticut: Wesleyan University Press, 1973); *The Fatal Environment: The Myth of the Frontier in the Age of Industrialization, 1800–1890* (New York: Atheneum, 1985); *Gunfighter Nation: The Myth of the Frontier in*

Twentieth-Century America (New York: Atheneum, 1992). For examples of the influence of wider cultural and mythic influences on the western, see Bruce A. Rosenberg, *Custer and the Epic of Defeat* (University Park: Pennsylvania University Press, 1974), and Lynn White, Jr., "The Legacy of the Middle Ages in the American Wild West," *American West* 3 (Spring 1966): 72–79, 95.

13. In *West of Everything*, for instance, Jane Tompkins recently analyzed the genre from a feminist perspective and took as her dominant theme the construction of sexual identity: "What is most interesting about Westerns at this moment is their relation to gender. . . ." Appearing simultaneously was Robert Murray Davis's *Playing Cowboy*. Westerns, Davis argued, are about "how to act like a man," and their answers are generally "more comprehensible and certainly more attractive" than any provided by family, church, or society at large. Davis began his epilogue in praise of Robert Bly's *Iron John*. Jane Tompkins, *West of Everything: The Inner Life of Westerns* (New York: Oxford University Press, 1992), 17; Robert Murray Davis, *Playing Cowboys: Low Culture and High Art in the Western* (Norman: University of Oklahoma Press, 1992), xxiii.

14. Jack E. Carver, "The Western Phenomenon," *Western English World*, May 1993.

15. Andrew W. H. Malcolm, "New Trees for Yellowstone; New Perspective in Newark," *New York Times*, 15 October, 1991, A-16.

16. Eric Dardel, *L'Homme et La Terre: Nature de Realite Geographique* (Paris: Presses Universitaires de France, 1952), 56, quoted in E. Relph, *Place and Placelessness* (London: Pion Limited, 1976), 41.

17. Richard F. Burton, *The City of the Saints and Across the Rocky Mountains to California* (New York: Alfred A. Knopf, 1963). His trip up the Platte is covered on pp. 16–103. The quotation is on p. 44.

18. Thomas Fitzpatrick to A. Cumming, 19 November, 1853, *Report of the Commissioner of Indian Affairs, 1853*, 370; Walter B. Sloan, *History and Map of Kansas and Nebraska . . .* (Chicago: Robert Fergus, 1855), 28.

19. William Lockwood Diary, 18 June, 1866, quoted in transcript of Samuel Finley Blythe Diary, 1866, Nebraska Historical Society; Julia Archibald Holmes, *A Bloomer Girl on Pike's Peak, 1858*, ed. Agnes Wright Spring (Denver: Denver Public Library, 1949), 15; Helen Stewart Diary, 1 May, 1853, Lane County Historical Society, Eugene, Oregon.

20. Ralph H. Pickett, "Friedrich von Holstein's Hunting Trips, 1865–1866," *Kansas Historical Quarterly* 32, no. 3 (Autumn 1966): 322.

21. John S. Fisher, *A Builder of the West: The Life of General William Jackson Palmer* (Caldwell, Idaho: The Caxton Printers, Ltd., 1939), 170–71.

22. Fisher, *Builder of the West*, 163–64, 202.

23. Mary Magdalene Bower Brulport Diary, 11 July, 16, 24, 26–30 August, 1877, Kansas State Historical Society.

24. Denis Cosgrove and Stephen Daniels, eds., *The Iconography of Landscape: Essays on the Symbolic Representation, Design, and Use of Past Environments* (Cambridge: Cambridge University Press), 318; Donald W. Meinig, *The Shaping of America: A Geographical Perspective on 500 Years of History* (New Haven: Yale University Press, 1986), and Donald W. Meinig, ed., *The Interpretation of Ordinary Landscapes: Geographical Essays* (New York: Oxford University Press, 1979); Edward

Relph, *Place and Placelessness* (London: Pion, 1976) and *Rational Landscapes and Humanistic Geography* (London: Croom Helm, and Totowa, New Jersey: Barnes & Noble, 1981); Douglas C. D. Pocock, ed., *Humanistic Geography and Literature: Essays on the Experience of Place* (London: Croom Helm, and Totowa, New Jersey: Barnes & Noble, 1981); Fred Lukerman, "Geography as a Formal Intellectual Discipline and the Way in Which It Contributes to Human Knowledge," *Canadian Geographer* 8: 167–72; Yi-Fu Tuan, *Space and Place: The Perspective of Experience* (Minneapolis: University of Minnesota Press, 1977), *Topophilia: A Study of Environmental Perception, Attitudes, and Values* (Englewood Cliffs: Prentice-Hall, 1974), and *Landscapes of Fear* (New York: Pantheon Books, 1979).

25. Ian Frazier, *Great Plains* (New York: Farrar, Straus, Girous, 1989); Gretel Ehrlich, *The Solace of Open Spaces* (New York: Viking Penguin, 1985); Merrill Gilfillan, *Magpie Rising: Sketches From the Great Plains* (Boulder: Pruett Publishing Co., 1988, and New York: Vintage Books, 1988); Dayton Duncan, *Miles From Nowhere: Tales From America's Contemporary Frontier* (New York: Viking Penguin, 1993); Pete Davis, *Storm Country: A Journey Through the Heart of America* (New York: Random House, 1992); Kathleen Norris, *Dakota: A Spiritual Geography* (New York: Ticknor and Fields, 1993). The quote from Frazier, *Great Plains* is on p. 15.

26. John W. Reps, *Cities of the American West: A History of Frontier Urban Planning* (Princeton: Princeton University Press, 1979) and *Town Planning in Frontier America* (Princeton: Princeton University Press, 1969). I am referring here to the earliest east-to-west settlement of the plains. Two recent works have emphasized the innovative influence of western cities, especially in the twentieth century and on the Pacific coast: John M. Findlay, *Magic Lands: Western Cityscapes and American Culture after 1940* (Berkeley: University of California Press, 1992), and Mike Davis, *City of Quartz: Excavating the Future in Los Angeles* (New York: Vintage Books, 1992).

27. Larry McMurtry, *The Last Picture Show* (New York: Dial Press, 1966), *Horseman, Pass By* (New York: Harpers, 1961), *Lonesome Dove: A Novel* (New York: Simon and Schuster, 1985), and *Buffalo Girls: A Novel* (New York: Simon and Schuster, 1990); Thomas Berger, *Little Big Man* (New York: Dial Press, 1964).

28. Gilfallin, *Magpie Rising*, 113; Norris, *Dakota*, 3; Ehrlich, *Solace of Open Spaces*, 15, 37.

29. Gary Snyder, *The Practice of the Wild: Essays* (San Francisco: North Point Press, 1990), 14.

30. Maurice Sendak, *Where the Wild Things Are* (New York: Harper and Row, 1963).

31. Richard West Sellars, "Manipulating Nature's Paradise: National Park Management Under Stephen T. Mather, 1916–1929," *Montana, The Magazine of Western History* 43, no. 2 (Spring 1993): 2–13.

32. Kerwin L. Klein, "Frontier Products: Tourism, Consumerism, and the Southwestern Public Lands, 1890–1990," *Pacific Historical Review* (1993): 43–44.

33. Mark David Spence, "Creating an American Wilderness: The Ideal of Preservation and the Dispossession of Native America," paper in possession of the author. Spence is currently working on a dissertation on this topic at the University of California, Los Angeles.

34. Klein, "Tourism, Consumerism, and the Southwestern Public Lands," 42.

35. Duncan, *Miles From Nowhere*, 91.

36. A recent article follows the business of rancher D. L. Taylor near Moab, Utah. Stymied by declining beef prices and poor grass, Taylor began charging tourists to work on his ranch and "act out their cowboy fantasies on his property." His fortunes turned around dramatically. "I don't really like doing it," he commented, "but it sure pays." *New York Times*, 18 September, 1994, 1, 15.

37. Roderick Nash, *Wilderness and the American Mind* (New Haven: Yale University Press, 1973), 271.

38. "Camping Catalogs Can Help Turn the Wild Into the Mild," *Denver Post*, 6 July, 1994, B-1.

39. Kathleen Meyer, *How To Shit in the Woods: An Environmentally Sound Approach to a Lost Art* (Berkeley: Ten Speed Press, 1989).

40. The recent surge in interest in Native American literature has brought with it a large and growing body of scholarly work on the many aspects of that literature, including autobiography and oral tradition. The curious ought to start with a relatively brief but excellent survey and bibliography: A. LaVonne Brown Ruoff, *American Indian Literatures: an Introduction Bibliographic Review and Selected Bibliography* (New York: Modern Language Association, 1990). For a selection of recent works, see Kenneth Lincoln, *Native American Renaissance* (Berkeley: University of California Press, 1983); Louis Owens, *Other Destinies: Understanding the American Indian Novel* (Norman: University of Oklahoma Press, 1992); Karl Kroeber, *Traditional Literatures of the American Indian: Texts and Interpretations* (Lincoln: University of Nebraska Press, 1981); Gerald Vizenor, ed., *Narrative Chance: Postmodern Discourse on Native American Indian Literatures* (Albuquerque: University of New Mexico Press, 1980); Andrew Wiget, ed., *Critical Essays on Native American Literature* (Boston: Hall, 1985); Kenneth Lincoln, *Indi'n Humor: Bicultural Play in Native America* (New York: Oxford University Press, 1993); Jarold Ramsey, *Reading the Fire: Essays in the Traditional Indian Literatures of the Far West* (Lincoln: University of Nebraska Press, 1983); Joseph Bruchac, III, ed., *Survival This Way: Interviews with American Indian Poets* (Tucson: University of Arizona Press, 1987); Arnold Krupat, *For Those Who Come After: A Study of Native American Autobiography* (Berkeley: University of California Press, 1985); Brian Swann and Arnold Krupat, eds., *I Tell You Now: Autobiographical Essays by Native American Writers* (Lincoln: University of Nebraksa Press, 1987); Brian Swann and Arnold Krupat, eds., *Recovering the Word: Essays on Native American Literature* (Berkeley: University of California Press, 1987); Brian Swann, ed., *Smoothing the Ground: Essays on Native American Oral Literature* (Berkeley: University of California Press, 1983).

41. N. Scott Momaday, *The Way to Rainy Mountain* (Albuquerque: University of New Mexico Press, 1969), 4.

42. On Cheyenne and Kiowa cosmology and mythic traditions and narratives, see George A. Dorsey, *The Cheyenne* (Chicago: Field Museum, 1905), Field Columbia Museum Publication 99 & 103, Anthropological Series, Vol. 9, no. 1–2; Karl. H. Schlesier, *The Wolves of Heaven: Cheyenne Shamanism, Ceremonies, and Prehistoric Origins* (Norman: University of Oklahoma Press, 1987); Mildred P.

Mayhall, *The Kiowas* (Norman: University of Oklahoma Press, 1952); Elsie Clews Parsons, *Kiowa Tales* (New York: G. E. Stechert and Co., 1929), Memoirs of the American Folk-Lore Society, Vol. 22; George B. Grinnell, *By Cheyenne Campfires* (New Haven: Yale University Press, 1926); Momaday, *Way to Rainy Mountain*; John Stands-in-Timber and Margot Liberty, *Cheyenne Memories* (New Haven: Yale University Press, 1967); Father John Peter Powell, *People of the Sacred Mountain: A History of the Northern Cheyenne Chiefs and Warrior Societies* (San Francisco: Harper and Row, 1981) and *Sweet Medicine: The Continuing Role of the Sacred Arrows, the Sun Dance, and the Sacred Buffalo Hat in Northern Cheyenne History* (Norman: University of Oklahoma Press, 1969).

43. Alice Marriott and Carol K. Rachlin, *Plains Indian Mythology* (New York: Thomas Y. Crowell Company, 1975), 96–97.

44. Keith H. Basso, *Western Apache Language and Culture: Essays in Linguistic Anthropology* (Tucson: University of Arizona Press, 1990), 122–40.

45. William W. Bevis, *Ten Tough Trips: Montana Writers and the West* (Seattle: University of Washington Press, 1990), 97.

46. Linda Hogan, *Mean Spirit* (New York: Atheneum, 1990).

47. James Welch, *Winter in the Blood* (New York: Harper and Row, 1974), 1. This point is well made by William Bevis in *Ten Tough Trips*, 120.

48. For a few examples from the central and southern plains, see Oello Ingraham Martin, "Father Came West," Frank Albert Waugh, "Pioneering in Kansas," Augusta Dodge Thomas, "Prairie Children," the Jessie K. Snell Collection, and reminiscences of George Hockderffer, Vallee McKee, Mary E. Murphy, Wallace A. Wood, Olive J. L. Bascom, and Effie Wood Conwell, all in the Kansas State Historical Society and the Edna Matthews Clifton, Ralla Banta Pinkerton, and Lydia Mooar reminiscences in the Southwest Collection, Texas Tech University. The Southwest Collection also houses extensive taped oral histories, some transcribed, from the southern plains.

49. Sanora Babb, *An Owl on Every Post* (New York: New American Library, 1972); Edward Everett Dale, *The Cross Timbers: Memories of a North Texas Boyhood* (Austin: University of Austin Press, 1966); Marquis James, *The Cherokee Strip: A Tale of an Oklahoma Boyhood* (New York: The Viking Press, 1960).

50. Mary Clearman Blew, *All but the Waltz: A Memoir of Five Generations in the Life of a Montana Family* (New York: Penguin Books, 1991); Ivan Doig, *This House of Sky: Landscapes of a Western Mind* (New York: Harcourt, Brace, Jovanovich, 1978); Teresa Jordan, *Riding the White Horse Home: A Western Family Album* (New York: Pantheon Books, 1993); Cyra McFadden, *Rain or Shine* (New York: Random House, 1986); William Kittredge, *Hole in the Sky: A Memoir* (New York: Alfred A. Knopf, 1992); Sallie Tisdale, *Stepping Westward: The Long Search for Home in the Pacific Northwest* (New York: Henry Holt, 1991); Terry Tempest Williams, *Refuge: An Unnatural History of Family and Place* (New York: Pantheon Books, 1991).

51. James Galvin, *The Meadow* (New York: Henry Holt and Company, 1992); Linda Hasselstrom, *Going Over East: Reflections of a Woman Rancher* (Golden, Colorado: Fulcrum Publishing, 1987).

52. William Kittredge, *Owning it All: Essays* (St. Paul: Graywolf Press, 1987), *The Van Gogh Field and Other Stories* (Columbia: University of Missouri Press, 1978),

We Are Not in This Together: Stories (Port Townsend, Washington: Graywolf
Press, 1984); Ivan Doig, *Dancing at the Rascal Fair* (New York: Atheneum, 1987),
English Creek (New York: Atheneum, 1984), and *Ride With Me, Mariah Montana*
(New York: Penguin, 1991); *Winter Brothers: A Season at the Edge of America*
(New York: Harcourt, Brace, Jovanovich, 1980); Mary Clearman Blew, *Lambing
Out, and Other Stories* (Columbia: University of Missouri Press, 1977) and
Runaway: A Collection of Stories (Lewiston: Confluence Press, 1990).

53. Terry Tempest Williams, *Pieces of White Shell: A Journey to Navajoland* (Albuquerque: University of New Mexico Press, 1987; originally published 1984), 3–5.

54. Noel Perrin, "Forever Virgin: The American View of America," in *On Nature:
Nature, Landscape, and Natural History*, ed. Daniel Halpern(San Fancisco: North
Point Press, 1986), 14–15.

55. Edward Abbey, *Desert Solitaire: A Season in the Wilderness* (New York: Ballantine
Books, 1971), 6.

56. Among Nabhan's works, see *The Desert Smells Like Rain: A Naturalist in Papago
Indian Country* (San Francisco: North Point Press, 1982), *Enduring Seeds: Native
American Agriculture and Wild Plant Conservation* (San Francisco: North Point
Press, 1989), and *Gathering the Desert* (Tucson: University of Arizona Press,
1985). On the gathering of saguaro fruit, see *The Desert Smells Like Rain*, 25–38.

57. Abbey, *Desert Solitaire*, xii.

58. Gary H. Holthaus, *Circling Back* (Salt Lake City: Peregrine Smith Books, 1984), 6.

59. Ron Hansen, *Nebraska: Stories* (New York: Atlantic Monthly Press, 1989), 191–93.

60. The term is taken from Bevis's essay on D'arcy McNickle in *Ten Tough Trips*, 92–108.

61. Wallace Stegner, "Finding the Place: A Migrant Childhood," in *Where the
Bluebird Sings to the Lemonade Springs: Living and Writing in the West* (New York:
Random House, 1992), 4, 19.

62. Donald Worster, "New West, True West: Interpreting the Region's History,"
Western Historical Quarterly 18, no. 3 (April 1987): 146.

63. On Webb, see Gregory M. Tobin, *The Making of a History: Walter Prescott Webb
and "The Great Plains"* (Austin: University of Texas Press, 1976); Necah Stewart
Furman, *Walter Prescott Webb: His Life and Impact* (Albuquerque: University of
New Mexico Press, 1976); Elliott West, "Walter Prescott Webb and the Search
for the West," in *Writing Western History: Essays on Major Western Historians*, ed.
Richard W. Etulain (Albuquerque: University of New Mexico Press, 1991), 167–
91; Walter Rundell, Jr., "Walter Prescott Webb: Product of Environment,"
Arizona and the West 5 (Spring 1963): 4–28.

64. Walter Prescott Webb, *The Great Plains* (Boston: Ginn and Company, 1931).

65. Walter Prescott Webb, "History as High Adventure," in *An Honest Preface and Other
Essays*, ed. Joe B. Frantz (Boston: Houghton Mifflin Co., 1959), 194–216. The
address that came closest to Webb's in its personal focus was Samuel Eliot Morison's
"Faith of a Historian," *American Historical Review* 56, no. 2 (January 1951): 261–75.

66. Frederick Turner, "Introduction," in Tom Turner, *Sierra Club: 100 Years of
Protecting Nature* (New York: Harry N. Abrams, Inc., 1991), 25.

67. For a recent book on the perils of treating parks as wildernesses, see Karl Hess, Jr.,
Rocky Times in Rocky Mountain National Park: An Unnatural History (Niwot:
University of Colorado, 1993).

68. "Tribes, Parks Trying to Settle Differences," *Denver Post*, 1 August, 1893, C-10. There is, of course, one great exception to the traditional approach of national parks: Colorado's Mesa Verde. Stewart Udall, former Secretary of the Interior, has suggested creating an Anasazi National Park, giving Canyon de Chelly National Monument back to the Navajos, and making another Indian-run national park out of Monument Valley. "Indian U.S. Parks Proposed by Udall," *Denver Post*, 6 August, 1991, B-3. The tourist appeal in effect would be inverted, with vacationers drawn to these western lands by their antiquity and their long, continuous history.

69. For the fullest account of the Poppers, their ideas, and responses to them, see Anne Matthews, *Where the Buffalo Roam* (New York: Grove Press, 1992).

70. "Where Many Elderly Live, Signs of the Future," *New York Times*, 7 March, 1993, A-12. Smith County, Kansas, has the highest percentage in the nation, just over five percent.

71. Matthews, *Where the Buffalo Roam*, 12–13, 122–23.

72. Ibid., 93, 54.

73. Barry Lopez, *Arctic Dreams: Imagination and Desire in a Northern Landscape* (New York: Charles Scribner's Sons, 1986), 176.

Bibliography

Unpublished Primary Sources

Barnitz, Alfred. Papers. Beinecke Library, Yale University, New Haven, Connecticut.

Beauvais, Geminian. File. Nebraska Historical Society, Lincoln, Nebraska.

Bell, Josias. "Sketches of a Journey From Smithsboro, Pa., to California and Return." Manuscript journal. Also typescript: "The Original Manuscript Diary of Josias Bell Detailing His Overland Experiences on the Santa Fe Trail . . . , 1841–1844." Newberry Library, Chicago, Illinois.

Bent-Hyde Papers. Western History Collections. University of Colorado Library, Boulder, Colorado.

Bent, George. Letters. Denver Public Library, Denver, Colorado.

———. Papers. Colorado State Historical Society, Denver, Colorado.

Blondeau, Barnard Silvaeir. Account Books, 1858–1867. Nebraska Historical Society, Lincoln, Nebraska.

Brainard, David. Journal. 1849. State Historical Society of Wisconsin, Madison, Wisconsin.

Bratt, John. Papers. Nebraska Historical Society, Lincoln, Nebraska.

Brooks, Alden. "Grand Trip Across the Plains." Manuscript journal. 1859. Newberry Library, Chicago, Illinois.

Brown, J. Robert. "Journal of a Trip Across the Plains of the U.S. from Mo. to Cal." Manuscript journal. Photocopy of original at Yale. Ayer Collection, 113. Newberry Library, Chicago, Illinois.

Brulport, Mary Magdalene Bower. Diary. 1877–1878. Kansas State Historical Society, Topeka, Kansas.

Clark, Calvin Perry. Diary. 1859. From Plano, Ill. to Pikes Peak. Denver Public Library, Denver, Colorado.

County Organizational Censuses. 1867–1887. Kansas State Historical Soceity, Topeka, Kansas.

Cozad, Justus L. Reminiscence. Handwritten. Nebraska Historical Society, Lincoln, Nebraska.

Cragin Notebooks. Denver Public Library, Denver, Colorado.

Faulkner, Harry. Diary. 1859. Denver Public Library, Denver, Colorado.

Fort Laramie. Sutler's books. 1858–1867. Denver Public Library, Denver, Colorado.

Fort Lyon. Papers. 1868–1889. Colorado State Historical Society, Denver, Colorado.

General Land Office. Survey reports, plats, field notes, for Colorado, Kansas. Bureau of Land Management Records. Denver, Colorado (for Colorado) and Santa Fe, New Mexico (for Kansas).

Gerry, Elbridge. Collection. 1854–1860. Colorado State Historical Society, Denver, Colorado.

Harvey, Augustus Ford. Journal. Copy of transcript. 1858. Kansas State Historical Society, Topeka, Kansas.

Hively, Sarah. Journal. 1863. Denver Public Library, Denver, Colorado.

Hurd, Charles W. Collection. Colorado State Historical Society, Denver, Colorado.

James Clyman. Memorandum book and diary. 1840. Manuscripts. Graff Collection. Newberry Library, Chicago, Illinois.

Lincoln, Lewis A. Papers. Denver Public Library, Denver, Colorado.

Mather, Colonel Thomas. "Diary of Colonel Thomas Mather, Santa Fe Road Commissioner." Typescript. Newberry Library, Chicago, Illinois.

McDonald, Charles. Papers. Correspondence and ledger books. 1862–1878. Nebraska State Historical Society, Lincoln, Nebraska.

Miller, Paul E. Papers. Colorado State Historical Society, Denver, Colorado.

Penniston and Miller General Store. Day Books, 1867–1871. Nebraska State Historical Society, Lincoln, Nebraska.

"The Plum Creek Area" and copy of military orders from post at Plum Creek. 1864–1865. Plum Creek File. Nebraska Historical Society, Lincoln, Nebraska.

Prowers, John Wesley. Collection. Colorado State Historical Society, Denver, Colorado.

Rogers, Henry Clay. Diary. Typescript. 1863. Nebraska State Historical Society, Lincoln, Nebraska.

Scott J. Anthony. Papers. Colorado State Historical Society, Denver, Colorado.

Sopris, William R. and Elizabeth Sopris file, Biographical Files, Colorado State Historical Society, Denver, Colorado.

Souders, J. A. Letter. To "Cousin Cora." 15 August, 1868. Copy. Kansas State Historical Society, Topeka, Kansas.

Tappan, Samuel F. Papers. Colorado State Historical Society, Denver, Colorado.

Webb, James Josiah. Papers. Missouri Historical Society, St. Louis, Missouri.

WPA Papers. Denver Public Library, Denver, Colorado.

Wynkoop, Edward W. Papers. Colorado State Historical Society, Denver, Colorado.

Published Primary Sources

Abbott, E. C. "Teddy Blue", and Helena Huntington Smith, *We Pointed Them North: Recollections of a Cowpuncher*. Chicago: The Lakeside Press; R. R. Donnelly and Sons, 1991.

Abel, Annie Heloise, ed. *Tabeau's Narrative of Loisel's Expedition to the Upper Missouri*. Trans. Rose Abel Wright. Norman: University of Oklahoma Press, 1939.

Bibliography 209

Abert, J. W. *Journal of Lieutenant J. W. Abert from Bent's Fort to St. Louis, in 1845.* U.S. Senate, 29th Cong., 1st sess., S. Doc. 438.

Babb, Sanora. *An Owl on Every Post.* New York: New American Library, 1972.

Baird, J. C. "First Gold Find in the Mountains." *The Trail* 14, no. 9 (February 1922): 3–10.

Barry, J. Nielson. "An Excerpt From the Journal of E. Willard Smith, 1839–1840." *Annals of Wyoming* 15, no. 3 (July 1943): 287–97.

Beadle, J. H. *The Undeveloped West; or, Five Years in the Territories . . .* Philadelphia: National Publishing Co., 1873.

Beauregard, Mrs. H. T., trans. "Journal of Jean Baptiste Trudeau Among the Arikara Indians in 1795." *Missouri Historical Society Collections* 4 (1912–1923): 9–48.

Bidwell, John. *A Journey to California, 1841: The First Emigrant Party to California by Wagon Train.* Berkeley: Friends of the Bancroft Library, 1964.

Bieber, Ralph P., ed. "Diary of a Journey to the Pike's Peak Gold Mines in 1859." *Mississippi Valley Historical Review* 14, no. 3 (December 1927): 360–78.

Bieber, Ralph P., ed. *Marching With the Army of the West, 1846–1848.* Glendale: Arthur H. Clark Company, 1936.

Bivens, Venola Lewis, ed. "The Diary of Luna E. Warner, a Kansas Teenager of the Early 1870s." *Kansas Historical Quarterly* 35, nos. 3, 4 (Autumn and Winter, 1969): 276–311, 411–441.

Bratt, John. *Trails of Yesterday.* Lincoln: The University Publishing Company, 1921.

Brown, George W. "Life and Adventures of George W. Brown." Kansas State Historical Society *Collections* 17 (1927–28): 98–134.

Bryant, Edwin. *What I Saw in California: Being the Journal of a Tour . . . in the Years 1846, 1847.* London: Richard Bentley, 1849.

Burton, Richard. *The Look of the West, 1860: Across the Plains to California.* Lincoln: University of Nebraska Press, n.d. Reprint of Burton's *The City of the Saints and Across the Rocky Mountains to California.* London: Longman, Green, Longman and Roberts, 1862.

Catlin, George. *Letters and Notes on the Manners, Customs, and Condition of the North American Indians,* Vol. I. London: Tosswill and Myers, 1841.

Clappe, Louise Amelia Knapp. *The Shirley Letters from California Mines in 1851–52.* San Francisco: T. C. Russell, 1922.

Clark, Olive A. "Early Days Along the Solomon Valley." Kansas State Historical Society *Collections* 17 (1927–28): 719–30.

Conard, Howard Louis. *Uncle Dick Wootton: The Pioneer Frontiersman of the Rocky Mountain Region.* Ed. Milo Milton Quaife. Chicago: Lakeside Press; R. R. Donnelley and Sons Company, 1957.

Conway, Cornelius. *The Utah Expedition; Containing a General Account of the Mormon Campaign, With Incidents of Travel on the Plains. . . . By a Wagon-Master of the Expedition.* Cincinnati: Safety Fund Reporter, 1858.

Cook, John R. *The Border and the Buffalo, An Untold Story of the Southwest Plains.* Topeka: Crane and Company, 1907.

Custer, Elizabeth B. *Following the Guidon.* Norman: University of Oklahoma Press, 1966.

Dale, Edward Everett. *The Cross Timbers: Memories of a North Texas Boyhood.* Austin: University of Texas Press, 1966.

Dodge, Colonel Henry. *Report of the Secretary of War . . . Journal of the March of a Detachment of Dragoons, Under the Command of Colonel Dodge, During the summer of 1835.* U.S. Congress, 24th Cong., 1st sess., H. E. Doc. 181.

Dodge, Richard Irving. *The Hunting Grounds of the Great West. A Description of the Plains, Game, and Indians of the Great North American Desert.* London: Chatto and Windus, 1877.

————. *Our Wild Indians: Thirty-three Years' Personal Experience Among the Red Men of the Great West.* Hartford: A. D. Worthington and Co., 1883.

Emory, W. H. *Lieutenant Emory Reports: A Reprint of Lieutenant W. H. Emory's Notes of a Military Reconnoissance* [sic]. Albuquerque: University of New Mexico Press, 1951.

Farnham, Thomas J. *Travels in the Great Western Prairies, The Anahuac and the Rocky Mountains, and in the Oregon Territory.* London: Richard Bentley, 1843.

Ferguson, Philip Gooch. "Diary of Philip Gooch Ferguson, 1847–1848." In Bieber, *Marching with the Army of the West.*

"Field Notes by Joseph C. Brown, United States Surveying Expedition, 1825–1827." *Eighteenth Biennial Report of the Board of Directors of the Kansas State Historical Society.* Topeka: State Printing Office, 1913.

Fouquet, L. C. "Buffalo Days." Kansas State Historical Society *Collections* 16 (1923–25): 341–52.

Fowler, Jacob. *The Journal of Jacob Fowler.* Ed. Elliott Coues. Lincoln: University of Nebraska Press, 1970.

Fulton, William. "Freighting and Staging in Early Days." *Proceedings and Collections of the Nebraska State Historical Society.* Series II, vol. V (1902): 261–64.

Galvin, John, ed. *Western America in 1846–1847: The Original Travel Diary of Lieutenant J. W. Abert, Who Mapped New Mexico for the United States Army.* San Francisco: John Howell, 1966.

Gardner, Hamilton, ed. "March of the 2nd Dragoons: Report of Lieutenant Colonel Philip St. George Cooke on the March of the 2nd Dragoons from Fort Leavenworth to Fort Bridger in 1857." *Annals of Wyoming* 27, no. 1 (April 1955): 43–60.

Garrard, Lewis H. *Wah-To-Yah and the Taos Trail.* Glendale: Arthur H. Clark Company, 1938.

Gass, Patrick. *A Journal of the Voyages and Travels of the Corps of Discovery, Under the Command of Capt. Lewis and Capt. Clarke* [sic] *of the Army of the United States. . . .* Minneapolis: Ross & Haines, Inc., 1958.

Gibson, George Rutledge. *Journal of a Soldier Under Kearny and Doniphan, 1846–47.* Ed. Ralph P. Bieber. Glendale: Arthur H. Clark Company, 1935.

Greene, J. Evarts. *The Santa Fe Trade: Its Route and Character.* Worcester, Mass: Charles Hamilton, 1893.

Hadley, C.B. "The Plains War in 1865." Nebraska State Historical Collections *Proceedings and Collections* II, no. 5 (1902): 273–78.

Hafen, LeRoy R., ed. *Colorado Gold Rush: Contemporary Letters and Reports, 1858–1859.* Glendale, California: Arthur H. Clark Co., 1941.

————. *Overland Routes to the Gold Fields, 1859, from Contemporary Diaries.* Glendale: Arthur H. Clark Company, 1942.

Hafen, Leroy R. and Ann W. Hafen, eds. *Rufus B. Sage, His Letters and Papers, 1836–1847* . . . Glendale: Arthur H. Clark Company, 1956.

———. *Relations with the Indians of the Plains, 1857–1861*. Glendale: Arthur H. Clark Company, 1959.

Hendricks, Carl Ludvig. "Recollections of a Swedish Buffalo Hunter." *Swedish Pioneer Historical Quarterly* 32:, no. 3 (July 1981): 190–204.

Holmes, Julia Archibald. *A Bloomer Girl on Pike's Peak, 1858*. Ed. Agnes Wright Spring. Denver: Denver Public Library, 1949.

Hopper, Silas L. "Diary Kept by Silas L. Hopper, Blandinsville, Illinois, 20 April, 1863." *Annals of Wyoming* 3, no. 2 (October 1925): 117–26.

Hulbert, Archer Butler, ed. *Southwest on the Turquoise Trail: The First Diaries on the Road to Santa Fe*. Colorado Springs: The Stewart Commission of Colorado College and Denver Public Library, 1933.

Hunt, Mrs. A. C. "Diary of Mrs. A. C. Hunt, 1859." *Colorado Magazine* 21, no. 5 (September 1944): 161–70.

Hunter, William W. *Missouri '49er: The Journal of William W. Hunter on the Southern Gold Trail*. Ed. David P. Robrock. Albuquerque: University of New Mexico Press, 1992.

Jackson, Donald, ed. *Journals of Zebulon Montgomery Pike, With Letters and Related Documents*. Norman: University of Oklahoma Press, 1966.

Jackson, Donald and Mary Lee Spence. *The Expeditions of John Charles Fremont. Volume 1, Travels from 1838 to 1844*. Urbana: University of Illinois Press, 1970.

James, Edwin. *Account of an Expedition From Pittsburgh to the Rocky Mountains, Performed in the Years 1819*. Philadelphia: H. C. Carey and I. Lea, 1823.

James, Marquis. *The Cherokee Strip: A Tale of an Oklahoma Boyhood*. New York: Viking Press, 1960.

"J.E.B. Stuart's Official Journal." In Hafen and Hafen, *Relations With the Plains Indians*. 217–244.

Kaiser, Leo M. and Priscilla Knuth, eds. "From Ithaca to Clatsop Plains: Miss Ketcham's Journal of Travel." *Oregon Historical Quarterly* 62, nos. 3–4 (September and December 1961): 237–87, 337–402.

Kellogg, Daniel. "Across the Plains in 1858." *The Trail* 5, no. 7 (December 1912): 5–12.

Latham, Dr. Hiram. *Trans-Missouri Stock Raising. The Pasture Lands of North America: Winter Grazing*. Denver: Fred A. Rosenstock and Old West Publishing Co., 1962.

"Letter of Thomas S. Twiss, Indian Agent at Deer Creek, U.S. Indian Agency on the Upper Platte." *Annals of Wyoming* 17, no. 2 (July 1945): 148–52.

Lewis, J. "Diary of a Pike's Peak Gold Seeker in 1860." *Colorado Magazine* 14, no. 6 (November 1937): 201–19, 15, no. 1 (January 1938): 20–33.

Lindsey, David, ed. "The Journal of an 1859 Pike's Peak Gold Seeker." *Kansas Historical Quarterly* 22, no. 4 (Winter 1956): 321–41.

Lowe, Percival G. *Five Years a Dragoon ('49 to '54) and Other Adventures on the Great Plains*. Kansas City, Missouri: Franklin Hudson Publishing Co., 1906.

Lyon, Herman Robert[?]. "Freighting in the 60s." *Proceedings and Collections of the Nebraska State Historical Society*. Series II, Vol. V (1902): 265–72.

Magoffin, Susan Shelby. *Down the Santa Fe Trail and Into Mexico. The Diary of Susan Shelby Magoffin, 1846–1847*. New Haven: Yale University Press, 1926.

Majors, Alexander. *Seventy Years on the Frontier. Alexander Majors' Memoirs of a Lifetime on the Border.* Minneapolis: Ross & Haines, Inc., 1965.

Marmaduke, M. M. "Santa Fe Trail. M. M. Marmaduke Journal." *Missouri Historical Review* 6, no. 1 (October 1911): 3–10.

Mattes, Merrill J., ed. "Capt. L. C. Easton's Report: Fort Laramie to Fort Leavenworth Via Republican River in 1849." *Kansas Historical Quarterly* 20, no. 6 (May 1853): 392–416.

McCoy, Joseph G. *Historic Sketches of the Cattle Trade of the West and Southwest.* Southwest Historical Series. Ed. Ralph P. Bieber. Vol. 7. Glendale: Arthur H. Clark Company, 1940.

Menefee, Arthur M. "Arthur M. Menefee's Travels Across the Plains, 1857." *Nevada Historical Society Quarterly* 9, no. 1 (Spring 1966): 3–28.

Messiter, Charles Alston. *Sport and Adventures Among the North-American Indians.* London: R. H. Porter, 1890.

Morgan, Lewis Henry. *The Indian Journals, 1859–62.* Ann Arbor: University of Michigan Press, 1959.

Napton, W. B. *Over the Santa Fe Trail, 1857.* Kansas City: Franklin Hudson, 1905.

Palmer, Joel. *Journal of Travels Over the Rocky Mountains, To the Mouth of the Columbia River; Made During the Years 1845 and 1846. . . .* Cincinnati: J.A. and U. P. James, 1847.

Parker, Wilbur Fiske. "'The Glorious Orb of Day Has Rose': A Diary of the Smoky Hill Route to Pike's Peak, 1858." Ed. Norman Lavers, *The Magazine of Western History* 36, no. 2 (Spring 1986): 50–61.

Pickett, Ralph H. "Friedrich von Holstein's Hunting Trips, 1865–1866." *Kansas Historical Quararterly* 32, no. 3 (Autumn 1966): 314–24.

Pierce, James H. "The First Prospecting of Colorado. Who Did It and What Lead [sic] to It." *The Trail* Part 1: 7, no. 5 (October 1914): 5–11.

———. "With the Green Russell Party." *The Trail* 13, no. 12 (May 1921): 5–14, 14, no. 1 ((June 1921): 5, no. 13.

Powell, Father John Peter. *People of the Sacred Mountain: A History of the Northern Cheyenne Chiefs and Warrior Societies.* San Francisco: Harper and Row, 1981.

Powell, H. M. T. *The Santa Fe Trail to California, 1849–1852. The Journal and Drawings of H. M. T. Powell.* Ed. Douglas S. Watson. San Francisco: The Book Club of California, 1931.

Riley, Paul D., ed. "A Winter on the Plains, 1870–1871—The Memoirs of Lawson Cooke." *Kansas Historical Quarterly* 37, no. 1 (Spring 1971): 33–40.

Rolfe, D. P. "Overland Freighting From Nebraska City." *Proceedings and Collections of the Nebraska State Historical Society.* Series II, vol. V (1902): 279–93.

Settle, Raymond W., ed. *The March of the Mounted Riflemen: First United States Military Expedition to Travel the full length of the Oregon Trail from Fort Leavenworth to Fort Vancouver, May to October 1849, as Recorded in the Journals of Major Osbourne Cross and George Gibbs and the Official Report of Colonel Loring.* Glendale: Arthur H. Clark Company, 1940.

Sloan, Walter B. *History and Map of Kansas and Nebraska: Describing Soil, Climate, Rivers, Prairies, Mounds, Forests, Minerals, Roads, Cities, Villages, Inhabitants, and Such Other Subjects as Relates to that Region—Politics Excepted.* Chicago: Robert Fergus, 1855.

Sloan, William K. "Autobiography of William K. Sloan, Western Pioneer." *Annals of Wyoming* 4, no. 1 (July 1926): 235–64.

Snell, Joseph W., ed. "Roughing It on Her Kansas Claim: The Diary of Abbie Bright, 1870–1871." *Kansas Historical Quarterly* 37, no. 3 (Autumn 1971): 233–68; 37, no. 4 (Winter 1971): 394–428.

Sopris, W. R. "My Grandmother, Mrs. Marcellin St. Vrain." *Colorado Magazine* 22, no. 1 (March 1945): 63–68.

Soule, George. "Pike's Peak, Valley of the Platte." *Western Reserve Chronicle* (September 21 1859): 2.

Stansbury, Howard. *An Expedition to the Valley of the Great Salt Lake of Utah.* . . . Philadelphia: Lippincott, Grambo and Co., 1855.

Steele, E. Dunsha. "In the Pike's Peak Gold Rush of 1859: Diary of E. Dunsha Steele." *Colorado Magazine* 29, no. 4 (October 1952): 299–309.

"Stock Raising on the Plains, 1870–71." *Annals of Wyoming* 17, no. 1 (January 1945): 55–63.

Toponce, Alexander. *Reminiscences of Alexander Toponce, Pioneer.* Salt Lake City: Century Printing Company, 1923.

Vox Buffalorem [pseud.] "Address. To the Hunters After the Ninety Days' Scout." *Dodge City Times,* 29 September, 1877. On sheet in John Cook, *The Border and the Buffalo.*

Waters, Lydia Milner. "Account of a Trip Across the Plains in 1855." *Quarterly of the Society of California Pioneers* 6, no. 2 (June 1929): 59–79.

Wells, Rev. Charles Wesley. *A Frontier Life, Being a Description of My Experience on the Frontier the First Forty-Two Years of My Life.* Cincinnati: Press of Jennings and Pye, 1902.

Richard L. Wilson. *Short Ravelings From a Long Yarn, or, Camp and March Sketches, of the Santa Fe Trail.* Chicago: Geer and Wilson, 1847.

Wislizenus, A. *Memoir of a Tour to Northern Mexico, Connected with Col. Doniphan's Expedition, in 1846 and 1847.* Washington: Tippin and Streeper, 1848.

Wislizenus, F. A. *A Journey to the Rocky Mountains in the Year 1839.* St. Louis: Missouri Historical Society, 1912.

Secondary Historical Sources

Barry, Louise. "The Ranch at Walnut Creek Crossing." *Kansas Historical Quarterly* 37, no. 2 (Summer 1971): 121–47.

———. *The Beginning of the West: Annals of the Kansas Gateway to the American West.* Topeka: Kansas State Historical Society, 1972.

Bean, Lee L., Geraldine P. Mineau, and Douglas L. Anderton. *Fertility Change on the American Frontier: Adaptation and Innovation.* Berkeley: University of California Press, 1990.

Biggers, Don H. "On the Buffalo Range of Texas." *Frontier Times* 18, no. 8 (May 1941): 369–76.

Branch, E. Douglas. *The Hunting of the Buffalo.* New York: D. Appleton and Company, 1929.

Burlingame, Merrill G. "The Buffalo in Trade and Commerce." *North Dakota Historical Quarterly* 3, no. 4 (July 1929): 262–91.

Burroughs, Jean M. "The Last of the Buffalo Hunters. George Causey: Hunter, Trader, Rancher." *El Palacio* 80, no. 4 (Winter 1974): 15–21.

Butler, Anne M. *Daughters of Joy, Sisters of Misery: Prostitutes in the American West, 1865–90.* Urbana: University of Illinois Press, 1985.

Byers, William N. *Encyclopedia and Biography of Colorado.* Chicago: Century Publishing and Engraving Co., 1901.

Clarke, H. T. "Freighting—Denver and Black Hills." *Proceedings and Collections of the Nebraska State Historical Society.* Series II, vol. V (1902): 299–307.

Cohen, Felix S. *Handbook of Federal Indian Law, With Reference Tables and Index.* Washington, D.C.: Government Printing Office, 1942.

Cronon, William. "A Place for Stories: Nature, History, and Narrative." *Journal of American History* 78 (March 1992): 1347–76.

Cronon, William, George Miles, and Jay Gitlin, eds. *Under an Open Sky: Rethinking America's Western Past.* New York: W. W. Norton and Co., 1992.

Dykstra, Robert R. *The Cattle Towns.* New York: Alfred A. Knopf, 1968.

Ellsworth, Lincoln. *The Last Wild Buffalo Hunt.* New York: Privately Printed, 1916.

Etulain, Richard W., ed. *Writing Western History: Essays on Major Western Historians.* Albuquerque: University of New Mexico Press, 1991.

Fink, Deborah. *Agrarian Women: Wives and Mothers in Rural Nebraska, 1880–1940.* Chapel Hill: University of North Carolina Press, 1992.

Fisher, John S. *A Builder of the West: The Life of General William Jackson Palmer.* Caldwell, Idaho: The Caxton Printers, Ltd., 1939.

Flores, Dan. "Bison Ecology and Bison Diplomacy: The Southern Plains from 1800 to 1850." *Journal of American History* 78, no. 2 (September 1991): 465–85.

Furman, Necah Stewart. *Walter Prescott Webb: His Life and Impact.* Albuquerque: University of New Mexico Press, 1976.

Gambone, Joseph G. "Economic Relief in Territorial Kansas, 1860–1861." *Kansas Historical Quarterly* 36, no. 2 (Summer 1970): 149–74.

Grinnell, George Bird. *The Fighting Cheyennes.* Norman: University of Oklahoma Press, 1985.

Hadley, James Albert. "A Royal Buffalo Hunt." *Transactions of the Kansas State Historical Society, 1907–1908.* Topeka: State Printing Office, 1908. 564–80.

Hafen, Leroy R., ed. *The Mountain Men and the Fur Trade of the Far West.* Vols. 3 and 6. Glendale, California: Arthur H. Clarke Co., 1966.

Hafen, LeRoy R. and Francis Marion Young. *Fort Laramie and the Pageant of the West, 1834–1890.* Glendale, California: Arthur H. Clark Company, 1938.

Hall, Frank. *History of the State of Colorado. . . .* 4 vols. Chicago: Blakely Printing Co., 1889.

Haywood, C. Robert. *Victorian West: Class and Culture in Kansas Cattle Towns.* Lawrence: University Press of Kansas, 1991.

Hollon, W. Eugene and Ruth Lapham Butler, eds. *William Bollaert's Texas.* Norman: University of Oklahoma Press, 1956.

Hudnall, Mary Prowers. "Early History of Bent County." *Colorado Magazine* 22, no. 6 (November 1945): 233–47.

Hurd, C. W. *Boggsville: Cradle of the Colorado Cattle Industry*. Las Animas, Colorado: Bent County Democrat, 1857[?].

Hutton, Paul Andrew. *Phil Sheridan and His Army*. Lincoln: University of Nebraska Press, 1985.

Kenner, Charles L. *A History of New Mexican-Plains Indian Relations*. Norman: University of Oklahoma Press, 1969.

Lavender, David. *Bent's Fort*. Garden City: Doubleday and Company, 1954.

Lecompte, Janet. "John Poisal." In LeRoy R.Hafen, *The Mountain Men and the Fur Trade of the Far West*. Glendale: Arthur H. Clark Company, 1968.

Lee, Wayne C. and Howard C. Raynesford. *Trails of the Smoky Hill: From Coronado to the Cowtowns*. Caldwell, Idaho: Caxton Printers, Ltd., 1980.

Leonard, Carol and Isidor Willimann, "Prostitution and Changing Morality in the Frontier Cattle Towns of Kansas." *Kansas History* 2, no.1 (Spring 1979): 34–53.

Lubers, H. L. "William Bent's Family and the Indians of the Plains." *Colorado Magazine* 13, no. 1 (January 1936): 19–22.

Malin, James C. *History and Ecology: Studies of the Grassland*. Ed. Robert P. Swierenga. Lincoln: University of Nebraska Press, 1984.

Matthews, Anne. *Where the Buffalo Roam*. New York: Grove Press, 1992.

McClung, Quantrille D. *Carson-Bent-Boggs Geneaology*. Denver: Denver Public Library, 1962. With Supplement, published in 1973.

McQuillan, D. Aidan. "The Mobility of Immigrants and Americans: A Comparison of Farmers on the Kansas Frontier." *Agricultural History* 53, no. 3 (July 1979):576–96.

Merriman. R. O. *The Bison and the Fur Trade*. Bulletin of the Departments of History and Political and Economic Science in Queen's University. Kingston, Ontario: Jackson Press, 1926.

Powers, Ramon and Gene Younger, "Cholera On the Plains: The Epidemic of 1867 in Kansas." *Kansas Historical Quarterly* 37, no. 4 (Winter 1971): 351–93.

Rath, Ida Ellen. *The Rath Trail*. Wichita: McCormick-Armstrong, Co., Inc., 1961.

Reps, John W. *Cities of the American West: A History of Frontier Urban Planning*. Princeton: Princeton University Press, 1979.

Reps, John W. *Town Planning in Frontier America*. Princeton: Princeton University Press, 1969.

Riggs, Thomas L. *The Last Buffalo Hunt*. Santee, Nebraska: Santee Normal Training School Press, 1935.

Roenigk, Adolph. *Pioneer History of Kansas*. Denver: Great Western Publishing Co., 1933.

Root, George A. and Russell K. Hickman. "Pike's Peak Express Companies." *Kansas Historical Quarterly* 13, no. 3–4 (August and November 1944): 163–95, 211–42.

Rundell, Walter Rundell, Jr. "Walter Prescott Webb: Product of Environment." *Arizona and the West* 5 (Spring 1963): 4–28.

Smith, Henry Nash. "Rain Follows the Plow: The Notion of Increased Rainfall for the Great Plains, 1844–1880." *Huntington Library Quarterly* 10, no. 2 (February 1947): 169–93.

Spence, Mark David. "Creating an American Wilderness: The Ideal of

Preservation and the Dispossession of Native America." Paper in possession
of the author.

St. Vrain, Paul Augustus. *Genealogy* [sic] *of the Family of De Lassus and Saint Vrain.*
Kirksville, Missouri: [s.n.], 1943.

Taylor, Morris F. "The Mail Station and the Military at Camp on Pawnee Fork,
1859–1860." *Kansas Historical Quarterly* 36, no. 1 (Spring 1970): 27–39.

Tobin, Gregory M. *The Making of a History: Walter Prescott Webb and "The Great
Plains."* Austin: University of Texas Press, 1976.

Unrau, William E. *The Kansas Indians: A History of the Wind People, 1673–1873.*
Norman: University of Oklahoma Press, 1971.

Webb, Walter Prescott. *An Honest Preface and Other Essays.* Ed. Joe B. Frantz.
Boston: Houghton Mifflin Co., 1959.

———. *The Great Plains.* Boston: Ginn and Company, 1931.

Welsh, Norbert. *The Last Buffalo Hunter, by Mary Weekes, As Told to Her by Norbert
Welsh.* New York: T. Nelson and Sons, 1939.

White, Richard. "The Winning of the West: The Expansion of the Western Sioux in
the Eighteenth and Nineteenth Centuries." *Journal of American History* 65, no. 2
(September 1978): 319–43.

Wishart, David J. *The Fur Trade of the American West, 1807–1840: A Geographical
Synthesis.* Lincoln: University of Nebraska Press, 1979.

Wyman, Walker. "Freighting: A Big Business on the Santa Fe Trail." *Kansas Historical
Quarterly* 1, no. 1 (November 1931): 17–27.

Secondary Environmental Sources

Alberston, F. W. and J. E. Weaver. "History of the Native Vegetation of Western
Kansas During Seven Years of Continuous Drought." *Ecological Monographs* 12:,
no. 1 (January 1942): 23–53.

Alberston, F. W., Andrew Riegel, and John L. Launchbauch, Jr. "Effects of Different
Intensities of Clipping on Short Grasses in West-Central Kansas." *Ecology* 34, no.
1 (January 1953): 1–20.

Allen, J. A. *The American Bisons, Living and Extinct.* Memoirs of the Museum of
Comparative Zoology, at Harvard College. Vol. 4, no. 10. Cambridge: University
Press, 1876.

Arthur, George W., comp. *A Buffalo Round-up: A Selected Bibliography.* Regina:
University of Regina, 1985.

Axelrod, D.I. "Rise of the Grassland Biome, Central North America." *Botanical
Review* 51 (1985): 163–202.

Bamforth, Douglas B. "An Empirical Perspective on Little Ice Age Climatic
Change on the Great Plains." *Plains Anthropologist* 35, no. 132 (November
1990): 359–66.

Beebe, J. D. and G. R. Hoffman. "Effects of Grazing on Vegetation and Soils in
Southeastern South Dakota." *American Midland Naturalist* 80, no. 1 (July 1968):
96–110.

Biswell, Harold H. and J. E. Weaver. "Effect of Frequent Clipping on the Development of the Roots and Tops of Grasses in Prairie Sod." *Ecology,* 14, no. 4
(October 1933): 368–90.

Blanchet, K., et al., comps. *An Abstract Bibliography on Shortgrass and Mixed-grass Prairie Ecosystems.* U.S. IBP Grassland Biome Tech. Rep. 236. Fort Collins: Colorado State University, 1973.

Boddicker, Major L. and Ernest J. Hugghins. "Helminths of Big Game Mammals in South Dakota." *Journal of Parasitology*, 55 no. 5 (October 1969): 1067–74.

Branson, Farrel and J. E. Weaver. "Quantitative Study of Degeneration of Mixed Prairie." *Botanical Gazette* 114, no. 4 (June 1953): 397, no. 416.

Bukey, F. S. and J. S. Weaver. "Effects of Frequent Clipping on the Underground Food Reserves of Certain Prairie Grasses." *Ecology* 20, no. 2 (April 1939): 246–52.

Carpenter, J. Richard. "The Grassland Biome." *Ecological Monographs* 10, no. 4 (October 1940): 617–84.

Clark, S. E. et al. "The Effects of Climate and Grazing Practices on Short-Grass Prairie Vegetation." Canadian Department of Agriculture Technical Bulletin 46. Ottawa, Canada, 1943.

Clements, F. E. and R. W. Chayney. *Environment and Life in the Great Plains.* Washington, D.C.: Carnegie Institution, 1936.

Clements, Frederick E. "Drought Periods and Climatic Cycles." *Ecology* 2, no. 3 (July 1921): 181–88.

Cole, James E. "Buffalo (*Bison bison*) Killed by Fire." *Journal of Mammalogy* 35, no. 3 (August 1954): 453–54.

Collins, Scott L. and Linda L. Wallace, eds. *Fire in the North American Tallgrass Prairies.* Norman: University of Oklahoma Press, 1990.

Coupland, Robert T. "The Effects of Fluctuations in Weather Upon the Grasslands, of the Great Plains." *Botanical Review* 24, no. 5 (May 1958): 273–317.

Creel, Darrell, Robert F. Scott IV, and Michael B. Collins. "A Faunal Record from West Central Texas and its Bearing on Late Holocene Bison Population Changes in the Southern Plains." *Plains Anthropologist* 35, no. 127 (February 1990): 55–69.

Day, T. A. and J. K. Detling. "Grassland Patch Dynamics and Herbivore Grazing Preference Following Urine Deposition." *Ecology* 71, no. 1 (February 1991): 180–88.

Detling, J. K. et al. "Examination of North American Bison Saliva for Potential Plant Growth Regulators." *Journal of Chemical Ecology* 7, no. 2 (March 1981): 239–46.

Dice, Lee R. "Methods for Estimating Populations of Mammals." *Journal of Wildlife Management* 5, no. 4 (October 1941): 398–407.

Frick, Edwin J. "Parasitism in Bison." *Journal of the American Veterinary Medical Asociation* 119, no. 896 (November 1951): 386–87.

Fryxell, John M., John Greever, and A. R. E. Sinclair. "Why Are Migratory Ungulates So Abundant?" *American Naturalist* 131, no. 6 (June 1988): 781–98.

Garretson, Martin S. *The American Bison: The Story of its Extermination as a Wild Species and its Restoration Under Federal Protection.* New York: New York Zoological Society, 1938.

Gernert, W. B. "Native Grass Behavior as Affected by Periodic Clipping." *Journal of the American Society of Agronomy* 28, no. 6 (June 1936): 447–56.

Hadwen, Seymour. "Tuberculosis in the Buffalo." *Journal of the American Veterinary Medical Association* 100, no. 778 (January 1942): 19–22.

Halpern, Daniel, ed. *On Nature: Nature, Landscape, and Natural History.* San Francisco: North Point Press, 1986.

Hanson, Jeffrey R. "Bison Ecology in the Northern Plains and a Reconstruction of Bison Patterns for the North Dakota Region." *Plains Anthropologist* 29 (May 1984): 93–113.

Hess, Karl, Jr. *Rocky Times in Rocky Mountain National Park: An Unnatural History.* Niwot: University of Colorado, 1993.

Hobbs, N. Thompson and David M. Swift. "Grazing in Herds: When Are Nutritional Benefits Realized?" *American Naturalist* 131, no. 5 (May 1988): 760–64.

Hornaday, William T. *The Extermination of the American Bison, With a Sketch of Its Discovery and Life History.* Washington, D.C.: United States National Museum, 1889.

James, S. W. "Soil Nitrogen, Phosphorus and Organic Matter Processing by Earthworms in Tallgrass Prairie." *Ecology* 72 (1991): 2101–10.

Johnson, Charles W. "Protein as a Factor in the Distribution of American Bison." *Geographical Review* 41, no. 2 (April 1951): 330–31.

Krueger, Kirsten. "Feeding Relationships Among Bison, Pronghorn, and Prairie Dogs: An Experimental Analysis." *Ecology* 67, no. 3 (June 1986): 760–70.

Larson, Floyd. "The Role of the Bison in Maintaining the Short Grass Plains." *Ecology* 21, no. 2 (April 1940): 113–21.

Lawson, Merlin Paul. *The Climate of the Great American Desert: Reconstruction of the Climate of Western Interior United States, 1800–1850.* Lincoln: University of Nebraska Press, 1974.

Liebig, Justus von. *Organic Chemistry and Its Applications to Agriculture and Physiology.* London: Taylor and Walton, 1840.

MacArthur, Robert. "Species Packing and Competitive Equilibrium for Many Species." *Theoretical Population Biology* 1, no. 1 (May 1970): 1–11.

Malin, James C. *History and Ecology: Studies of the Grassland.* Ed. Robert P. Swierenga. Lincoln: University of Nebraska Press, 1984.

May, Robert M. *Stability and Complexity in Model Ecosystems.* Princeton: Princeton University Press, 1973.

McHugh, Tom. *The Time of the Buffalo.* New York: Alfred A Knopf, 1972.

McNary, David C. "Anthrax in American Bison, 'Box Bison L'." *Journal of the American Veterinary Medical Association* 112, no. 854 (May 1948): 378.

Morgan, R. Grace. "Bison Movement Patterns on the Canadian Plains: An Ecological Analysis." *Plains Anthropologist* 25, no. 88, Part 1 (May 1980): 143–60.

Osborn, Alan J. "Ecological Aspects of Equestrian Adaptations in Aboriginal North America." *American Anthropologist* 85, no. 3 (September 1983): 563–91.

Peden, D. G. et al. "The Trophic Ecology of *Bison Bison* L. on Shortgrass Plains." *Journal of Applied Ecology* 11, no. 2 (August 1974): 489–97.

Reher, Charles A. "Buffalo Population and Other Deterministic Factors in a Model of Adaptive Process on the Shortgrass Plains." *Plains Anthropologist* 23, no. 83, Part 2 (November 1978): 3–39.

Roe, F. G. "The Numbers of the Buffalo." *Transactions of the Royal Society of Canada.* Third Series. Section 2, 31 (1937): 1171–203.

Roe, Frank Gilbert. *The North American Buffalo: A Critical Study of the Species in its Wild State.* 2nd Ed. Toronto: University of Toronto Press, 1970.

Sala, O. E. et al. "Primary Production of the Central Grassland Region of the United States." *Ecology* 69 (1988): 40–45.

Sauer, Carl O. "Grassland Climax, Fire and Man." *Journal of Range Mangagement* 3 (1950): 16–21.

Schulman, Edmund. *Dendroclimatic Changes in Semiarid America.* Tucson: University of Arizona Press, 1956.

Schwartz, Charles C. and James E. Ellis. "Feeding Ecology and Niche Separation in Some Native and Domestic Ungulates on the Shortgrass Prairie." *Journal of Applied Ecology* 18, no. 2 (August 1981): 343–53.

Shelford, Victor E. *The Ecology of North America.* Urbana: University of Illinois Press, 1978.

Sherow, James. "Workings of the Geodialectic: High Plains Indians and Their Horses in the Region of the Arkansas River Valley, 1800–1870." *Environment History Review* Summer, 1992.

Singh, J. S. *U.S. IBP Grassland Biome Tech. Rep. No. 155.* Fort Collins: Colorado State University, 1972.

Soper, J. Dewey. "History, Range, and Home Life of the Northern Bison." *Ecological Monographs* 11, no. 4 (October 1941): 348–412.

Telfer, Edmund S. and John P. Kelsall. "Adaptation of Some Large North American Mammals for Survival in Snow." *Ecology* 65, no. 6 (December 1984): 1828–34.

Tessaro, Stacy V. "Review of the Diseases, Parasites and Miscellaneous Pathological Conditions of North American Bison." *Canadian Veterinarian Journal* 30, no. 5 (May 1989): 416–22.

Thomas, Lewis. *Lives of a Cell: Notes of a Biology Watcher.* New York: Viking Press, 1974.

Wali, Mohan K., ed. *Native Grassland Ecosystems East of the Rocky Mountains in North America: A Preliminary Bibliography. A Supplement to Prairie: A Multiple View.* Grand Forks: University of North Dakota Press, 1975.

Weakly, Harry. "A Tree Ring Record of Precipitation in Western Nebraska." *Journal of Forestry* 41 (1943): 816–19.

Weaver, J. E. "Underground Plant Development in its Relation to Grazing." *Ecology* 11:, no. 3 (July 1930): 543–57.

———. "Replacement of True Prairie by Mixed Prairie in Eastern Nebraska and Kansas." *Ecology* 24, no. 4 (October 1943): 421–34.

———. "Summary and Interpretation of Underground Development in Natural Grassland Communities." *Ecological Monographs* 28, no. 1 (January 1958): 55–78.

Weaver, J. E. *North American Prairie.* Lincoln: Johnsen Publishing Co., 1954.

Weaver, J. E. and F. W. Albertson. "Nature and Degree of Recovery of Grassland From the Great Drought of 1933 to 1940." *Ecological Monographs* 14, no. 4 (October 1944): 393–479.

———. *Grasslands of the Great Plains.* Lincoln: Johnsen Publishing Co., 1956.

Weese, A. O. "The Effect of Overgrazing on Insect Population." Oklahoma Academy of Science *Proceedings* 19 (1939): 95–99.

Secondary Anthropological and Sociological Sources

Anderson, Karen. "Commodity Exchange and Subordination: Montagnais-Naskapi and Huron Women, 1600–1650." *Signs* 11, no. 1 (Autumn 1985): 48–62.

Bamforth, Douglas B. "Historical Documents and Bison Ecology on the Great Plains." *Plains Anthropologist* 32, no. 115 (February 1987): 1–16.

———. *Ecology and Human Organization on the Great Plains: Interdisciplinary Contributions to Archaeology.* New York: Plenum Press, 1988.

Basso, Keith H. *Western Apache Language and Culture: Essays in Linguistic Anthropology.* Tucson: University of Arizona Press, 1990.

Beider, Robert E. "Scientific Attitudes Toward Indian Mixed-Bloods in Early Nineteenth Century America." *Journal of Ethnic Studies* 8, no. 2 (Summer 1980): 17–30.

Byler, William. "Removing Children: The Destruction of American Indian Families." *Civil Rights* 9, no. 4 (Summer 1977): 18–28.

Conrad, Lawrence A. "Comment: An Early Eighteenth Century Reference to 'Putting a woman on the Prairies' Among the Central Algonquians and Its Implications for Moore's Explanation of the Practice Among the Cheyenne." *Plains Anthropologist* 28, no. 100 (May 1983): 141–42.

Creel, Darrell. "Bison Hides in Late Prehistoric Exchange in the Southern Plains." *American Antiquity* 56, no. 1 (1991): 40–49.

Daniels, John D. "The Indian Population of North America in 1492." *William and Mary Quarterly*, 3rd series 49, no. 2 (April 1992): 298–320.

Davis, Leslie B. *Lifeways of Intermontane and Plains Montana Indians: In Honor of J. Verne Dusenberry.* Occasional Papers of the Museum of the Rockies No. 1. Bozeman: Montana State University, 1979.

Devens, Carol. "Separate Confrontations: Gender as a Factor in Indian Adaptation to European Colonization in New France." *American Quarterly* 38, no. 3 (1986): 460–80.

Dillehay, Tom D. "Late Quaternary Bison Population Changes on the Southern Plains." *Plains Anthropologist* 19, no. 65 (August 1974): 180–96.

Doring, Jurgen. *Kulturwandel bei den Nordamerikanischen Plainsindianern: Zur Rolle des Pferdes bei den Comanchen und den Cheyenne.* Berlin: Dietrick Reimer, 1984.

Dorsey, George A. *The Arapaho Sun Dance: The Ceremony of the Offerings Lodge.* Field Columbian Museum Publication 75, Anthropological Series, Vol. 4. Chicago: Field Columbian Museum, 1903.

———. *The Cheyenne.* Field Columbia Museum Publication 99 and 103, Anthropological Series, Vol. 9, nos. 1–2. Chicago: Field Museum, 1905.

Downs, James F. "Comments on Plains Indian Cultural Development." *American Anthropologist* 66, no. 2 (April 1964): 421–22.

Easterlin, Richard A. "Factors in the Decline of Farm Family Fertility in the United States: Some Preliminary Research Results." *Journal of American History* 63, no. 3 (December 1976): 600–14.

Eggan, Fred, ed. *Social Anthropology of North American Tribes.* Chicago: University of Chicago Press, 1955.

Ekvall, Robert Brainerd. *Fields on the Hoof: Nexus of Tibetan Nomadic Pastoralism.* New York: Holt, Rinehart and Winston.

Etienne, Mona and Eleanor Leacock, eds. *Women and Colonization: Anthropological Perspectives.* New York: Praeger, 1980.

Ewers, John C. "Contraceptive Charms among the Plains Indians." *Plains Anthropologist* 15, no. 49 (August 1970): 216–18.

———. "The Influence of Epidemics on the Indian Populations and Cultures of Texas." *Plains Anthropologist* 18, no. 60 (May 1973): 104–15.

————. "Climate, Acculturation, and Costume: A History of Women's Clothing among the Indians of the Southern Plains." *Plains Anthropologist* 25, no. 87 (February 1980): 63–82.

Fletcher, Alice C., and Francis La Flesche. *The Omaha Tribe*. Lincoln: University of Nebraska Press, 1972.

Frischo, A. Robert, Jane E. Klayman, and Jorge Matos. "Symbiotic Relationship Between High Fertility, High Childhood Mortality and Socio-Economic Status in an Urban Peruvian Population." *Human Biology* 48, no.1 (February 1976): 101–11.

Galaty, John G. *The World of Pastoralism: Herding Systems in Comparative Perspective*. New York: Belhaven Press, 1991.

Grinnell, George B. *By Cheyenne Campfires*. New Haven: Yale University Press, 1926.

Hafen, Leroy R. and Zachary Gussow. *Arapaho-Cheyenne Indians* [Reports and findings of United States Indian Claims Commission]. New York: Garland Publishing Inc., 1974.

Hall, Stephen A."Environment and Archaeology of the Central Osage Plains." *Plains Anthropologist* 33, no. 120 (May 1988): 203–18.

Hanna, Margaret G. "Do You Take This Woman? Economics and Marriage in a Late Prehistoric Band." *Plains Anthropologist* 29, no. 104 (May 1984): 115–29.

Hanson, Wynn. "The Urban Indian Woman and Her Family." *Social Casework: The Journal of Contemporary Social Work* 61, no. 8 (October 1980): 476–83.

Henning, Elizabeth R. P. "Western Dakota Winter Counts: An Analysis of the Effects of Westward Migration and Culture Change." *Plains Anthropologist* 27, no. 95 (February 1982): 57–65.

Hickerson, Harold. "The Virginia Deer and Intertribal Buffer Zones in the Upper Mississippi Valley." In Leeds and Vayda, eds., *Man, Culture, and Animals*. 43–66.

Hoebel, E. Adamson. *The Cheyennes: Indians of the Great Plains*. Fort Worth: Harcourt Brace Jovanovich, 1978.

————. "On Cheyenne Sociopolitical Organization." *Plains Anthropologist* 25, no. 88, Part 1 (May 1980): 161–69.

Homewood, Katherine and W. A. Rodgers. "Pastoralism and Conservation." *Human Ecology* 12, no. 4 (1984): 431–41.

Hyde, George E. *Indians of the High Plains: From the Prehistoric Period to the Coming of Europeans*. Norman: University of Oklahoma Press, 1959.

Ingold, Tim. *Hunters, Pastoralists, and Ranchers: Reindeer Economics and their Transformations*. Cambridge: Cambridge University Press, 1980.

Jablow, Joseph. *The Cheyenne in Plains Indian Trade Relations, 1795–1840*. Monographs of the American Ethnological Society, XIX. New York: J. J. Augustin, 1951.

Jacobsen, R. Brooke and Jeffrey L. Eighmy. "A Mathematical Theory of Horse Adoption on the North American Plains." *Plains Anthropologist* 25, no. 90 (November 1980): 333–41.

Kehoe, Alice B. "The Function of Ceremonial Sexual Intercourse Among the Northern Plains Indians." *Plains Anthropologist* 15, no. 48 (May 1970): 99–103.

Kemnitzer, Luis S. "Adjustment and Value Conflict in Urbanizing Dakota Indians Measured by Q-Sort Technique." *American Anthropologist* 75, no. 3 (June 1973): 687–707.

Kuznar, Lawrence A. "Transhumant Goat Pastoralism in the High Sierra of the

South Central Andes: Human Responses to Environmental and Social Uncertainty." *Nomadic Peoples* 28 (1991): 93–104.

Leacock, Eleanor. "Women's Status in Egalitarian Society: Implications for Social Evolution." *Current Anthropology* 19 (1978): 247—75.

Leed, Anthony and Andrew P. Vayda, eds. *Man, Culture, and Animals: The Role of Animals in Human Ecological Adjustments*. Washington, D.C.: American Association for the Advancement of Science, 1965. Publication No. 78.

Liberty, Margot. "Hell Came With Horses: Plains Indian Women in the Equestrian Era." *Montana, The Magazine of Western History* 32, no. 3 (Summer 1982): 10–29.

———. "Plains Indian Women Through Time: A Preliminary Overview." In Leslie B. Davis, ed. *Lifeways of Intermontane and Plains Montana Indians*. Occasional Papers of the Museum of the Rockies No. 1. Bozeman: Montana State University, 1971.

———. "Population Trends Among Present-Day Omaha Indians." *Plains Anthropologist* 20, no. 69 (August 1969): 225–30.

Liberty, Margot, David V. Hughey, and Richard Scaglion. "Rural and Urban Omaha Indian Fertility." *Human Biology* 48, no. 1 (February 1986): 59–71.

Mallery, Garrick. *Picture-Writing of the American Indians*. New York: Dover Publications, 1972.

Marquis, Thomas B. *The Cheyennes of Wyoming*. Ed. Thomas D. Weist. Algonac, Michigan: Reference Publications, 1978.

Marriott, Alice and Carol K. Rachlin. *American Indian Mythology*. New York: Thomas Y. Crowell Company, 1968.

———. *Plains Indian Mythology*. New York: Thomas Y. Crowell Company, 1975.

Maxwell, Joseph A. "The Evolution of Plains Indian Kin Terminologies: A Non-Reflectionist Account." *Plains Anthropologist* 23, no. 79 (February 1978): 13–28.

Mayhall, Mildred P. *The Kiowas*. Norman: University of Oklahoma Press, 1952.

May, Philip A. "Contemporary Crime and the American Indian: A Survey and Analysis of the Literature." *Plains Anthroplogist* 27, no. 97 (August 1982): 225–38.

Mayhall, Mildred P. *The Kiowas*. Norman: University of Oklahoma Press, 1952.

Mishkin, Bernard. *Rank and Warfare among the Plains Indians*. Monographs of the American Etnological Society, no. 3. New York: Augustin, 1940.

Momaday, N. Scott. *The Way to Rainy Mountain*. Albuquerque: University of New Mexico Press, 1969.

Mooney, James. *Calendar History of the Kiowa Indians*. Washington, D. C.: Smithsonian Institution Press, 1979.

Moore, John H. and Gregory R. Campbell. "An Ethnohistorical Perspective on Cheyenne Demography." *Journal of Family History* 14, no. 1 (1989): 17–42.

Moore, John H. "Cheyenne Political History, 1820–1894" *Ethnohistory* 21, no. 4 (Fall 1974): 329–59.

———. "Evolution and Historical Reductionism." *Plains Anthropologist* 26, no. 94, Part 1 (November 1981): 261–69.

———. *The Cheyenne Nation: A Social and Demographic History*. Lincoln: University of Nebraska Press, 1987.

———. "The Developmental Cycle of Cheyenne Polygyny." *American Indian Quarterly* 15 (Summer 1991): 311–28.

Morgan, Lewis H. *Ancient Society, or Researches in the Lines of Human Progress from Savagery, Through Barbarism to Civilization.* New York: Henry Holt and Company, 1877.

Netting, Robert. *Balancing on an Alp: Ecological Change and Continuity in a Swiss Mountain Community.* Cambridge: Cambridge University Press, 1981.

O'Brien, Patricia J. *Archaeology in Kansas.* Lawrence: University of Kansas Museum of Natural History, 1984.

Orser, Charles E., Jr. and Larry J. Zimmerman. "A Computer Simulation of Euro-American Trade Good Flow to the Arickara." *Plains Anthropologist* 29, no. 105 (August 1984): 195–210.

Ottaway, Harold. "A Possible Origin for the Cheyenne Sacred Arrow Complex." *Plains Anthropologist* 15, no. 48 (May 1970): 94–98.

Parsons, Elsie Clews. *Kiowa Tales.* New York: G. E. Stechert and Co., 1929.

Perry, Richard J. "The Fur Trade and the Status of Women in the Western Subarctic." *Ethnohistory* 26 (1979): 363–75.

Petter, Rodolphe C. *English-Cheyenne Dictionary* . . . Kettle Falls, Washington: Valdo Petter, 1915.

Pope, Polly. "Trade in the Plains: Affluence and Its Effects." Kroeber Anthropological Society Publication No. 34 (Spring 1966): 53–61.

Red Horse, John G. et al. "Family Behavior of Urban American Indians." *Social Casework* 59, no. 2 (February 1978): 67–82.

Reiter, Rayna B., ed. *Toward an Anthropology of Women.* New York: Monthly Review Press, 1975.

Renaud, E. B. *Archaeological Survey of Eastern Colorado.* Reports 1–3. Denver: University of Denver, 1931–33.

Renaud, Etienne B. "Archaeology of the High Western Plains: Seventeen Years of Archaeological Research." Publication of the Department of Anthroplogy, University of Denver, 1947.

Richardson, Jane. *Law and Status Among the Kiowa Indians,* Monographs of the American Ethnological Society No. I. New York: J. J. Augustin, Publisher, 1940.

Sanday, Peggy R. "Toward a Theory of the Status of Women." *American Anthropologist* 75, no. 5 (October 1973): 1682–1700.

Schlesier, Karl. H. *The Wolves of Heaven: Cheyenne Shamanism, Ceremonies, and Prehistoric Origins.* Norman: University of Oklahoma Press, 1987.

Simms, S. C. "A Crow Monument to Shame." *American Anthropologist* 5 (1903): 374–75.

Singh, K. P. "Child Mortality, Social Status and Fertility in India." *Social Biology* 21 (Winter 1974): 285–88.

Smith, Andrew B. *Pastoralism in Africa: Origins and Development Ecology.* London and Athens: Hurst & Co., and Ohio University Press, 1992.

Smith, G. Hubert. "Notes on Omaha Ethnohistory, 1763–1820." *Plains Anthropologist* 18, no. 62 (November 1973): 257–70.

Soliday, Gerald L., ed., with Tamara K. Hareven, Richard T. Vann, and Robert Wheaton. *History of the Family and Kinship: A Select International Bibliography.* Millwood, New York: Kraus-International Publications, 1980.

"Some of the Ancestors and Descendants of Quanah Parker." *Journal of American Indian Family Research* 1, no. 1 (1980): 23–33.

Spicer, Edward H., ed. *Perspectives in American Indian Culture Change,* Chicago:
    University of Chicago Press, 1961.
Spielmann, Katherine B., ed. *Farmers, Hunters, and Colonists: Interaction Between the
    Southwest and the Southern Plains.* Tucson: University of Arizona Press, 1991.
Stands-in-Timber, John and Margot Liberty. *Cheyenne Memories.* New Haven:
    Yale University Press, 1967.
Stoltman, James B., ed. *Archaeology of Eastern North America: Papers in Honor of
    Stephen Williams.* Archaeological Report No. 25. Jackson, Mississippi: Mississippi
    Department of Archives and History, 1993.
Sweet, Louis E. "Camel Pastoralism in North Arabia and the Minimal Camping
    Unit." In Leeds and Vayda, *Man, Culture and Animals,* 129–52.
Szalay, Lorand B., and Bela C. Maday. "Implicit Culture and Psychocultural
    Distance." *American Anthropologist* 85, no. 1 (March 1983): 110–18.
Thornton, Russell. *American Indian Holocaust and Survival: A Population History
    Since 1492.* Norman: University of Oklahoma Press, 1987.
Townsend, Patricia K. and Ann McElroy. "Toward an Ecology of Women's
    Reproductive Health." *Medical Anthropology* 14, no. 1 (1992): 9–34.
Vehik, Susan C. "Late Prehistoric Plains Trade and Economic Specialization."
    Plains Anthropologist 35, no. 128 (May 1990): 125–45.
Verano, John W. and Douglas H. Ubelaker, eds. *Disease and Demography in the
    Americas.* Washington, D.C.: Smithsonian Institution Press, 1992.
Watrall, Charles. "Virginia Deer and the Buffer Zone in the Late Prehistoric-Early
    Protohistoric Periods in Minnesota." *Plains Anthropologist* 13 (1968): 81–86.
Webster, Steven. "Native Pastoralism in the South Andes." *Ethnology* 12 (April
    1973): 115–33.
Wedel, Waldo R. "Some Problems and Prospects in Kansas Prehistory."
    Kansas Historical Quarterly 7 (May 1938): 115–32.
———. *Prehistoric Man on the Great Plains.* Norman: University of Oklahoma Press,
    1961.
———. "Toward a History of Plains Archeology." *Great Plains Quarterly* 1
    (Winter 1981): 16–38.
———. *Central Plains Prehistory: Holocene Environments and Culture Change in the
    Republican River Basin.* Lincoln: University of Nebraska Press, 1986.
Wells, Philip V. "Scarp Woodlands, Transported Grassland Soils, and Concept of
    Grassland Climate in the Great Plains Region." *Science* 148 (1965): 246–49.
Western, David. "The Environment and Ecology of Pastoralists in Arid Savannas."
    Development and Change 13, no. 2 (1982): 159–82.
Wilson, H. Clyde. "An Inquiry into the Nature of Plains Indian Cultural Develop-
    ment." *American Anthropologist* 65, no. 2 (April 1963): 355–69.

Secondary Literary and Other Sources

Abbey, Edward. *Desert Solitaire: A Season in the Wilderness.* New York: Ballantine
    Books, 1971.
Berger, Thomas. *Little Big Man.* New York: Dial Press, 1964.
Bevis, William H. *Ten Tough Trips: Montana Writers and the West* Seattle: University
    of Washington Press, 1990.

Bruhac, Joseph, III, ed. *Survival This Way: Interviews with American Indian Poets.* Tucson: University of Arizona Press, 1987.

Cosgrove, Denis and Stephen Daniels, eds. *The Iconography of Landscape: Essays on the Symbolic Representation, Design, and Use of Past Environments.* Cambridge: Cambridge University Press, 1988.

Hansen, Ron. *Nebraska: Stories.* New York: Atlantic Monthly Press, 1989.

Holthaus, Gary H. *Circling Back.* Salt Lake City: Peregrine Smith Books, 1984.

Kroeber, Karl. *Traditional Literatures of the American Indian: Texts and Interpretations.* Lincoln: University of Nebraska Press, 1981.

Krupat, Arnold. *For Those who come After: A Study of Native American Autobiography.* Berkeley: University of California Press, 1985.

Lincoln, Kenneth. *Native American Renaissance.* Berkeley: University of California Press, 1983.

————. *Indi'n Humor: Bicultural Play in Native America.* New York: Oxford University Press, 1993.

Lopez, Barry. *Arctic Dreams: Imagination and Desire in a Northern Landscape.* New York: Charles Scribner's Sons, 1986.

Luckerman, Fred. "Geography as a Formal Intellectual Discipline and the Way in which it Contributes to Human Knowledge." *Canadian Geographer* 8: 167–72.

McMurtry, Larry. *Horseman, Pass By.* New York: Harpers, 1961.

————. *The Last Picture Show.* New York: Dial Press, 1966.

————. *Lonesome Dove: A Novel.* New York: Simon and Schuster, 1985.

————. *Buffalo Girls: A Novel.* New York: Simon and Schuster, 1990.

Meinig, Donald W. *The Shaping of America: A Geographical Perspective on 500 Years of History.* New Haven: Yale University Press, 1986.

Meinig, Donald W., ed. *The Interpretation of Ordinary Landscapes: Geographical Essays.* New York: Oxford University Press, 1979.

Nabhan, Gary Paul. *The Desert Smells Like Rain: A Naturalist in Papago Indian Country.* San Francisco: North Point Press, 1982.

————. *Enduring Seeds: Native American Agriculture and Wild Plant Conservation.* San Francisco: North Point Press, 1989.

Owens, Louis. *Other Destinies: Understanding the American Indian Novel.* Norman: University of Oklahoma Press, 1992.

Pocock, Douglas C. D., ed. *Humanistic Geography and Literature: Essays on the Experience of Place.* London: Croom Helm, and Totowa, New Jersey: Barnes & Noble, 1981.

Ramsey, Jarold. *Reading the Fire: Essays in the Traditional Indian Literatures of the Far West.* Lincoln: University of Nebraska Press, 1983.

Relph, Edward. *Place and Placelessness.* London: Pion, 1976.

————. *Rational Landscapes and Humanistic Geography.* London: Croom Helm, and Totowa, New Jersey: Barnes & Noble, 1981.

Ruoff, A. LaVonne Brown. *American Indian Literatures: An Introduction, Bibliographic Review and Selected Bibliography.* New York: Modern Language Association, 1990.

Stegner, Wallace. *Where the Bluebird Sings to the Lemonade Springs: Living and Writing in the West.* New York: Random House, 1992.

Swann, Brian, ed. *Smoothing the Ground: Essays on Native American Oral Literature.* Berkeley: University of California Press, 1983.

Swann, Brian and Arnold Krupat, eds. *Recovering the Word: Essays on Native American Literature.* Berkeley: University of California Press, 1987.

———. *I Tell You Now: Autobiographical Essays by Native American Writers.* Lincoln: University of Nebraska Press, 1987.

Tuan, Yi-Fu. *Topophilia: A Study of Environmental Perception, Attitudes, and Values.* Englewood Cliffs: Prentice-Hall, 1974.

———. *Space and Place: The Perspective of Experience.* Minneapolis: University of Minnesota Press, 1977.

———. *Landscapes of Fear.* New York: Pantheon Books, 1979.

Turner, Tom. *Sierra Club: 100 Years of Protecting Nature.* New York: Harry N. Abrams, Inc., 1991.

Vizenor, Gerald, ed. *Narrative Chance: Postmodern Discourse on Native American Indian Literatures.* Albuquerque: University of New Mexico Press, 1980. '

Wiget, Andrew, ed. *Critical Essays on Native American Literature* Boston: Hall, 1985.

Newspapers

[Columbia] *Weekly Missouri Statesman.*

Daily Kansas City [Missouri] *Journal of Commerce.*

Denver [Colorado] *Field and Farm.*

Denver [Colorado] *Post.*

[Denver, Colorado] *Rocky Mountain News.*

Hannibal [Missouri] *Messenger.*

Hays [Kansas] *Republican.*

Nebraska City News.

New York Times

[St. Louis] *Daily Missouri Democrat.*

[St. Louis] *Missouri Republican.*

Government Documents

"Abstract of Journals kept by Lt. Turner, adjutant 1st dragoons, and Lt. Franklin, Top. Eng., during an expedition performed in the summer of 1845, by five companies of the 1st dragoons under the command of Colonel S. W. Kearny." U.S. Congress, 29th Cong., 1st sess., H. E. Doc. 2, 214–17.

Annual Report of the Commissioner of Indians Affairs. . . 1855. Report to Secretary of the Interior. Washington, 1856.

Annual Report of the Commissioner of Indian Affairs, Transmitted with the Message of the President . . . 1849–1850. Washington: Gideon and Co., 1850.

Biennial Report of the Secretary of State of the State of Nebraska . . . Omaha: Omaha Republic Company, 1887.

Fourth Annual Report of the State Board of Agriculture to the Legislature of the State of Kansas, For the Year Ending November 30, 1875.

Morse, Jedediah. *A Report to the Secretary of War of the United States on Indian Affairs.* New Haven, 1822.

Report of the Commissioner off Indian Affairs . . . 1856. Washington, 1857. Report to
    Secretary of Interior.
Report of the Commissioner of Indian Affairs. 1847. E. Doc. 8.
Report of the Commissioner of Indian Affairs. 1848. E. Doc. 1.
Report of the Commissioner of Indian Affairs. 1853. H. Doc. 1.
Report of the Commissioner of Indian Affairs. 1850. Doc. 1.
Report of the Commissioner of Indian Affairs. 1845. 29th Cong., 1st sess. H. E. Doc. 2.
Report of the Secretary of War. 1857. 35th Cong., 1st sess. H. E. Doc. 2. Appendix H.
    Report of Lt. Francis T. Bryan, 455–520. Serial Set 943.
S. W. Kearny. "Report of a Summer Campaign to the Rocky Mountains, &c., in
    1845." U.S. Congress, 29th Cong., 1st sess., H. E. Doc. 2, 210–13.
U.S. Census Office. *Statistics of the Population of the United States at the Tenth Census,
    June 1, 1880.* Washington: Government Printing Office, 1883.
U.S. Census Office. *Report on the Productions of Agriculture as Returned at the Tenth
    Census, June 1, 1880.* Washington: Government Printing Office, 1883.
U.S. Commissioner of Indians Affairs. Annual Report of the Commissioner of Indian
    Affairs . . . 1854. Washington: A. O. P. Nicholson, 1855.

Theses and Dissertations

Grosser, Roger Douglas. "Late Archaic Subsistence Patterns from the Central Great
    Plains." Ph.D. dissertation. University of Kansas, 1977.
Hill, Clifford Clinton. "Wagon Roads in Colorado, 1858–1876." M.A. thesis.
    University of Colorado, 1949.
Huggard, Christopher James. "The Role of the Family in Settling the Cherokee
    Outlet." M.A. thesis. University of Arkansas, 1987.
Smith, Honora DeBusk. "Early Life in Trinidad and the Purgatory Valley." M.A.
    thesis. University of Colorado, 1930.
Trindell, Roger Thomas. "Sequent Occupance of Pueblo, Colorado." M.A. thesis.
    University of Colorado, 1960.

Index

229